Bathsheba Survives

Bathsheba Survives

Sara M. Koenig

scm press

© Sarah M. Koenig 2019

This edition published in the UK 2019 by SCM Press
Editorial office
3rd Floor, Invicta House,
108–114 Golden Lane,
London EC1Y 0TG, UK
www.scmpress.co.uk

SCM Press is an imprint of Hymns Ancient & Modern Ltd
(a registered charity)

Hymns Ancient & Modern® is a registered trademark of
Hymns Ancient & Modern Ltd
13A Hellesdon Park Road, Norwich,
Norfolk NR6 5DR, UK

Published in the United States in 2018 by
The University of South Carolina Press

British Library Cataloguing in Publication data

A catalogue record for this book is available
from the British Library

978 0 334 05854 0

Printed and bound by
CPI Group (UK) Ltd

Dedicated to Ehud and Heidi, who told me,
"Just write the book."

CONTENTS

ILLUSTRATIONS

ACKNOWLEDGMENTS

This work grew out of my dissertation, and it has been in progress for longer than I like to admit. During that time, I have been helped by many people in many different ways. In particular, I acknowledge and thank Margaret Diddams, the former director of the Center for Scholarship and Faculty Development at Seattle Pacific University, for awarding me a Faculty Research Grant. That grant funded my work at the Getty Research Institute (GRI) in Los Angeles where I researched Bathsheba's depiction in medieval iconography. I also thank Tracey Shuster and the Getty Research Institute for their assistance while I was there. My initial research for the medieval era was funded by a Summer Fellowship through the Wabash Center for Teaching and Learning in Theology and Religion. I am grateful to Paul Myhre, Dena Pence, and all of my colleagues in the Workshop for Pre-Tenure Religion Faculty for charades, karaoke, and support.

I am privileged to include art from various museums around the world. Thanks go to the Bibliothèque nationale de France; the British Library; the Trustees of the Chester Beatty Library, Dublin; the J. Paul Getty Museum; the Koninklijke Bibliotheek in The Hague, Netherlands; the Metropolitan Museum of Art; the Morgan Library and Museum; the Royal Library Copenhagen; and the Vatican Library for allowing me to include depictions of Bathsheba from their collections.

I am grateful for Jennifer McKinney, Karen Snedker, and Rob Wall, my colleagues who read drafts and offered suggestions. My "write club" partners Amy Erickson and G. Brooke Lester deserve a special shout-out. Owen Ewald and Rick Hebron assisted me in translating Latin, French, and Hebrew. Seattle Pacific University's librarian extraordinaire, Steve Perisho, was tireless and thorough in offering help. I am also grateful to student workers Danica Eisman, Scot Bearss, and Rachel Douglass. The following individuals cheered me on and prayed for me: Ann, Becky, Deb, Larie, Laurie, Christie, Jen B., Jen K., Julie, Elna, Laura, Shannon, Emily, Tracey, Meda, Ruth, James, Lauren, Brittney, Marilyn, Anika, Lisa, and Kristin. I appreciate you all!

My family has been very supportive, especially my parents, Jon and Jean Malmin, and my in-laws, Sandy and John Stokely. I thank Jan Morris, who hosted me during my Los Angeles research time. Thank you. My children

Madeleine and Max give me both support and diversions from my work, and I'm grateful for them. I simply could not do what I do without the encouragement and support of my husband, Matthew. Thank you for loving me so well.

The rough places have been made smooth by my editors James Crenshaw and Jim Denton, and it has been a pleasure to work with them both.

Over the years, I have enjoyed being involved in the Pacific Northwest Regional Society of Biblical Literature's Hebrew Bible section. There is a level of collegiality and support in that group that is rarely found in academia, and a large part of that can be attributed to the leadership of Ehud Ben Zvi and Heidi M. Szpek. After I had done my second presentation on Bathsheba at one of our regional meetings, they both told me, "Sara, just write the book." I did, and I dedicate it to them with my thanks.

Introduction

Why Bathsheba?

"On the Scriptures, everyone quite indiscriminately undertakes some
enterprise on his own account . . . the old gossip, the old fool, the wordy
sophist, all of them take it up and tamper with it, teaching others
before they learn themselves."

Ep. 53:7, Jerome

"With a sensible degree of historical perspective, we will observe that
the Bible has never known a period of unanimity in interpretation."

A. K. M. Adam, Faithful Interpretation, *9*

When people have found out that I am researching Bathsheba, responses
have ranged from frank curiosity to rude dismissiveness. One student
asked me, "Why do you like her so much?" while a colleague—in an attempt
at a joke—said, "And your book can be titled *Everything You Never Wanted to
Know about Bathsheba.*" While I think the colleague in particular could have
used some etiquette tips on how not to devalue another's research interests, I
understand these responses because Bathsheba is a minor biblical character. She
appears in a grand total of merely 76 verses: just four chapters in Samuel–Kings,
mentioned in the superscription to Psalm 51, and only alluded to in the genealogy that begins the New Testament. Moreover, the texts that do speak about
Bathsheba are riddled with gaps, or holes in the narrative where details are
lacking. Even allowing that the entire biblical narrative is severely gapped, Meir
Sternberg described the story of David and Bathsheba in 2 Sam 11 as "frugal
to excess even relative to the biblical norm."[1] If that chapter, where Bathsheba
first appears, does not tell much about her, neither does the final chapter in her
story; she fades away in 1 Kings 2 without a report of her death.[2]

However, the post-biblical reception of Bathsheba is rich and extensive.
She has not only been characterized on the spectrum from helpless victim to

unscrupulous seductress; but also, she has filled that spectrum. It might seem that the sparse profile of biblical Bathsheba stands in stark contrast to the varying interpretations of her through the centuries, but they are, in fact, related. This book demonstrates how the minor character Bathsheba has invited a succession of gap-filling that has gone on through the centuries. Tracing the history of Bathsheba's reception through different eras illustrates how enigmatic and multidimensional the varying views of her have been over time.

Though Bathsheba is admittedly a minor character, King David obviously is not, and Bathsheba's role in David's story is significant. Walter Brueggemann was not exaggerating when he described David as "the dominant figure in Israel's narrative,"[3] and Bathsheba first appears at a high point in David's story, just four chapters after the glorious Davidic covenant in 2 Sam 7. Her reappearance comes at David's lowest point in 1 Kgs 1–2 when the formerly virile king cannot even keep his own body warm, and is not interested in (or able to have?) sexual relations with a young, beautiful woman who lies in his bed. In some ways, Bathsheba is in counterpoint to David; she is relatively powerless when he is enjoying the heights of power, and using her power and authority to help her son succeed David on the throne when he is weak and near death. Of course, it is also the child Solomon, the son of David and Bathsheba, who lives, who builds the first temple for Yahweh in Jerusalem. Interpreters over the years give much more time and space to David, as does the Bible itself, but discussions about David also lend insight into Bathsheba's character. Moreover, minor means manageable; to trace David's reception history, for example, would be overwhelming, but because there is relatively little information about Bathsheba, she can serve as a north star in an interpretive sea. Focusing on her enables us to chart the currents and tides of how the Bible has been read and appropriated over time.

Gaps: Promise and Peril

Gaps in any text give it both peril and promise. At times, readers have filled in the gaps concerning Bathsheba in such ways that the story becomes a tool for either anti-Judaism or misogyny; such consequences are more evident with the benefit of hindsight. But the gaps in the text are what make the text more interesting and curious, and what invite the reader to participate dynamically, in making meaning of the text.[4] In fact, without the involvement of the reader, there is so little to Bathsheba that she is—as has often been the case—completely overshadowed by the richer, more complex, and dominant characters in the chapters: David and Solomon, and even Joab and Nathan. Were it not for readers filling in the gaps, Bathsheba would be a mere parenthesis, or footnote, to the grand story. If there is no active reader, there is no Bathsheba surviving through the centuries.

Shlomith Rimmon-Kenan has suggested that gaps are necessary for a story, that the answer to the question of how you make a story is to start with a hole.[5] No story can include every single detail, and a text that buttons up every answer and possibility is no longer really a story; it is something else, more akin to a dictionary entry than a narrative. Wolfgang Iser asserted that a story gains dynamism through its omissions or gaps, which the reader must then fill.[6] In Erich Auerbach's comparison of Gen 22 to Homer's *Odyssey*, Auerbach noted how for Homer, all the events are set in a definite time and place, and connected together "without lacunae in a perpetual foreground; thoughts and feeling completely expressed." By contrast, Auerbach described the narrative in Gen 22 as follows: "the externalization of only so much of the phenomena as is necessary for the purpose of the narrative, all else left in obscurity; the decisive points of the narrative alone are emphasized, what lies between is nonexistent; time and place are undefined and call for interpretation; thoughts and feeling remain unexpressed, are only suggested by the silence and the fragmentary speeches; the whole, permeated with the most unrelieved suspense . . . remains mysterious and 'fraught with background.'"[7] Auerbach concludes, "Homer can be analyzed, as we have essayed to do here, but he cannot be interpreted. . . . It is all very different in the Biblical stories."[8] Though Auerbach may be overstating the contrast between Homer and the biblical narrative, it is the "background" that calls for interpretation, inviting a reader to enter the open spaces and explain the meaning. Moreover, because interpretation is a way to solve problems in the text, those texts which are obscure and undefined allow for a surfeit of solutions.

Music provides an analogy, with a recent study in Denmark demonstrating that the most danceable music is that which has "gaps" in the percussive beats. Maria Witek, the chief author of the article explained, "Gaps in the rhythmic structure . . . [provide] us with an opportunity to physically inhabit those gaps and fill in those gaps with our own bodies."[9] The researchers created an online survey with different drumming patterns, which included a spectrum of complexity in rhythm. Some of the music had extremely regular, even predictable beats, while others had extremely complex rhythms, with pauses where one would expect beats. Across the globe, survey participants agreed that the most danceable rhythms were those that fell in the middle, with a balance of predictability and complexity to their beats. There must be enough syncopation to allow for, and even invite, the bodies to move, but not so many gaps that it becomes awkward.

The narrative of Bathsheba strikes that kind of balance. While she says very little, she does speak. Not much is known about her, but she is no Jane Doe: we know her name, and the name of her father and her husband. She is acted upon, but she also acts. With the gaps that are present (for example, why does she send the message of her pregnancy to David in 2 Sam 11:5? Why does she ask Solomon to give Abishag to Adonijah in 1 Kgs 2:18–21?), the reader is invited to answer the questions that are left unanswered by the taciturn Hebrew narrative.[10] Without the gaps in Bathsheba's motives and feelings, her character would be so predictable or so functionary that she would not be worth noting.[11] Bathsheba's character is given dry bones by the narrator; it is up to the reader to flesh out her character, to give her breath and sinew, and to allow her to live. It is Bathsheba's sparely drawn character that makes the reader's activity so significant.

Reception History: Terminology and Methodology

Because the reader's activity in Bathsheba's reception is so significant, it is helpful to clarify what is meant by "reception history." The term has two semantic flaws: first, "reception" can seem passive, and second, as Hans Robert Jauss, one of the early, major proponents of "reception theory," humorously noted in 1979, the term "may seem more appropriate to hotel management than to literature."[12] Jauss's "aesthetics of reception," developed in the 1960s and 1970s suggested that the meaning of a text is neither located solely in the text nor in the experience of the reader, but in the relationship between the two.[13] The reception history of Bathsheba therefore considers both what the text says and how a reader has interpreted the text.

Though Jauss was interested in the overlap, reception history has been critiqued for focusing either too much on the reader, or too much on the text. For example, Jim West expressed concern that the focus on reading "allows scholars to talk 'around' the text without ever having to talk 'about' the text,"[14] while Timothy Beal, on the other hand, critiqued "reception history" for being too tied to the text. Beal was concerned that such attention to the text itself bracketed off critical attention to the economic aspects of scriptural production, marketing, and consumption, and to the way those processes trade in various unstable forms of social, cultural, financial, and sacred capital.[15]

Beal also was concerned that "reception" implies that there was an "original," but in biblical studies, in particular, the single original text is elusive at best, and probably never existed.[16] Beal would rather see a focus on cultural history that could "shift from hermeneutical reception to cultural production."[17] The second shift Beal would like to see is "from interpreting scripture via culture to interpreting culture, especially religious culture, via scripture. As such it presumes that the proper academic context for biblical studies is religious studies, and more generally, the academic humanities."[18] In other words, scripture could be seen as a facet of cultural studies, instead of cultural study being used as a tool in the service of exegesis.[19]

Bears, Nomads, and Tigers

Brennan Breed agreed with Beal that texts are generated and regenerated in particular cultural contexts. He also affirmed Beal's awareness of how problematic it is to focus on a text as abstracted from its cultural embedding, and he noted that such a move is "the danger of Gadamerian and Jaussian readings."[20] But Breed expressed concerned that Beal's call to move "beyond reception history" in cultural studies could end up focusing on a text's singular meaning in a singular culture, and thus obscure the diachronic meanings of a text. Reception history has highlighted connections between the different meanings given to a text over time. Breed asserted that "even an attempt to break from the past and reconstruct a text in a new way will never quite exorcise the spirits of past interpretations."[21] Additionally, any singular cultural (re)construction and (re) production of a text does not exhaust the "resources" of the text. To illustrate this point, Breed drew on Giles Deleuze's distinction between the "virtual" and the "actual" and offered an analogy of "virtual" potentials for what might happen if one were to encounter a sleeping bear. The bear might wake up and maul the one who has disturbed it; it might wander away disinterestedly; it might remain in slumber.[22] If any one of these occurrences is "actualized," it does not mean that the other "virtual" potentials were not also real.[23] We cannot directly perceive these latent, virtual potentials; we can only perceive the actual. But if we observe what happens when sleeping bears are encountered over time, in different contexts, we are able to indirectly intuit that there are real, virtual potentials which may be initially only abstract.[24] In the same way, Breed explained, a text has varying potentials for meaning. For example, the text about Bathsheba has the potential to be interpreted in such a way as to depict her as a seductress, as happens in the medieval period. But, that does not mean that the text does not also have the resources to be read in such a way as to interpret Bathsheba as a victim. The cultural context that produced such a reading of Bathsheba in the medieval period—its increased use of art as an interpretive medium, its focus on sexual sin and penance—is worthy of study and attention, as are other cultural and historical contexts which produced other readings of her. Breed affirmed such a both/and approach: cultural history should not attempt to exclude entirely the perspective of reception history. Whereas Beal encouraged biblical scholars to tell the story of a particular culture through its construction of biblical texts, reception history encourages scholars to tell the story of the biblical text through its diachronic interactions with particular cultures. Beal analyzed the irreducible differences between bibles, while reception history analyzes the shared process that creates, sustains, and disseminates these irreducible differences. Breed explains that neither perspective is *the* perspective, and scholars would do well to learn from both.[25]

Breed's overarching analogy suggested that texts, and their meanings, ought to be viewed as nomads. Nomads are material and embodied, with a physical origin. They may be particularly tied to a geographic region and have observable patterns of behavior; but they do not remain fixed and sedentary. They are on the move, resisting singular locations, and even resisting being too closely identified with political structures. Breed used this analogy to illustrate that the meaning of a text is not simply its original, historical meaning.[26] Though a text—like a nomad—did have a particular historical starting point, its meaning is not limited to what it meant in its original historical context. It would be utterly anachronistic to argue that the original scribes understood Bathsheba's bath to be a sign of baptism, but the early church read it as such because of their ontology of scripture.

To this point—that a text's meaning is often limited to its original historical context—Breed has offered another analogy. Texts are like tigers that keep escaping the "cages" of their original context,[27] and biblical scholars are zookeepers whose job is to capture the loose animals and return them to their contextual cages. When the animals keep escaping, it calls into question the efficacy of the cages meant to hold them.[28] Breed's use of a tiger in his analogy is suggestive of the dangerous nature of a text which can and has done harm; the hope is that a proper cage, particularly its historical context, can tame and protect. When the story of Bathsheba is read in a way that blames a victim of rape, it does harm. Protection comes from the "cage" of the historical context of kingship in the Iron Age, when the power differential between kings and subjects was so great that one could not refuse a king's command.

Nyasha Junior agreed that texts may overrun their boundaries, asserting that texts do not have agency on their own. "Texts do not swim, slither, or run, and biblical scholars are not chasing them down wearing pith helmets and waving butterfly nets. . . . Instead, texts are repurposed, corralled, and coerced into new contexts."[29] But to Junior's point (and to stretch the analogy), tigers are not like chimpanzees who are known for escaping cages;[30] if a tiger gets loose, it would likely be let out. Who does so, and why? Or, who made the cage in the first place? Who gets to reinforce a particular cage? Junior encouraged those practicing reception history to ask "who has (re)used this text, how, and for what purpose," in order to identify more clearly the interpreters and their agendas.[31]

Consequences

Because the interpreter's agenda may not always be readily identifiable, I question the ethical implications and the effects of interpretation. For example, when Leonard Cohen wrote in his song "Hallelujah" that David saw Bathsheba "bathing on the roof," Cohen may not have had the agenda of implicating Bathsheba as an exhibitionist or seductress; but, his interpretation may have had that effect. Leong Seow urged interpreters to pay attention to such effects when he defined his term "history of consequences." Seow explained that he was referring to consequences both in the sense of what comes after (including any interpretation of the text) and, in the sense of application, the work's use, influence, and impact. The term "consequences" also carries with it the connotation of effects, as in the ethical implications of certain readings or use of the text.[32]

If we pay attention to the ethical consequences or implications of a given interpretation, we can avoid three common critiques of reception history. First, seeking to understand both a text and its meaning as "produced" instead of merely as "received" means that reception history may no longer seem passive. Production need not be planned by the interpreter; production of this sort is less like a carpenter producing a cabinet, and more akin to a car accident producing smoke. Second, reception history is often criticized for being practiced uncritically. Rachel Nicholls noted that many biblical reception histories resemble "scrapbooks of effects" that simply display what the author finds interesting, meaningful, or memorable.[33] When reception history pays attention to the consequences of interpretations, it can avoid being highly sentimentalized.[34] Third, as Davis Hankins noted, using the term "consequences" "underscores a dual agency. The text is not simply received; it has consequences for those who use it."[35] As Jauss's reception theory indicated, the primary point of reference is not simply the text itself, but also includes the reader.[36]

"Consequences" also benefit from being grounded in Deleuze's distinction between the virtual and the actual. A patristic interpretation of the Old Testament has the virtual potential to be anti-Judaic, but actually, it might not be. When there was a supersessionist, anti-Judaic reading of 2 Sam in the Patristic period, this did not exhaust the potential virtual meaning of the text. But those readings did have negative consequences for Jews living at the time that reading was produced.

Ultimately, Breed urged those practicing reception history to move away from questions like, "What are the essential features of the text?" and instead ask, "What can this text do?"[37] Following Junior, I would clarify the question as, "What can an interpreter do with a text?" Interpreters can do many things with the story of Bathsheba. When a text is on the loose from a singular context, there are more possibilities for meaning. In the zoological world, cages are helpful and even necessary; but, when something is caged, it can become less alive, less free. I used to be quite exasperated by interpretations that placed Bathsheba on a roof. I was the biblical scholar-cum-zookeeper, trying with every class I taught to return the interpretation to the text of 2 Sam 11:2, which clarifies that it was *David* on the roof, not her. The songs about Bathsheba, such as Cohen's "Hallelujah," or Sting's "Mad About You," have rewritten the text into poetic lyrics, adding melody and percussion that have allowed the text to do things it would not have done if it had remained locked in its historical-critical or textual-linguistic cage.

Thus, the chapters to follow look at Bathsheba's reception history, including the "history of consequences" of how she has been interpreted. Each chapter focuses on how Bathsheba has been interpreted during a discrete historical period, with an eye toward how the different meaning potentials in this text become evident over time. Though the different historical eras use distinct hermeneutical methods, they also overlap and inherit from one another. This structure provides a diachronic sense of how Bathsheba has been interpreted, but not only; I also highlight points of connection through the different eras.[38] Additionally, I hope to beware of "chronocentrism," the idea that my own time is the golden age of interpretation, and therefore to recognize and even to appreciate the hermeneutical methods of the different historical eras. Such an appreciation of other hermeneutic methods must not preclude critical evaluation of their consequences. Eric Repphun et al have explained, "It is not just that the past shapes the present: the present also shapes the past, or at least what we can understand about the past . . . There is, then, an inescapable ideological-critical dimension to reception history."[39]

General Trends and Themes over Time

General trends are visible through the years. First, David has always been the focus, but the different views of David have led to different and corresponding views of Bathsheba: when David is a type of Christ, for example, Bathsheba is the bride of Christ, the church. When David is a type of sinful humanity, Bathsheba is the object with which David sinned. Marti Steussy observed that David can be read either cynically or optimistically,[40] and Bathsheba is correspondingly cast as either a victim or a seductress. Second, different genres also allow for different interpretations of Bathsheba. When she is written about in commentaries or homilies, different aspects of her are highlighted; when she is the main subject of a novel, her inner life is expanded. In paintings and films, other aspects of her character come to light.[41] Third, in early interpretations there is often a sort of benign neglect of Bathsheba, where she is simply not mentioned. The more negative interpretations of her as a seductress begin in the medieval period, and continue into the contemporary world. During the enlightenment, the benign neglect shifts to a both/and approach, where interpreters maintain that David is in the wrong, but also do not remove blame from Bathsheba for their sexual liaison.

Because I take seriously Junior's admonition to pay attention to who is re-purposing texts, I am aware that this work is less representative than I would like it to be. For example, the book does not include information about Bath-sheba's reception in Islam.[42] Neither is this study very globally diverse. It is mostly western and white, reflecting my own cultural position, though I do include in the final chapter some descriptions of how Bathsheba is interpreted in online newspapers from Nigeria, Jamaica, and India. Bathsheba's story has been explored by German and French authors. Andreas Kunz examined David's vari-ous wives and wrote several sections about Bathsheba. He noted the connection between David's comfort of Bathsheba in 2 Sam 12:24 and Solomon's ascension in 1 Kgs 1:30, going so far as to claim that Solomon's birth ends Bathsheba's misery.[43] Additionally, Kunz has suggested similarities between Bathsheba and Abishag, in particular that neither of them are official wives of David when they first appear in the narrative.[44] Maria Häusl compares Bathsheba and Abishag in her book about the roles of the two women in the succession narrative of 1 Kgs 1–2.[45] Another German study on Bathsheba is Elisabeth Kunoth-Liefels's *Über die Darstellungen der «Bathsheba im Bade,"* which focuses on the artistic representations of Bathsheba bathing, but which also includes detailed com-ments on implications of Bathsheba's "Darstellung," that is, how she has been depicted, presented, and even characterized in art.[46] Studies of Bathsheba in French include Maria Besançon's look at how Bathsheba appears in the different accounts of Jesus's genealogy in Matthew and Luke.[47] In 2004, Daniel Bodi and Masha Itzhaki edited an interdisciplinary study, *L'Historie de David et Bethsabée.* Topics included how David and Bathsheba appear in modern Yiddish literature, Bathsheba's nakedness in European paintings, and a historical-critical approach to David and Bathsheba and "la maison de David"[48] [David's house].

These studies notwithstanding, Bathsheba is rarely the focus of scholarly discussion. Still, she survives throughout the various historical eras, and with all these varying ways to fill in the gaps concerning her. Certainly, the gaps make Bathsheba's story narratologically interesting. We can see meaning potentials over time in the texts where she appears, which makes her story a good test-case for reception history. Additionally, this story and its reception have signifi-cant ethical implications, inviting us to consider the consequences for how a text is received, and how its characters are read.

"Here's why I like Bathsheba," I told my student. "She reminds me not to make assumptions about people when I know only part of their story." If I saw that student today, I would add that Bathsheba's character also serves as a reminder that the future can be different from the present. She reminds me to keep asking, "What happens next?" This and the reasons mentioned above make the reception history of this minor, enigmatic biblical character something worthy of study and reflection.

1

Bathsheba in the Bible
Identifying Gaps

B ecause the story of Bathsheba in the Hebrew Masoretic Text (hereafter MT) is so heavily gapped, the gaps within the story must also be examined.[1] Most of the breaks involve what motivates a character to act a certain way, but there are also gaps regarding what happens.

Is David in the Wrong Place at the Wrong Time?

The first gap occurs in the very first verse in 2 Sam 11, and though it has to do with David, it does affect Bathsheba. Why does David stay in Jerusalem? It is the spring, when the kings go to war, and everyone (Joab, and his servants, and all Israel) is off fighting the Ammonites, but David—possibly alone—remains in Jerusalem. This could be wise military strategy. Moshe Garsiel pointed out that while a king's presence on the battlefield would have raised morale, it also would have given the enemy an opportunity to win the battle outright by killing him (see 1 Kgs 22:31–36).[2] In 2 Sam 10, the chapter preceeding, David sent out Joab and the whole army against the Ammonites and Arameans (2 Sam 10:7), and only joined the battle after he had been informed that the Arameans had come to Helam (2 Sam 10:17). In 2 Sam 18:2–4 when David's army is about to face the army of Absalom, David's men tell him not to come and fight with them.

David's staying could also point to some lack in his leadership. If it is true that *kings*[3] go to war, it is striking that Israel's king remains back, especially because one of the reasons the Israelites wanted a king was to lead their battles (1 Sam 8:20). In the fourteenth century preacher's handbook, *Fasciculus Morum,* the author wrote, "For just as stagnant water rots of itself, so does idleness generate sin, and particularly lust. As a type of this, King David did not fall into adultery as long as he was engaged in warfare, but when he gave himself to idleness at home, he slept with Bathsheba and afterwards committed murder."[4] In this interpretation, David would have been better off at war.

Gaps regarding David's "timing" continue in 2 Sam 11:2, when David gets up "late in the day," and walks around the roof of his house. Is David sleeping in because of indolence or depression, or is this merely a custom on hot days?[5]

Although a stroll on a roof can be benign (see Dan 4:26), Randall Bailey noted that the three other occurrences of the hithpael (a particular Hebrew verbal pattern) of הלך in Samuel are in contexts in which David has problems with the local inhabitants of Judah (1 Sam 23:13, 25:15, 30:31). Bailey therefore suggested that David's "walking around" in 2 Sam 11:2 should signal that questionable conduct is about to occur.[6] Novelists in the twentieth and twenty-first centuries fill these gaps by suggesting that David is not at battle and sleeping during the day because he is suffering from grief or depression; and therefore, he is in a place of emotional vulnerability when he sees Bathsheba.[7]

Does Bathsheba Know David Can See Her Bathing?
How Much of Her Can He See? What Type of a Bath Is This?

The gaps in this story are related: if the people in Jerusalem expected their king to be away at war, they might suppose that he would not be on his roof during that time. Whether or not Bathsheba knows that David can see her may be one of the most central gaps regarding her characterization, and the answer one gives will have a domino effect for understanding her. The text gives no indication, and other studies, including intertextual comparisons, are less than definitive. Susanna, in the deuterocanonical text of Daniel, is taking a bath in a place she thinks is private when the evil elders spy on her, but Susanna could be similar to Bathsheba, or different. Archeological studies that attempt to identify the proximity of Bathsheba's house to David's are tentative at best, and sociological studies of bathing practices of the time are quite limited. Understood one way, Bathsheba is an exhibitionist, displaying her nakedness publicly where she could be seen. Understood another way, David is a Peeping Tom, spying on a woman who is unaware that she is being watched.

The gap regarding Bathsheba's awareness that she is seen is related to the one about how much David can see. Does he have a full view of her, or only glimpses? Is she taking a sponge bath or is she fully immersed? Is she completely naked? The visual interpretations of Bathsheba over time—in art, but also in film—fill in these gaps quite differently. In *The Bible* television miniseries, David peers through a lattice fence, only able to see hints of Bathsheba. In the 1951 movie *David and Bathsheba,* Susan Hayward as Bathsheba bathes behind a screen, while in the 1985 film *King David,* David can see Bathsheba's naked body. J. Cheryl Exum has paid close attention to Bathsheba's portrayal in these various media, both in article form and in a chapter in a book which includes other biblical women in addition to Bathsheba.[8] Exum asserted that even if David cannot see much of Bathsheba, the bathing scene is shot in film and painted in such a way that the viewers become voyeurs of the naked woman. Exum drew on the work by film theorist Laura Mulvey, who considered the idea of "scopophilia," or "pleasure in looking," in films from the 1950s. Mulvey argued that two distinct modes of the male gaze—the voyeuristic and the fetishistic—view the female body as an object of sexuality and desire meant to stir up visual pleasure.[9]

Exum explained that she intended to "problematize our position as consumers of images, to draw attention to its gendered nature, and to make it difficult to view unreflectively both texts and images that invite our collusion in voyeurism."[10] In certain medieval Books of Hours, Bathsheba is illustrated bathing naked in the open, either in a courtyard or a fountain. Other medieval works of art, however, have her clothed and only washing her feet. Hans Memling's 1485 painting "Bathsheba at her Bath" depicts Bathsheba topless and stepping out of the bath (a strategically placed towel covers her pubic area), but David could see virtually nothing of her: he is too far away in the far right corner of the image, and the towel is between them.

Because the text does not specify the type of Bathsheba's bath, interpreters fill this gap, also. If Bathsheba is taking a sponge bath or a footbath, it seems obvious that that would have less sexual innuendoes than if she is bathing naked or cleaning her genitals.[11] There is a clause in 2 Sam 11:4 which reads, "and she was sanctifying herself from her impurity" which interpreters commonly understand to refer back to Bathsheba's bath in 2 Sam 11:2 as a ritual bath for purification after menstruation.[12] However, Lev 15, which does deal with purification from bodily discharge, says nothing about a bath or any other cleansing ritual; instead, after a woman waits for seven days, she is automatically clean (Lev 15:28). It is in later rabbinic law that bathing is prescribed for purification after menstruation, and Tikvah Frymer-Kensky suggested that it is anachronistic to interpret Bathsheba's bath in 2 Sam 11:2 as such purification. She asserted that the bath discussed in 2 Sam 11:4 is a second bath in which Bathsheba is "washing off the impurity that comes from all sexual relations, even licit ones . . . the phrase does not refer back to the bath that she was taking when she was first introduced, but to postcoital purification."[13] Helen Leneman observed that the version of 2 Sam 11 found at Qumran leaves out the phrase "from her impurity" in verse 4. Leneman suggested that the phrase was added by a later editor, reflecting changing attitudes toward menstruation and impurity.[14]

What Prior Interaction, If Any, Have David and Bathsheba Had?

In 2 Sam 11:3, when David asks about Bathsheba, an anonymous source identifies her by her name, "Bathsheba"; her patronym, "the daughter of Eliam"; and her marital status, "wife of Uriah the Hittite." Though this identification is threefold, it is still somewhat tentative, placed in a question, "Isn't this Bathsheba . . . ?" Marti Steussy suggested that David is the one who identifies Bathsheba in such a way. She observed that the Hebrew has three consecutive verbs followed by a rhetorical question without any indication of a change in subject, and therefore translates 2 Sam 11:3 as "David sent . . . and inquired . . . and said . . . 'Isn't this Bathsheba?'"[15] If David is not the one who asks the question, the gap about the identity of the person who identifies Bathsheba remains open throughout most of interpretive history; only in the genre of novels in the contemporary world is David's source named. This might be what Meir Sternberg referred to not as a "gap," but a "blank," a detail that is intentionally omitted and need not be filled in for the story still to signify.[16] In other words, it does not matter so much who tells David about Bathsheba's identity as it matters that before he takes her, he knows who she is: married to one of his elite fighting men, and the daughter of another (2 Sam 23). In many novels in the contemporary world, David and Bathsheba do interact with each other prior to him seeing her bathe.[17]

What Is the Nature of Their Sexual Interaction: Forced, Or Consensual?

2 Sam 11:4, in particular, could be a poster child for Auerbach's phrase "fraught with background,"[18] as it leaves out most of the details that would explain what is happening. It is rich in plot, narrating four events in quick succession (he sent messengers to get her, she came to him, he lay with her, and she returned to her house), but without any indication of feelings or motives.[19] A lot of interpretive weight is placed on the phrase in 2 Sam 11:4, "and she came to him." The phrase's relatively small narrative size—only three Hebrew words—does not match the enormity of the implication that Bathsheba is either complicit or compliant in the act of adultery.

Moreover, was it adultery, or rape?[20] Bathsheba's action, coming to David, can be explained with reference to David's power as king, for it is unlikely that she could refuse to come when summoned. Whether Bathsheba was raped or committed adultery is a debate that illustrates Breed's analogy of texts as no-mads. By considering the verbs used in comparative narratives about rape in the MT, it appears that David's sin was not rape. There is no single Hebrew word that precisely corresponds to contemporary understandings of rape,[21] but in the three narratives about rape (of Dinah in Gen 34, the Levite's concubine in Judg 19, and Tamar in 2 Sam 13), the piel (another Hebrew verbal pattern) of ענה is present. That word does not occur in 2 Sam 11; it only says that David "lies with" (שכב) Bathsheba after he takes (לקח) her.[22] Mark Gray is an interpreter who has pointed out the differences in the language used in 2 Sam 11–12 and 2 Sam 13, and he has concluded that the sexual encounters are not the same.[23]

However, as Breed asserted, the meaning of this text does not remain in that linguistic cage; it is a hermeneutical nomad. Others explain that Amnon treats Tamar as he does because David treated Bathsheba similarly.[24] Even the legal material in the Hebrew Bible does not definitively answer the question of rape or adultery. The rape laws in Deut 22:23–27 connect the legal decision about rape with the location where the violation occurred: if in the city, the woman is presumed to have consented for she did not cry for help. If it took place in the country, she presumably resisted.[25] Therefore, because David "lay with" Bathsheba in Jerusalem, the ancient legal standpoint would indicate that it was not rape. However, both Deut 22:22 and Lev 20:10 clarify that both parties who commit adultery—the adulterer and adulteress—are to be put to death. Steussy wrote, "The fact that no one mentions a death penalty for Bathsheba . . . suggests that she was not considered at fault."[26] The variety of interpretations about the sexual act demonstrates the meaning potentials of the clause, "and he lay with her," in 2 Sam 11:4 (later discussed).

In the Greek Septuagint (hereafter LXX), 2 Sam 11:4 says, "και εισηλθεν προς αυτην" (and *he* went in to her), which differs from MT (and the manuscript of Samuel found in Qumran, 4QSam^a), "and she came to him." This translation—an early reception of the story—makes David into the one who takes all initiative in the verse; he sent for her, he came to her, he lay with her. Bathsheba is not the subject of the verb "to come," she is merely the object of David's actions. In the LXX, Bathsheba does nothing until she returns to her house. By making the change, these early Greek interpreters highlight that she was victimized, especially in contrast with the MT, which is more open to different possibilities regarding Bathsheba's motivations.

David's Punishment in 2 Sam 12

The gap about the nature of David and Bathsheba's sexual relationship is not necessarily closed in 2 Sam 12 when David's punishment is discussed. In 2 Sam 12:5–6, David passes a sentence on "the man"—who is, of course, David himself (2 Sam 12:7)—that he is "a son of death" and that he must make fourfold compensation for the ewe lamb. The first phrase is often interpreted as a death sentence; that the man deserves death, as would be the punishment for adultery or murder. But fourfold restitution is what gets mandated in the Book of the Covenant (Exod 21:37; ET 22:1) for the theft of a sheep.[27] Where the MT has ארבעתים "fourfold," the LXX has επταπλασιονα "sevenfold," a number Roland de Vaux suggested ought not to be taken literally, but which reflects perfect restitution.[28] Nathan's parable and David's sentence raise the question: what has David done? Did he commit murder, adultery, rape, theft, or a combination of all of the above?[29] Nathan mentioned two specific acts when he describes what David did: killing Uriah, and taking Uriah's wife as his own wife (2 Sam 12:9–10). That language of "taking" seems to refer to theft, but could also refer to adultery.[30] Even YHWH's punishments—that the sword will remain in David's house, that his wives will be taken by another, and that the child born to Bathsheba and him will die—do not close the gap about what happened.[31] However, David does respond by acknowledging his sin (2 Sam 12:13). David Gunn comments, "the stunning simplicity of David's response to Nathan . . . functions powerfully to reinstate him in the reader's estimation."[32] Bathsheba, in contrast, has no words. Is that because she did not sin and only David did? Her silence and David's confession demonstrate that one potential for meaning is that the responsibility is entirely his, which would again point to rape, not adultery. But she is silent, and such an argument is correspondingly made from silence. In the enlightenment, many interpreters affirm that David is wrong, but they do not declare that Bathsheba is victimized, or that she is innocent: they argue that she also has done something wrong.[33]

Why Does Bathsheba Tell David She Is Pregnant?

Bathsheba's announcement of her pregnancy can be explained in different ways. Among other things, it could be the triumphant announcement of a woman who has succeeded in entrapping a man as a "baby daddy," or she might have sent David the message because she expects he will solve "the problem" for her. Enlightenment scholars ascribe to Bathsheba the emotion of fear, as Joseph Benson explained, "She was afraid of infamy, and perhaps of the severity of her husband, who might cause her to be stoned."[34] Centuries earlier, Josephus described the events in 2 Sam 11:5 as follows, "she became pregnant and sent to the king, asking him to contrive some way of concealing her sin, for according to the laws of the fathers she was deserving of death as an adulteress."[35] Contemporary novels often have Bathsheba planning with David to make it appear that Uriah is the father of her child. But the biblical text leaves the gap open as to whether Bathsheba wanted to cover up the paternity of her child. Helen Leneman observed how this verse continues to hold open the gap about David and Bathsheba's feelings for each other: "The question of whether David ever loves Bathsheba (or vice versa) is left unanswered. The minute she announces her pregnancy, his interest is in the paternity of the child, conceding her to Uriah from the start, which does not suggest great love."[36] Chloe Sun observed that Bathsheba did not speak directly to David, but instead sent someone else to do so, suggesting that she might have been afraid to confront David.[37] Another possible interpretation holds that Bathsheba is expressing some power when she sends this message to David.[38]

What Sort of Relationship Did Uriah and Bathsheba Have?
Does Uriah Know What Happened Between David and Bathsheba?

The question about the relationship between Uriah and Bathsheba is a thoroughly contemporary one, but there was interest in the "love" between David and Bathsheba in eras as early as the patristic, with John Chrysostom's assertion that Solomon's parents were in love.[39] However, the text does not specify why Uriah stays at the entrance of the palace instead of doing what David commands, "Go down to your house and wash your feet" (2 Sam 11:8–9).[40] Interpreters through the years have demonstrated that this gap has a number of possibilities. Uriah could be a dedicated soldier, unwilling to enjoy the luxuries of his home and his wife while the ark and the rest of the soldiers are camping in open fields during battle (2 Sam 11:11). But, it could also be that he knows about Bathsheba's pregnancy, and he refuses to participate in David's attempt at a cover-up. Perhaps some of the servants with whom Uriah stayed (2 Sam 11:9) knew what happened in the palace and told him about it. Another possibility that would explain Uriah's motives is that he did not care for Bathsheba; in certain contemporary movies, he is portrayed as loveless and even abusive to her.[41]

The question of what Uriah knows remains a gap in 2 Sam 11:14–17, when David writes a letter to Joab that essentially contains a death warrant for Uriah, and Uriah is the one who brings that letter to Joab. In the 2012 *Bible* miniseries, David seals the letter in a dramatic scene, but no seal is mentioned in the text. Uriah could be so trusting of David, or so obedient to the chain of command, that he would not read a letter written by David. Perhaps Uriah did read the letter and knew that he would die because the king wanted his wife, but still went to his death.

Does Joab Know Why David Commands Uriah's Death?

Joab and Bathsheba do not have direct interaction in the MT, but Joab's reference to Abimelech in his message to David (2 Sam 11:21) could suggest that Joab knows—and disapproves—of Bathsheba's role in this imbroglio. Abimelech dies after a woman threw a millstone on him from the wall (Judg 9:50–55), and though Bathsheba does not throw a millstone on either Uriah or David, Sternberg explained, "Both kings, David and Abimelech, fall because of a woman. (So does Uriah, in still another sense.) What is more, the notorious incident of Abimelech's death bears—for both Joab and the reader—connotations of royalty disgraced at the hand of a woman."[42]

The "disgrace" is noted by Abimelech when, after his skull is cracked, he calls to his armor bearer, "Draw your sword and kill me, lest they say of me, 'A woman killed him!'" (Judg 9:54). In a manner similar to Sternberg, Jan Fokkelman explained that the comparison between Abimelech's death and what happened at the Ammonite front rests on six motifs, "death-woman-wall-battle-shame-folly," and that its inclusion in the narrative has to do with an unconscious fear of the woman.[43] Mieke Bal, however, warns against making the connection between Bathsheba and the woman in Judges 9 (and 2 Sam 11:21) too simplistic.[44]

The manner in and the level to which Joab supports David is debatable. Most often, Joab directly follows David's orders, as when Joab goes to battle (2 Sam. 10:7, 11:1), and when he sends Uriah back to Jerusalem (2 Sam. 11:6). But despite Adam Clarke's description of Joab as "the wicked executor of the base commands of his fallen master,"[45] Joab only partly obeys David's instructions to put Uriah at the front and then withdraw from him: Uriah is killed, but so are other Israelite soldiers (2 Sam. 11:17).[46] It could be that killing Uriah in such a manner would be too obvious or too destructive of the morale of the other soldiers, but accompanied by Joab's reference to Abimelech, Joab's refusal to do what he was commanded hints at something more. Joab is not the only one to communicate in code; David responds to Joab using other loaded phrases, including, "Do not let this thing be evil in your eyes" (2 Sam 11:25), which resonates with Judg 21:15[47] and "the sword devouring" (תֹאכַל הַחֶרֶב) phrase that Abner said to Joab after Abner had murdered Joab's brother in 2 Sam 2:26. David and Joab have a complex relationship that extends beyond the narrative where Bathsheba appears,[48] but Joab's role in the Ammonite war—the context in which David meets Bathsheba—is significant.[49]

How Does Bathsheba Feel: About Uriah's Death, About Getting Married to David, About the Death of Her First Child?

It might seem strange to include these questions when the first and third get narrated in the text: Bathsheba mourns over Uriah for a period of time (2 Sam 11:26–27) and needs comfort when the child dies (2 Sam 12:24). The reception of this text throughout history, however, demonstrates that even when Bathsheba's feelings are narrated, readers understand them in different ways. Some wonder how genuine is Bathsheba's grief over Uriah, such as John Calvin, who described Bathsheba's tears as merely for show.[50] In a similar vein, an Enlightenment era commentary explains, "What vile mockery! Only God knows how often the outward 'mourning' over the departed is but a hypocritical veil to cover satisfaction of heart for being rid of their presence."[51] By contrast, several contemporary novels assume that Bathsheba is honestly grieved at Uriah's death.[52] As before, the filling in of previous gaps has a domino effect: if a reader understands Bathsheba's marriage with Uriah to be a good one, that same reader will likely interpret Bathsheba's grief as genuine. Though 2 Sam 11:26 simply has one verb to describe Bathsheba's mourning,[53] the verse repeatedly highlights the marriage relationship between Uriah and Bathsheba, as it says, "And the *wife* of Uriah heard that her *husband* was dead, she mourned for her *husband*" (emphasis added).[54]

There is less debate over Bathsheba's feelings when her child dies, likely because any death of a child is simply tragic, while the death of a spouse could be more complicated. Cheryl Kirk-Duggan observed that, "the narrator silences her grief by describing only David's pain at the loss of their first child,"[55] but Bathsheba's grief gets acknowledged—if not directly narrated—when David comforts Bathsheba in the description in 2 Sam 12:24.[56] But certainly, Kirk-Duggan is correct to have noted that David is the focus, with several verses devoted to describing his response to the child's sickness and subsequent death.[57] If Bathsheba's grief can be easily assumed, it is not explicitly stated.

Bathsheba's feelings about her marriage are nowhere addressed in the text, though there is a domino effect from how previous gaps are filled. If an interpreter understands Bathsheba as wanting to be seen by David, then that interpreter is likely to also understand that Bathsheba is happy to be his wife. In *The Women's Bible Commentary* from 1895, suffragist Elizabeth Cady Stanton did not say anything about Bathsheba's feelings for David, but more practically observed that "to be transferred from the cottage of a poor soldier to the palace of a king was a sufficient compensation for the loss of the love of a true and faithful man."[58]

What Is Bathsheba's Relationship Like with Nathan?

Nathan confronts David in 2 Sam 12, without any mention of whether Nathan interacts directly with Bathsheba. In 1 Kgs 1, Bathsheba and Nathan dialogue. While it could be that their first personal interaction is in 1 Kgs when it is explicitly narrated, it is likely that they have some sort of relationship before that point, perhaps from the time when Nathan gives Solomon his second name; or, perhaps from before that time. In the Copenhagen Psalter's illuminated initial M of Psalm 50 as well as in the Crusader Bible held at the Morgan Museum, Bathsheba is illustrated as being with David when Nathan comes to confront him. In Francine Rivers's *Unspoken*, Nathan is one of the few people whom Bathsheba trusts,[59] but in Madeleine L'Engle's *Certain Women,* she is frightened by him.[60] Again, the question about their relationship will be more pressing in 1 Kgs 1 when Nathan tells Bathsheba what to say to David regarding her son Solomon's succession. Is she Nathan's pawn or co-conspirator? Is she in charge?

What Motivates Bathsheba's Grandfather Ahithophel to Support Absalom?

Bathsheba fades from the story before the end of 2 Sam 12; the final thing she does in that chapter is to bear a son and name him Solomon (2 Sam 12:24). Bathsheba, however, lingers in the story commonly referred to as "the Succession Narrative"[61] before she reappears in 1 Kgs 1. It is easy to read those tragic chapters about David's children as the enactment of the punishment Nathan spoke of in 2 Sam 12, for the sword is very present in David's house. In particular, Absalom having sex with David's concubines on the roof before the eyes of all Israel (2 Sam 16:22) is a direct fulfillment of the prophet's words in 2 Sam 12:12.[62]

Absalom was advised to act as he did by Bathsheba's grandfather, Ahithophel (2 Sam 16:21–23), whose own motivation is a gap. Some contemporary commentators fill this gap by suggesting that Ahithophel was taking revenge on David for his mistreatment of Ahithophel's granddaughter. For example, Stephen McKenzie wrote, "Ahithophel may have acted against David as revenge for Uriah's death and the humiliation of Bathsheba."[63] In contrast, A. F. Kirkpatrick, who filled in the gaps regarding Ahithophel by describing him as "ambitious and unscrupulous," and by explaining that Ahithophel "would be more likely to regard the elevation of his granddaughter to the position of the king's favorite as an honour, than to feel aggrieved at the circumstances by which it was effected."[64] Different recent novels portray Bathsheba's relationship with Ahithophel in varying ways.[65]

Solomon's Succession

The main drama in 1 Kgs 1–2 is about David's successor, who is not David's eldest living son, Adonijah, but rather is Bathsheba's son Solomon.[66] Adonijah assumes the throne in 1 Kgs 1:5–10, but the chapter ends with Solomon anointed as king after the intervention of Nathan and Bathsheba. The gaps in this part of the story have to do with each character's motivation and knowledge.

Did David Promise Bathsheba That Solomon Would Succeed to the Throne? Is David Being Manipulated? Is Bathsheba Being Manipulated?

The central question of this section is posed in the text when Nathan tells Bathsheba to say to David, "Did you not, my lord the king, swear to your maidservant saying, 'Solomon your son will be king after me, and *he* will sit on my throne?'" (1 Kgs 1:13). The question, "did not?"[67] can be answered with a "yes" or a "no" by David, or by subsequent readers of the text as they actualize the varying potentials of meaning. It could be that David did promise Bathsheba that Solomon would be king. If so, Nathan must have known of it: either he was present when David made that promise to Bathsheba, or he was told about it.[68] Perhaps David—in his old age—has forgotten, and needs a reminder.

But the question also has the potential to be answered negatively; David did not promise Bathsheba that Solomon would be king. If that is the case, perhaps Nathan invented it because of his ties with Solomon. Perhaps Bathsheba invented it because she wanted her son to be the one to be king. Or, perhaps Solomon wisely invented it so there would be divine sanction for his rule. Because the text of Samuel-Kings never records such a promise many say that it never occurred.[69] However, in 1 Chronicles, David gives Solomon building plans for the temple, and tells him that he will be king (1 Chron 22:7–16); and, David makes this promise known to the assembly of Israel in 1 Chron 28. Readers who approach the biblical text more atomistically will likely not turn to Chronicles to explain Samuel-Kings. The rabbis, however, viewed disparate verses as connected, and therefore read the texts together to mean that David did make such a promise that Solomon would be king.

Related to the question of whether David made a promise are questions about how much each character knows and does not know, especially David and Bathsheba. How guileless, or manipulative, is each character? What is the nature of the relationship between David, Bathsheba and Nathan?[70] David's physical state at the beginning of 1 Kgs is clearly not good; he is so old and infirm that Abishag the Shunammite is brought to David to keep him warm. Abishag is described as "young and beautiful," but the text explains that David "did not know her" (1 Kgs 1:4). What is not explained is why: Does David choose to refrain from sexual relations with a beautiful young girl put under his covers to help keep him warm? Or, is he impotent, and unable to "know" her? In Talmud tractate *b. Sanh.* 22a, Rab Judah affirms David's continued virility as evidenced by the fact that after he tells Abishag that she is forbidden to him, David has sex with Bathsheba thirteen times in a row.

If David's physical and sexual state is received in different ways, so, too is his mental state. The narrator says that David did not "know" Abishag (1 Kgs 1:4), and then Nathan says that David did not "know" that Adonijah has become king.[71] David is clearly elderly: is he also senile, unaware and able to be manipulated? Such a characterization of him is a potential in the text, but hard to sustain in its extreme, especially because before he dies, David gives brutal and astute advice to Solomon about how to set things in order (1 Kgs 2:1–9). Therefore, another potential interpretation of David is that he was aware of Adonijah's actions, but rather than directly opposing him, David allowed or even asked others to put Solomon on the throne instead.

There are also various potentials as to why Nathan plays the role that he does in Solomon's appointment. Nathan could be self-interested: he took a particular interest in Solomon from his birth (2 Sam 12:25), and he was snubbed by Adonijah (1 Kgs 1:7–8). Nathan's function in helping Solomon take the throne could also be an extension of his prophetic role, something commanded by YHWH. In 2 Sam 12 when Nathan confronted David, he did so directly. In 1 Kgs 1, however, Nathan only talks with David after he first speaks with Bathsheba, and after Bathsheba tells David about Adonijah's claim to the throne. While Nathan could have colluded with many people—Zadok, Benaiah, Shimei, Rei, or "the fighting men" mentioned in 1 Kgs 1:8—he chooses to go to Bathsheba. Does Nathan need Bathsheba's help to influence David, or is he using and directing her? As Seow put it, "Is Bathsheba merely a nice old woman who is easily manipulated? Or is she coldly calculating and shrewder than she seems at first blush?"[72] The different potentials of meaning are actualized by different inter-preters. Nehama Aschkenasy wrote, "Although Natan and the uninitiated reader may think that the prophet is manipulating her, perhaps the opposite is right. By playing the helpless mother, Batsheba empowers Natan to take a bolder, more decisive action in her favor and force the issue on David."[73] In contrast, Brueggemann has maintained that Nathan has scripted the entire scenario, even giving Bathsheba the lines she is to speak to David.[74] The question Nathan asks Bathsheba in 1 Kgs 1:11, "Haven't you heard?" is part of the gap; Bathsheba could have heard already of Adonijah's plans, or, she could be ignorant to his political jockeying.[75]

Why Does Bathsheba Wish David Eternal Life?

After David vows to put Solomon on the throne Bathsheba says, "May my Lord the king David live forever" (1 Kgs 1:31), and those words can be read in varying ways. Before speaking, Bathsheba bows in homage to David; Seow suggested that her statement is "surely not an expression of hope for David's physical immortality, but a wish that David would live on through his lineage upon the throne, as promised by the deity in Nathan's oracle (2 Sam 7:12–16)."[76] Bruegge-mann, however, has maintained that her wish "is less than earnest."[77] In Joseph Heller's novel *God Knows,* Bathsheba no longer cares about David and is wait-ing for him to die, but in Jill Eileen Smith's novel—that casts their relationship as a romance—Bathsheba does not want to lose the husband who has become precious to her.[78]

Why Does Adonijah Ask Bathsheba to Ask Solomon to
Give Him Abishag as a Wife? Why Does She Agree to Do So?

The question about Adonijah's motivation can be read as having two levels: first, why does he ask this; what is he after? And second, why does he ask *Bathsheba?* Adonijah asks for Abishag to be his wife after he says that the kingdom was his, but that it was given to Solomon because of God's plan (1 Kgs 2:15–17). Taken at face value, it seems that Abishag is a sort of consolation prize for his loss; En-lightenment interpreter James Montgomery referred to this as Adonijah's "love-affair."[79] Yet, taking women from previous rulers was a way to claim authority over another's throne, as happened with Abner in 2 Sam 3:7 and Absalom in 2 Sam 16:21–22. Certainly, this is how Solomon understands Adonijah's request; he sees it as tantamount to a request for the throne (1 Kgs 2:22) and therefore he has Adonijah put to death.

Adonijah answers why he approaches Bathsheba to make the request when he expresses his confidence that Solomon will not refuse the request if it comes from her (1 Kgs 2:17), something Solomon confirms in 1 Kgs 2:20. Indeed,

Solomon's response to his mother—arising to meet her, bowing to her, setting a throne for her at a position of honor on his right—signifies Bathsheba's status and power.[80] Perhaps Adonijah also thinks that Bathsheba is more easily persuaded than her son; or, perhaps Adonijah assumes that Bathsheba will not hear his request in the same way that Solomon does, as a bid for the kingdom. Her response to Adonijah is part of this gap; she says, "Good, *I* will speak to the king about you" (1 Kgs 2:18).[81] The word "good" (טוב) could mean that Adonijah's request is a good one in that it is appropriate, or fair. It could also mean that what will happen to Adonijah—his death—is a good thing for her son. Or, it could mean simply that she will relay Adonijah's position. A similar gap is present with Bathsheba's description of the request to Solomon in 1 Kgs 2:20; she explains that she has "one small request." She may be trying to minimize something that she knows is major; she may honestly believe the request is not a large one; she may also be speaking sarcastically. Several scholars acknowledge the gap: Nancy Bowen stated, "What cannot be determined is if Bathsheba is acting in good faith or with cunning deviousness."[82] Others argue more specifically for one or the other. Robert Whybray described Bathsheba as "a good-natured, rather stupid woman who was a natural prey both to more passionate and cleverer men,"[83] while George Nicol and Nehama Aschkenasy both view Bathsheba as clever, resourceful, and cunning, knowing that Adonijah's request for Abishag will give her son Solomon the warrant for deposing his half-brother and consolidating his reign.[84]

At this point in the text—when Solomon vows to kill Adonijah—Bathsheba disappears. Her son Solomon is king, and in some way she has helped him attain the throne and get rid of his enemies. There is no mention of her exiting the throne room, and there is no record of her death. Bathsheba gets brought up in the superscription to Psalm 51, but after that, she is not mentioned by name again in the text.[85] What happens to Bathsheba after 1 Kgs 2 cannot even really be described as a mystery because the text's focus on Solomon is so absolute. But she, as a character, remains mysterious, and the gaps in the story invite readers to fill in her characterization in different ways. Frank Kermode explained that regarding the filling of gaps, "we may have to content ourselves with coexistent possibilities."[86] These coexistent possibilities for Bathsheba are not necessarily present in a single reader's reception of her, but can be seen more clearly with a diachronic review of Bathsheba's reception. Her surprising afterlife begins in the Jewish midrash's imaginative descriptions of her.

2

Bathsheba Revealed in
Rabbinic Literature

"Is not my word like . . . a hammer that breaks the rock in pieces?"

Jer 23:29

As the hammer splits the rock into many splinters,
so will a scriptural verse yield many meanings.

B. Sanh 34a

The heavily gapped texts about Bathsheba are imaginatively interpreted in the Talmud and midrash by readers who are particularly interested in filling the gaps.[1] There is even a rabbinic saying that illustrates such an interest: "this verse cries out, 'interpret me!'"[2] Many of the verses in 2 Sam 11–12 and 1 Kgs 1–2 must have been crying out particularly loudly because Bathsheba's character is quite clearly filled out beyond the biblical text, particularly in reference to her role as Solomon's mother. A natural catalyst for this is the Talmud and midrash's interest in David, an interest that is quite understandable. After all, he is the king of Israel par excellence, the one by whom all subsequent kings are measured. The rabbis assess David's actions in 2 Sam 11–12 in ways that can be plotted along a continuum. On one end of the continuum, David is a sinner. Even if the rabbis—like the reformers—affirm that David's penitence is exemplary, the bottom line is that what he did was wrong. On the other end of the continuum, the rabbis exonerate David's sins, or at least justify them based on extenuating circumstances.[3]

By contrast, the rabbis never present Bathsheba as the seductress who tempted David to sin. Even in places where Bathsheba might be referenced negatively—such as in the Talmudic discussion of women's sexual desire when their husbands are away (*b. 'Erubin* 100b), or in the commentary about the bathing (such as *b. Pesahim* 51a, *b. Meg* 5a)—she is not held up as an example of one whose sexual desire for her absent husband got the best of her, nor is she named as an immodest bather.[4] This chapter will trace the ways that Bathsheba's character is received in the midrash and Talmud, noting in particular how her afterlife in these texts extends beyond 1 Kgs 2 to imagine her presence at Solomon's coronation.

How to Read the Rabbis/How the Rabbis Read

Delving into the texts of the Talmud and midrash may seem at first akin to a trip through the looking glass into a bizarre and perplexing world where, for example, paragraphs are devoted to calculating Bathsheba's age when Solomon was born. But this textual world has its own rules and logic. Once those are understood, we are better able to make sense of its imaginative, deeply intertextual hermeneutic. As mentioned above, the rabbis were particularly interested in gaps in the text, and in explaining things either problematic or unclear. Those "problems" could be at a textual level, such as a lack of vowel points, or they could be larger theological issues, such as God's actions or lack thereof. Both the Talmud and midrash are, in short, a collection of answers to those "problems."[5]

Rabbinic Assumptions: Two Sets of Four

To acknowledge that the biblical text might have "problems" requires making an assumption about the nature of the text that other interpreters might not share.[6] James Kugel and Ben Sommer both describe four other rabbinic assumptions about the nature of the biblical text, and there is some overlap in their heuristic. For Kugel the biblical text is first, fundamentally cryptic insofar that there is a hidden meaning beyond the apparent meaning; second, it is fundamentally relevant to each reader's present situation; third, it is perfect and perfectly harmonious, such that any apparent mistake will be clarified by proper interpretation; and fourth, it is divinely sanctioned, which can mean that it is of divine provenance, or divinely inspired.[7] Sommer's four characteristics provide a logical progression to explain how the rabbis interpreted. First, because scriptural language is understood to be divine, it differs from human language insofar as human language has a fairly limited number of meanings, whereas God's language is "supercharged with meaning" so that it has unlimited potentials for meaning. Kugel uses the term "omnisignificant" to describe this quality of the biblical text.[8] Sommer noted secondly that especially for the earliest rabbis, the primary unit of expression for midrash is a single verse, or at most a group of about three verses.[9] Third, all parts of scripture are related to each other. As Kugel explained, "Midrash is an exegesis of biblical verses, not of books. . . . One of the things this means is that each verse of the Bible is in principle as connected to its most distant fellow as to the one next door."[10] Contemporary biblical scholars may wonder if Bathsheba or Nathan invented David's promise that Solomon would be king, but the rabbis do not because they read 1 Kgs 1:13, 17 along with 1 Chron 22:5–9, when David himself discusses Solomon's succession. Fourth, connections are made not only between verses, but also between other rabbinic commentaries.[11] In *b. Šabb.* 56a, Rabbi Shemuel b. Nahman's comment that David did not sin is followed by another rabbi's explanation that the former was a descendant of David and had his own personal motivations to excuse David. Many scholars have noted the dialogic nature of midrash,[12] where instead of a single voice presenting a systematic, coherent interpretation, there is heteroglossia. When one rabbi's interpretation is juxtaposed with another's interpretation of the same text, this dialogue (which has been collected and codified in the Talmud and Midrash) can often contradict.[13] One reason for this is that the individual rabbis come from different historical and social contexts, which allows them to see different things and to make different kinds of arguments. And, the conversations happen over time. In some ways this relates to Breed's hope that reception history considers not just diachronic reception of texts, but pays attention to the "semantic nodes" of meaning.[14] Because Jewish interpretations are not limited to a tight historical period, the conversations can be more robust. To those seeking a single "true" interpretation, the multitude and variety of rabbinic interpretations can seem surprising if not shocking.[15] But when it is understood that this hermeneutical system allows for—and even relishes in—the myriad ways to interpret, it is not surprising that there is more than one way to explain why David had sex with Bathsheba.

This interpretive expansiveness, or excessiveness, was not done simply to proliferate dialogue: it was done to produce new understandings of how the ancient text could be situated in a new social context.[16] Karin Zetterholm characterizes Jewish tradition as in "constant tension between commitment to the Bible on the one hand, and a considerable freedom in interpreting and adapting its meaning on the other."[17] The Bible and the legal tradition that came from that text is understood as divine, as (omni)significant, as always relevant. But it is only constantly relevant if a hermeneutic generates its relevance anew. "Relevance" is not just a logical proposition, something to be intellectually assented to as the text itself remains sealed in a pristine package; the biblical text and its legal tradition continues to be relevant when it is applied in each new setting.

Even the aforementioned characteristics of rabbinic reading cannot be pressed into some totalizing schema. We ought not to be surprised at that; in a system that codified and even celebrated dialogue, there is no singular hermeneutic. This is particularly true diachronically. The rabbis who produced the Talmud and Midrash date roughly to the 2nd to 5th centuries, but the Karaites in the medieval Islamic world rejected "Talmudic literature and its interpretive methodology" and called for more attention to what we would call scientific, historical, linguistic, or literary methods of study. They understood the language of the biblical texts as "governed by conventions that rule all forms of human communication and which can be analyzed through the use of specific tools, mainly, those of grammar."[18]

Again, a wide range of interpretations of David arise out of these varying interpretive methods. Two general points on a continuum emerge: one accepts David's sin and the other downplays or denies his sin. These are not entirely mutually exclusive, and offer comment, debate, and even disagreement on one another. Yet again, with this tendency toward dialogue and difference in interpretive possibilities, it is noteworthy that there is a relatively unified position on Bathsheba.[19] Simply put, she is not blamed for seducing David. As with other chapters this one will begin with considering how David is interpreted, and will note the implications for understanding Bathsheba.

David as a Sinner

Even as many of these texts affirm that David did indeed sin with Bathsheba, some of the same texts offer explanations for those sins. For example, Redak[20] comments on Ps 51:4 that the reason David would say that his sin was against God, and God alone, was because David committed his sin in secret, and no one not even his servants—knew why he called Bathsheba, or why he brought about Uriah's death. Redak has David confessing, "Only You knew that my intentions in both cases were evil, and I do not deny my sins."[21] Clearly, according to Redak, David did not deny that he had sinned. But Redak went on to have David explain, "Although I did sin, it was because the evil inclination[22] overwhelmed me; it never entered my mind or my reins to rebel against You or Your commandments. My lust enticed me to transgress, but it was not done in a rebellious manner, for I knew that I was doing evil by transgressing your commandments and I now regret it deeply. My regret is a sign that I did not mean to rebel against You or provoke You. I only wanted to gratify my overpowering desires."[23] Such a description of David's regret, that his sinfulness was not full out rebellion against God, can help maintain a high view of David and still acknowledge that he did wrong. Thus, even in this category that affirms David's sinfulness, there are often comments which explain—and in some cases ameliorate—his sin. The "evil inclination" also appears in the sections that assert that David did not sin.

In the Talmud, David's interaction with Bathsheba gets variously described as a "stumbling block" (*b. Meg.* 14b) and a "trial." The latter comes from *b. Sanh.* 107a, a text worth quoting in its entirety.

David said to God, "Sovereign of the Universe! Why do we say [in prayer] 'The God of Abraham, the God of Isaac, and the God of Jacob,' but not the God of David?" He replied, "They were tried by me, but thou wast not." Then, replied he, "Sovereign of the Universe, examine and try me,"—as it is written, *Examine me, O Lord, and try me* [Ps 51:1]. He answered, "I will test thee, and yet grant thee a special privilege, for I did not inform them [of the nature of their trial beforehand], yet, I inform thee that I will try thee in a matter of adultery." Straightaway, *And it came to pass in an eveningtide, that David arose from his bed, etc.* R. Johanan said: He changed his night couch to a day couch, but he forgot the *halachah:* there is a small organ in man which satisfies him in his hunger but makes him hunger when satisfied. *And he walked upon the roof of the king's house: and from the roof he saw a woman washing herself; and the woman was very beautiful to look upon.* Now Bath Sheba was cleansing her hair behind a screen,[24] when Satan came to him, appearing in the shape of a bird. He shot an arrow at him, which broke the screen, thus she stood revealed, and he saw her. Immediately, *And David sent and enquired after the woman. And one said, Is not this Bath Sheba, the daughter of Eliam, the wife of Uriah the Hittite? And David sent messengers, and took her, and she came unto him, and he lay with her; for she was purified from her uncleanliness: and she returned unto her house.* Thus it is written, *Thou hast proved my heart; thou hast visited me in the night; thou hast tried me, and shalt find nothing; I am purposed that my mouth shall not transgress.* [Psalm 17:3] He said thus: 'Would that a bridle had fallen into the mouth of mine enemy [i.e. himself], that I had not spoken thus.'

On the basis that David's association with God is not added to the typical tripartite recollection of the ancestors Abraham, Isaac, and Jacob, he did not pass this trial. Though David was warned in advance, he still was unable to not commit adultery.

Some commentators have read this passage as excusing David from sin, such as when Shulamit Valler asserted that because Satan is part of the story, David has no agency.[25] Immediately following the story in *b. Sanh.* 107a, Raba the sage expounds on different verses from Psalms. He first draws on Ps 51:6 to explain that David deliberately chose not to suppress his lust in order that the people would not say that he, David, was greater than his master, God. Valler wrote, "The first homily eradicates David's sin altogether. Whatever he did he did for the glory of God, not for his own gratification."[26] Second, Raba explained Ps 38:18 as meaning that Bathsheba was "predestined for David from the six days of Creation, but that she came to him with sorrow."[27] The school of Rabbi Ishmael shares that view and adds the detail that David "enjoyed her before she was ripe." Valler read this as reducing David's sin, that "in taking her from Uriah,

David put things back into their natural order (even though much pain was involved)."[28] And in reference to Ps 35:15, Raba has David responding to those who taunt him by saying that the punishment for those who publically put their neighbor to shame is greater than the punishment for one who seduces a married woman, which Valler interpreted as saying that adultery with Bathsheba was the only sin David committed during his whole lifetime.[29]

Because the Talmud is codified dialogue, it seems in keeping with the spirit of the Talmud that its contemporary interpreters including Valler and myself would disagree about the meaning of the rabbinic statements. When Raba explained the story of David and Bathsheba with reference to the verses in Psalms, I agree that he is attempting to give some reason or excuses for David's sin. But the bottom line is that *b. Sanh.* 107a does not deny that David did sin with Bathsheba, even if David did wrong for a good reason or for some good purpose. The tractate itself continues with a conversation with David and God: "He pleaded before him, 'Sovereign of the Universe! Pardon me that sin completely [as though it had never been committed].' He replied, 'It is already ordained that thy son Solomon should say in his wisdom, Can a man take fire in his bosom, and his clothes not be burned? Can one go upon hot coals, and his feet not be burned? So he that goeth in to his neighbour's wife, whoseoever toucheth her shall not be innocent [Prov 6:27ff]. He lamented, 'Must I suffer so much?' He replied, 'Accept thy chastisement,' and he accepted it."

David is not pardoned, but punished. In fact, immediately after the above reference in *b. Sanh 107a*, Rab Judah explained in Rab's name that David's punishment included three things: he was deserted by the *Shechinah,* the Sanhedrin held aloof from him, and he was smitten with leprosy for six months. *B. Yoma* 22b also mentions that David was punished with leprosy. Such punishments go beyond those mentioned by Nathan in 2 Sam 12, and suggest that even if there were reasons for David's sin, he suffered for what he did.

In his comments on Ps. 51, Redak explained the plural "my transgressions" (פְּשָׁעַי in v. 2, 5) as possibly including the two transgressions, "the taking of Bathsheba and the slaying of Uriah."[30] In contrast, Abarbanel calculated David's major offenses as five:

> [First] He had relations with Bathsheba who was the lawful wife of another man; [second] He shamelessly attempted to distort the ancestry of the child he fathered by recalling Uriah from the battlefront in order to have it appear that Bathsheba's own husband had impregnated her. This ploy, if successful, would have allowed an otherwise illegitimate child to feel free to marry within the ranks of the Israelites when the Torah strictly prohibits this (Deut 23:2); [third] He added the enormous sin of bloodshed to the previous act of adultery by

placing Uriah at the battlefront to be killed. Furthermore he was undoubtedly responsible for the death of other innocents who were forced to accompany Uriah to the front; [fourth] David did not allow Uriah the dignity of being killed on his own soil and by his own people but chose to bring about the death at the hands of Israel's enemies; [fifth] Apparently devoid of any feelings of shame or guilt, David took Bathsheba as a wife immediately after her period of mourning over the death of her husband.[31]

Abarbanel concluded that only David's sincere repentance allowed him to enter back into the grace of God. He also contended, regarding David's fasting in 2 Sam 12, that "David knew he had no hope of revoking God's decree, but feigned prayer and fasting so that people would not guess that the child had died as punishment for his affair with Bathsheba."[32]

Abarbanel was unflinching in his recital of David's wrongdoings, but other rabbis have noted the difference between God's dealing with David and with other "sinners." For example, in *b. Yoma* 22b, R. Huna contrasts Saul and David, explaining that though Saul sinned once, it brought calamity upon him; while David sinned twice, but because God supported David, David's actions did not bring evil upon him. Saul's singular sin is identified as not killing Agag (1 Sam 15), and David's two sins are "the sin against Uriah" and the sin of the census (2 Sam 24; 1 Chron 21). But then, R. Huna mentioned "the matter of Bathsheba," explaining, "for that he was punished, as it is written, And he shall restore the lamb fourfold: the child, Amnon, Tamar and Absalom," as was mentioned earlier. In other words, David's murder of Uriah seems to be separated from "the matter of Bathsheba." The murder is referred to as "sin," though apparently this did not bring evil upon David. David was punished for "the matter of Bathsheba" with the death of three of his children, the unnamed child in 2 Sam 12, Amnon in 2 Sam 13, and Absalom in 2 Sam 18. Tamar is not killed, but is raped, which is arguably a form of death.

In *Gen. Rab.* 32.1, David responds to God's pardon spoken by Nathan in 2 Sam 12:13 by referring to Doeg (1 Sam 21–22) and Ahithophel, Bathsheba's grandfather who supports Absalom in his revolution.[33] David describes them as people who "permitted incest and bloodshed. . . . As they have acted so have I acted; yet what is the difference between me and them? Only that you have shown me love and said to me, *The Lord also hath put away thy sin: thou shalt not die* (2 Sam 12:13)."[34] The difference between David's sins and those of Doeg and Ahithophel (whom the *Gen. Rab.* explains "will neither be resurrected nor judged") is not qualitative; God favored and pardoned David. Instead of excusing David's sins, such a text highlights God's mercy in light of David's sins.

Two separate places in the Talmud explain that it is not until after Solomon has built the temple—and, therefore, after David has died—that God finally forgives David for his sins with Bathsheba. *B. Mo'ed Qat.* 9a describes the exact moment of forgiveness of the "misdeed" against Uriah and Bathsheba.

> At the moment when Solomon wanted to bring the Ark into the Temple, the gates held fast together. Solomon recited [a prayer of] four and twenty [expressions of] intercession but had no response. He began [anew] and said: *Lift up your heads, O ye gates* [Ps 24:7, 9] and again he had no response. As soon as [however] he said: [*Now therefore arise O Lord God . . . Thou and the Ark of Thy strength . . .*] *O Lord, turn not away the face of Thine anointed, remember the good deeds of David Thy servant,* he was answered forthwith. At that moment the faces of David's foes turned [livid] like the [blackened] sides of a pot and all became aware that the Holy One, blessed be He, had pardoned David that misdeed.

Whereas *b. Mo'ed Qat.* focuses on the response from David's foes who were angered at David's pardon, when this story is repeated in *b. Šab.* 30a the emphasis is on the joy of the Israelites when they hear that God has forgiven David. It could be argued that these tractates suggest that the forgiveness was contingent on Solomon's building of the temple, but the length of the time it took for David to be pardoned points to the seriousness of David's sins.

Of course, Solomon the temple builder is also Solomon the lover of a thousand foreign women, who turn his heart away from YHWH. Rabinowitz made the link between Solomon's end and his parents' beginning as follows: "While, on one hand, we must consider it one of the wonders of God's conduct that so many good things come through such a complicated and tortuous path, on the other hand, had David waited for Bathsheba perhaps Solomon's rule would have been a perfect one, unblemished by its rather dour end."[35]

Rabinowitz named Bathsheba here, but still put the weight of the act on David, attributing wrong to him. Additionally, according to Rabinowitz, the consequences for David continued beyond David's rule into Solomon's. David's wrong in not waiting for Bathsheba had influences on their son.

Within the general category that considers David's actions to be sin is a strain of interpretation that emphasizes the pedagogical and theological purposes of David's sins. *B. 'Abod. Zar.* 4b–5a explains that David was not the kind of man to commit adultery with Bathsheba in the same way that the Israelites were not the kind of people to make a golden calf. In both cases, God predestined their sinful actions to teach individuals and communities about the effects of repentance.[36] Some may understand predestination as an explanation for sin. Certainly, "predestination" gives David less agency and less choice, unlike Raba's explanation in *b. Sanh.* 107a, that David deliberately chose not to conquer his lust. Still, even if the weight of interpretation is on why David did this (or, why God made David do this), it does not erase that a sin was committed.[37]

David Did Not Sin

R. Shemuel b. Nahman clearly attempts to exonerate David in *b. Šab.* 56a, when he said, "Whoever says that David sinned is plainly mistaken, for it is said, 'And David behaved himself wisely in all his ways, and the Lord was with him' [1 Sam 18:14]. Is it possible that sin came to his hand yet the Divine presence was with him? Then how do I interpret, 'Why have you despised the word of the Lord, to do that which is evil in his sight?' [2 Sam 12:9] He wished to do (evil) but did not."[38] In other words David only wished or had the desire to do evil, but he did not. R. Shemuel places a lot of weight on the latter half of the verse, assuming that God's presence would not be able to remain with David if he sinned, such that the implied answer to the rhetorical question is "no, it is not possible that sin came to his hand and the Divine presence was still with him." R. Shemuel, however, was a descendant of David, and immediately following R. Shemuel's explanation, Rab comments that R. Shemuel sought to absolve David out of a desire to defend his ancestor. Sandra Shimoff has argued that all the rabbinic defenses of David can be attributed to social motivations or political motivations. In addition to R. Shemuel, who would want to defend his ancestor, Shimoff mentions Raba, who wrote those homilies in *b. Sanh* 107a. Shimoff explained that Raba was a wealthy man, a friend of the Persian royal family and a frequent guest of the Exilarch, and his "defense may well reflect his general admiration for the ruling class."[39]

An interpretive thread that runs more consistently through the Talmud is that David did not commit adultery with Bathsheba because Bathsheba was not married to Uriah. In *b. Met.* 58b, Bathsheba is referred to as a "doubtful married woman"; that is, it is doubtful that she was married at the time to Uriah. This theme is repeated in *b. Ketub.* 9b[40] and *b. Šabb.* 56a: "For R. Samuel b. Naḥmani said in R. Jonathan's name: Every one who went out in the wars of the house of David wrote a bill of divorcement for his wife, for it is said, *and bring these ten cheeses unto the captain of their thousand, and look how thy brethren fare, and take their pledge* ['arubatham] (1 Sam 17:18). What is meant by 'arubatham? R. Joseph learned: The things which pledge man and woman [to one another]."[41] The point being made is that every soldier who went out to war divorced his wife, and Uriah was no exception to that practice. Thus, when David encountered Bathsheba, she was not technically married, and therefore David did not commit adultery (2 Sam 12:9–10 notwithstanding). There is some disagreement as to how the marriage was renewed: Rabbeinu Tam, grandson of Rashi, has argued that the divorce was granted outright but was accompanied by a firm verbal pledge that the couple would renew upon the safe return of the husband. Because no such renewal is recorded, the idea is that Bathsheba and Uriah were divorced.[42] Rabinowitz, however, made the point that the divorce would have been made invalid merely through Uriah's return, and suggested that perhaps one of the reasons why Uriah refused to go home was because he knew he would have to re-issue Bathsheba a divorce when he returned to the battlefield.[43]

R. Jacob Pidanki wrote, "It was undoubtedly to assure himself that such a divorce was indeed granted that David launched the inquiry of v. 3, for if we should assume that David was prepared to commit adultery, it would be rather ludicrous to think that at the height of his passion he should seek to investigate Bathsheba's family background. Clearly it was only after he was fully assured that her husband had totally complied with the customary procedure of granting a divorce that he allowed Bathsheba to be brought to him."[44] Rabbi Meir Leibush Malbim also agrees that Bathsheba and Uriah were not married, based on 2 Sam 11:26, which says that "When Bathsheba heard that her husband (אישה) was dead, she mourned for her master (בעלה)." Malbim explained that it was outsiders whom Bathsheba heard speaking of the death of her husband (אישה), but she knew that Uriah had granted her a divorce and mourned only her master (בעלה), the one who had in the past enjoyed rights to her, but to whom she was no longer attached.[45]

If we allow that there was no adultery, what about Uriah's murder? In two places, that is also justified. In B. Šabb. 56a, the text wherein R. Shemuel explained that anyone who said David sinned was mistaken, continues by explaining that David ought not be punished for murdering Uriah, because Uriah had been "rebellious against royal authority, saying to him, *and my lord Joab, and the servants of my lord, are encamped in the open field* [2 Sam 11:11]." It allows that David should not have had killed Uriah on the battlefront because the prescribed procedure was to have him tried by the Sanhedrin, but that Uriah actually deserved death is not called into question. Midrash Samuel also has argued that David is not guilty for Uriah's death, based on 2 Sam 23:39, which reads "Uriah the Hittite; all the thirty-seven." R. Joshua ben Levi and R. Jonah Boṣriah explain, "They reduced [Uriah] from his greatness for he was worthy to be appointed after thirty-six, and they appointed him after thirty-seven." In other words, Uriah had been denigrated from being the thirty-sixth most mighty man to the thirty-seventh, and therefore David is not guilty of his blood.

These rabbis seem to be grasping at straws to provide evidence that David did not wrong Uriah. Though not as egregious as the allegorical interpretation of Uriah in the Patristic period that turns him into Lucifer, it is still hard to square this rabbinic dismissal of David's deed with the textual presentation in 2 Sam 11–12.[46] But again, in rabbinic interpretation, a text can be explained with another verse, and not even one that is literarily close. Thus, it is justified to use a reference in 2 Sam 23 to explain David's action in 2 Sam 11, especially if both refer to Uriah.

Another way to argue that David did not sin is by drawing on the "evil inclination" (יצר הרע), which itself is a complicated concept in Judaism.[47] In Nathan's parable, three different words are utilized to refer to the visitor who comes to the rich man and whose visit precipitates the taking of the ewe-lamb. Rashi explained how the three different terms illustrate different aspects of the evil inclination: "The Evil Inclination is first like a wayfarer who passes a man by and does not take lodging with him. But after this he is like a traveler who passes a man and does take lodging with him. And then he is like a house-holder in that he has power over the man."[48]

Obviously, if a יצר הרע [evil inclination] has power over a man, the power to choose good and not evil is limited, which could be taken to mean that David was unable to choose to not sleep with Bathsheba. But in Redak's commentary on Ps 51, David himself evoked the "evil inclination" as an explanation of why he sinned, and there the word "sin" was used, so that the concept of "evil inclination" and "sin" were linked. This is similar to the way Rabinowitz referred to the term, as discussed above. Daniel Boyarin referred to a Talmudic story that demonstrates how "the evil inclination is good," insofar as without it, there would not be fertility and reproduction.[49] Therefore, the "evil inclination" can be explained in multiple ways: like the character of David.

Bathsheba's Action and Intention

Bathsheba's character also gets explained in multiple ways, but throughout the rabbinic texts she is not an active agent of seduction. In some ways this fits with general rabbinic views of women, sexuality, and seduction, which are overall less concerned with the sexuality of the woman than that of the man.[50] There are some limited exceptions, three of which will be mentioned here: first, *b. Šab* 62b and *b. Yoma* 9b both refer to Isa 3:16 which describes the daughters of Zion as "haughty" and flirtatious, but men are also chastised in this reference. Second, A. Tanna taught in *b. Keth.* 65a the formula of what happens when women drink: "One cup [of wine] is becoming to a woman, two are degrading, three she solicits publicly, four she solicits even an ass in the street and cares not." Third, the fear of female infidelity became institutionalized in the *ṣotah* ritual, and takes up an entire Talmud tractate.[51] The places where women are described as seductive or unfaithful do not mention Bathsheba.[52] However, Bathsheba is explained as active in her sexual relations with David in two places, in differing ways.

First, she was active in abstaining from David after the first child died. Kimchi and Abarbanel explained that Bathsheba estranged herself from David because she was afraid that if a healthy (second) child was born, that child would be humiliated for being born "from a sinful union." Bathsheba forced David to swear that any child born from their union would be heir to his throne before she agreed to have sexual relations with him.[53] Second, Bathsheba is active in taking sexual initiative with David when she is pregnant with Solomon. In *Numbers Rabbah*, Bathsheba tells Solomon, "All the other women of thy father's house, when once they had become pregnant, saw the king's face no more, but I forced my way through and entered, so that my son might be fair complexioned and active!"[54] Both examples have Bathsheba's active sexual agency connected to concern for her son: she withholds sex from David in order to secure the promise of succession, and she "forced her way through" to have sex with David for the benefit of her unborn child.

Such interpretations depict Bathsheba as smart and cunning: she understands the potential humiliation for a bastard son, and knows conventions regarding sexuality.[55] In *b. Sanh.* 69b, the rabbis posit that Bathsheba first conceived with the child who died when she was six years old, and was only eight when she bore Solomon.[56] Though rabbinic interpretations are not meant to be read systematically, the overall implications for Bathsheba are that she is very young and yet wise.

In addition to describing Bathsheba as having had agency—or lack thereof—in her sexual relations with David, the rabbinic readings of Bathsheba also highlight her responsibility in naming Solomon. As mentioned earlier, 2 Sam 12:24 is a Masoretic *Kethib/Qere;* what is written is "she called," but what is to be read is "he called." Kimchi follows what is written and connects this verse to 1 Chron 22:9, where God is the one who gives Solomon his name to indicate that peace will be ushered in during Solomon's time; and, Kimchi asserted, "We must therefore assume that here Bathsheba named him שלמה [Solomon] based on God's command to do so."[57] Certainly, Kimchi overstated the necessity of this assumption, but in his explanation of this textual problem, he presented Bathsheba as obedient to God's command, even in conversation with God. In this example, as with the previous one, Bathsheba's actions were connected to Solomon. These events occurred within the storyline narrated in 2 Samuel, but the rabbis were also quite interested in events connected with Solomon's rule that are narrated in 1 Kgs 1–2 and beyond.

Queen Mother and Teacher

As 1 Kgs 1 begins, David is introduced as so old that he cannot keep himself warm and is therefore in need of the beautiful young virgin Abishag to keep him warm. The text simply states, "he did not know her" (1 Kgs 1:4), but the rabbis give explanations which relate to Bathsheba. Rashi explained that a virgin is better for warming than a non-virgin,[58] and it was because Abishag was a virgin that David refrained from sexual relations with her; he was still virile. *B. Sanh.* 22a describes the following series of events: first, Abishag says to David, "Let us marry"; second, he tells her she is forbidden to him; third, Abishag insults David's courage; fourth, David tells his servants to call Bathsheba; and fifth, when Bathsheba came, David had sex with her thirteen times in a row, according to Rab Judah who spoke in Rab's name. In the same section of the Talmud, the Oruch Lanair asserts, "David has still not forgotten his original sinful affair with Bathsheba. He therefore intentionally sought [in Abishag] a young and beautiful girl for this purpose in order to arouse his temptation to a maximum. By resisting this strong enticement, his repentance for that incident with Bathsheba would be so much more complete."[59] The rabbinic willingness to talk about sex and sexuality is part of their worldview that the body—and bodily functions—are an important part of being human and spiritual.[60]

Beyond the description of David and Bathsheba's sex life, the rabbis were interested in Bathsheba's role in helping Solomon take the throne. Because the rabbis connected Samuel with Chronicles, they could argue that Solomon's succession was intended all along, even though the account in the narrative of 1 Kgs 1–2 is more dramatic and less certain. When Bathsheba speaks to David about Adonijah's claims to the throne in 1 Kgs 1:22 she says that she and Solomon will be considered "sinners" (חטאים). When Rashi worked with this word, he departed from the literal—something his work rarely does—and translated it to say that if Adonijah attains the throne, Bathsheba and Solomon can never expect any dignity or honor, "Instead they will always be lacking and restrained from any greatness."[61] Abarbanel and Redak, though coming from different historical periods, both understand "sinners" more literally, and highlight its rhetorical force in her speech to David as follows:

> She intended to impress David with the danger she and her son faced if Adoniahu would ascend the throne. She claimed that Adoniahu might even recall the first affair between David and herself, before Uriah was killed, and condemn her to death as an adulteress. Solomon, as the fruits of this affair would also be killed.[62] Mother and son would thus be publicly proclaimed sinners. On the other hand, should Solomon be made king, this act would convince the people of their innocence and purity, and prove to all future generations that this entire episode had been inspired by God.[63]

It is not clear exactly what "this entire episode" refers to because Abarbanel consistently highlighted David's sinfulness in 2 Sam. The phrase might reference only the crowning of Solomon as king as having been inspired by God. Consistently in rabbinic interpretation, Bathsheba is not someone who seeks to have her son on the throne out of her own desire; the theological direction of the succession is without doubt. In Midrash Ecclesiastes, the "threefold cord" (Ecc 4:16) is identified as Bathsheba, Nathan, and David, who together enabled Solomon to take the throne.[64]

Most of the commentators describe Bathsheba as naïve about Adonijah's request in 1 Kgs 2 for her to ask Solomon to give him Abishag as a wife. Abarbanel believed that Bathsheba did not grasp that Adonijah's request was for Abishag, which is why she responded as she did in 2:18 by saying "Good, I will speak for you."[65] Similarly, Malbim explained:

> Bathsheba was so deeply impressed by his sincerity that it never occurred to her that she might be instrumental thereby in harming her own son. On the contrary, she was convinced that were she able to persuade Solomon to grant Adoniahu this seemingly innocent request, she would be strengthening his kingdom immeasurably. She felt he would gain the loyalty of his strongest adversary thereby. The word לו would then be rendered 'for him.' Bathsheba came to Solomon to discuss a subject beneficial to Solomon himself (for him), but she was speaking in place of Adoniahu.[66]

R. Jacob explained in *b. Sanh.* 22a that Abishag was not permitted to Adonijah, although she would have been permitted to Solomon to marry because Solomon inherited the throne and subsequently the rest of David's harem. This reference supports the idea that Adonijah's request for Abishag was indeed tantamount to requesting the throne, as Solomon himself said (1 Kgs 2:22). R. Jacob's explanation focuses on the legalities regarding Abishag, but does not directly address why Bathsheba would ask Solomon to give Abishag to Adonijah. The rabbis do not argue that she intentionally and cunningly gave her son a reason to depose Adonijah; such an interpretive thread won't come until later.

The portraits of Bathsheba as ignorant to the implications of Adonijah's request must be balanced with other portraits of her that highlight her wisdom. In the Midrash to Leviticus and Numbers, Bathsheba is identified as responsible for Prov 31; Solomon is King Lemuel,[67] and as Solomon's mother she is therefore the one who teaches the proverbial words. In the Midrash to Leviticus and Numbers, Bathsheba admonishes Solomon using the words from Prov 31:2–4. She also admonishes him based on Deut 17:17, "Neither shall he multiply wives to himself," warning him "Be cautious in these things, for they are the ruination of kings." The setting for Bathsheba's sagacious words to Solomon is the day of the dedication of the temple. The rabbis explained that Solomon had been sleeping until late in the day, because Pharaoh's daughter had spread a canopy over him in which all sorts of jewels and stones glittered like constellations, and when Solomon intended to rise, he would lie back down. "R. Levi said: On that day the continual offering was sacrificed at four hours of the day. Now Israel were grieved, for it was the day of the dedication of the Temple, and they could not perform the service because Solomon was asleep and they were afraid to wake him, out of their awe of royalty. They went and informed Bathsheba his mother, and she came and woke him up and reproved him."[68]

In addition to the words from Prov 31 and Deut 17, Bathsheba tells Solomon, "All the women of thy father's house, when they became pregnant, would make vows and say: 'May we have a son worthy of kingship,' but I made a vow and said: 'May I have a son diligent and learned in the Torah and worthy of prophecy!'"[69] The text in *Lev. Rab.* 12.5 is similar, but adds the detail that when Bathsheba corrected Solomon, "She took her slipper and slapped him this way and that." Moreover, she explains that when Nathan had prophesied that Solomon would be born, Bathsheba tells him, "every one [of David's wives] said: 'If I bring Solomon into the world, I shall offer up all the sacrifices mentioned in the Torah,' and now I stand with my sacrifices [ready] in my hands and you are sleeping!"[70]

Bathsheba exercises a great deal of authority over Solomon. According to these texts, she is the only one in Israel not afraid to wake up Solomon. She reproves him, even using physical force. Moreover, Bathsheba is a woman of faith who is more interested in her son being "diligent and learned in the Torah and worthy of prophecy" than she is interested in his becoming king. She quotes from the Deuteronomic law of the king to her son. And, while she is concerned for her own reputation and for the reputation of David, she nonetheless gives Solomon advice about how to live with integrity and rule with justice. In the Midrash Rabbah to Numbers 10:4, there is an alternate exposition that the "mother" who corrected Solomon was not Bathsheba, but the Torah.[71] The bulk of the textual evidence, though, is given to Bathsheba, who speaks with strength, power, and authority to encourage her son to act wisely.

According to the Midrash to Song of Songs, and specifically based on Song 3:11, Bathsheba also crowned Solomon.[72] This text, which was used in certain places as evidence that the character Bathsheba was responsible for crowning her son, is also used allegorically in *Exodus Rabbah*, which states:

R. Simeon b. Yoḥai asked R. Eleazar, the son of R. Jose: 'Perhaps thou hast heard an explanation from thy father of "Upon the crown wherewith his mother hath crowned him" [Song 3:11]? He replied: "Yes, it can be compared to a king who possessed an only child—a daughter. He loved her so dearly, that he called her 'my daughter,' and when his love increased he called her 'my sister,' and finally 'my mother.' Similarly, the Holy One, blessed be He, first addressed Israel as 'daughter' . . . when He loved Israel more, He called them 'my sister' . . . and when he loved them even still more, he called them 'mother.'[73]

As the analogy progresses, Bathsheba and Solomon become symbols for Israel and God, respectively. In *Midrash Song of Songs,* on the day when the tabernacle was established, Song 3:11 was recited to compare the tabernacle to a crown because it was designed as beautifully and with as much intricate detail as a crown.[74] By and large, the rabbinic move was not to allegorize Bathsheba; they tended to treat her as a character in the narrative instead of as a spiritual trope. But this example demonstrates the overlap with the allegorizing tendencies in the Patristic Era.

Bathsheba as a Type and
Trope in the Patristics

"When I was a monk I was a master in the use of allegories . . .
I allegorized everything, even a chamber pot."

Martin Luther, Luther's Works, *54:46.*

How is Bathsheba portrayed in the exegesis of the church fathers? Not surprisingly they—like the rabbis, and like the biblical text—are more interested in David than in Bathsheba; but, we get glimpses of how they understood her when they discuss him. Like the Bible and Jewish interpreters, they did not deny David's sinfulness; in fact, they used him both as a cautionary example of sinfulness and as an exemplar of penitence. Bathsheba is mostly of interest only insofar as she is the one with whom David sinned, and much less as a character in her own right. When the church fathers did discuss Bathsheba, it was often as a type: of sinful flesh, of the law, or of the gentile church. In their interpretations we can see the potential of Bathsheba to take on different significances. She transcends literary characterization to become something more, such as a virtue, or a vice, or an exemplar of some kind.

In fact, without the typological reading of Bathsheba, there would be very little about her in patristic exegesis; those allegorical interpretations of her are what cause her to survive. In that way the hermeneutical strategy applying to Bathsheba in this time mirrors the hermeneutical strategy that applies to the Old Testament. For the church fathers to demonstrate that the Old Testament was the Christian Church's book, and not only that of the Jews, a common strategy was to read the texts allegorically and typologically as pointing to Jesus Christ. And while all texts could potentially be read allegorically, the selection criterion included characters and events in the Old Testament that enabled Christians to reflect on the significance of Jesus Christ. Additionally, not all of the Old Testament was read with equal attention. Genesis, Exodus, Psalms, and Isaiah (and systematically only parts of those) were the books that were commented on by the church fathers, while other books were largely ignored.[1] Here is another analogy to Bathsheba's story, in that most of the attention is paid to David's sin with Bathsheba and to her bath, while her role as Solomon's mother is largely disregarded.[2]

The interpretations of Bathsheba provide a focused lens through which to view the broad hermeneutical approaches in the Patristic era. And yet, the reverse is also true: when looking at these specific interpretations of Bathsheba, it is necessary to understand the patristic theology of scripture and their consequent exegetical strategies. Unlike the Jewish interpreters, the church fathers did blame Bathsheba for David's sins, and their exegesis is the beginning of a trajectory of negative characterizations of her. But, they were not simplistically negative; in all the varying typological interpretations of her, that typology is largely positive. Again, by interpreting her as something more than a literary character or a historical figure,[3] the church fathers elevated her into representing the church or the law.

Patristic Exegesis: Alexandrians and Antiochenes

During the Patristic period, there were two major "schools" of interpretation: the Alexandrian and the Antiochene. The Alexandrian school was known for using allegorical interpretation, while the Antiochene school read the text using more literary and historical approaches. This categorization, however, is not without its complications, because different authors alternated literal and allegorical interpretations depending on their purposes and agendas. For example, in response to Jewish interpretations, a church father would read the Old Testament allegorically and Christologically. In response to the Gnostics, who have been characterized as practicing "exaggerated allegorism,"[4] a church father saw fit to interpret texts more literally. Methodological consistency was not the priority; refuting the doctrinal argument of an opponent was the primary concern. Therefore, an author who might be part of the so-called Antiochene school still practiced allegorical interpretation. However, the categories are still helpful heuristically, to distinguish between them, and historically, because the more historical and literal approaches to exegesis were a later response to what was seen as excessive allegorical interpretation practiced by Christians.[5]

Alexandrians and Allegory

Though the existence of an Alexandrian school as a continuous institution has been called into question, tradition holds that Origen was a leader of a catechetical school in Alexandria that followed the educational and theological practices of Clement of Alexandria, and there were several generations of successive teachers with a common approach to Scripture.[6] Origen did not ignore textual details; his work with the Hexapla demonstrates his commitment to philology. But Origen's *On First Principles* understands Scripture as a text that is inspired by God's Spirit. Such an ontology raises the question of how one is to interpret a text whose very nature is divinely inspired. Origen's solution was to speak of texts having a body, soul, and spirit. The bodily nature of a text inclines its readers to pursue its literal sense, or its plain meaning. But a text's spiritual sense—and subsequent theological meaning—is what forms faith. Allegory is the reading strategy that can mine the spiritual meanings of the text. Allegory also was (and still is) a strategy for reading problematic texts when there is a clash between the world of the text and a reader's own world. By explaining the meaning of the text as something other than the literal meaning, readers can harmonize the tradition with their own philosophies.[7] Some of those "problems" might include divine anthropomorphisms, contradictions with other sections of the canon, or unethical actions by biblical characters.[8]

Augustine, in his *Confessions,* expressed a sense of relief in hearing Ambrose explain that the Old Testament had a meaning beyond its plain sense.

> I rejoiced that at last I had been shown how to interpret the ancient Scriptures of the law and the prophets in a different light from that which had previously made them seem absurd, when I used to criticize your saints for holding beliefs which they had never really held at all. I was pleased to hear that in his sermons to the people Ambrose often repeated the text, "The letter kills, but the spirit gives life" [2 Cor 3:6], earnestly commending it as a rule. For once the mysterious veil had been lifted, he disclosed in spiritual fashion things that seemed perverse if taken literally.[9]

Boniface Ramsey asserted, "It would not be too much to suggest that the belief in a spiritual meaning preserved the Old Testament for the church."[10]

Again, Bathsheba's survival as she is interpreted allegorically is a focused example of what happens more broadly for the Old Testament as the church fathers read it allegorically, as more than the literal or literary text. Some of these spiritual meanings may seem as far away from the textual details as the east is from the west. And yet as a hermeneutical method, allegory was disciplined by the "Rule of Faith," which held that Scriptures always were to be construed in a manner consistent with apostolic teaching. The "Rule of Faith" provided a hermeneutical guide in two ways: it guided interpretation of given texts and guided the canonical process and creedal formulations of the church.[11] Additionally, Kugel and Rowan Greer explain that while the "Rule of Faith" excluded "incorrect" interpretations, it did not require one single correct one. They write: "Of a given passage there may be many interpretations that are valid because they do not contradict the Rule of Faith . . . Unity of belief in the early church is never confused with uniformity of belief or with assent to a definite list of theological propositions. And by the same token, the unity of valid scriptural interpretation does not require uniformity."[12]

Antiochenes and Literal/Historical

Though the Rule of Faith provided hermeneutical checks and balances to allegorical interpretations, there was still some reservation about the allegorical method.[13] Those in the so-called Antiochene school of the 4th and 5th centuries sought to understand and interpret texts in light of those texts' historical context and literary details, and not only insofar as it might connect with Christ and the church.[14] For example, in reference to Theodore of Mopsuestia's exegesis, Manlio Simonetti commented, "It is indisputable that Theodore has reduced the presence of Christ in the Old Testament to the barest necessary minimum."[15] In addition to focusing more on the historical and literary details of the text than the Alexandrians, the Antiochene position is also noted for favoring typology over allegory, though the distinction between typology and allegory is debated.[16] Certainly, the church fathers did not clearly distinguish the two.

Both typology and allegory look for a spiritual meaning that connects the Old Testament to the New.[17] For example, Bathsheba is described as a type of the Christian church, and the story about her relationship with David can also be read allegorically as referring to the relationship between Christ and the church. A fine point between them would be that the allegorical reading understands the meaning of the text as referring directly (albeit only allegorically) to Christ, while the typological reading would see in the literal story a "type" of character which relates to something in the New Testament.[18]

Continuities and Discontinuities with Jewish Interpretations

Patristic exegesis has some interesting continuities and discontinuities with Jewish interpretations. The church fathers and the rabbis both understood the Bible to be divinely inspired, though they differ on how that gets expressed.[19] Both groups make connections between one text and another, though the church fathers jump between the Old and New Testaments as they explicate texts,[20] and the Jewish interpreters obviously do not. Both the rabbis and the church fathers wanted to make the text applicable to their own time and context.[21] Gerald Bruns observed that that application to the contemporary setting is what makes patristic exegesis continuous with the Jewish practices of *midrash* and *pesher*. And yet, Bruns also noted the "frequently anti-Jewish point" of patristic typology,[22] an example of which can be seen in how the allegories about Bathsheba glorify the church and denigrate the synagogue. Other specifically patristic interpretations of Bathsheba and David, however, are very similar to those interpretations done by the rabbis, including the emphasis on David as an example of human fallibility and God's grace and mercy.

David Is Viewed as a Cautionary Example

Indeed, a common theme with the church fathers—as in other eras—is that David demonstrates how even the great ones of faith can fall into sin. In Jerome's treatise "Against Jovinianus," he challenges the latter's high view of David by reminding him of David's sins of killing Uriah and committing adultery with Bathsheba, explaining that because of these acts David was not permitted to build the temple for the Lord.[23] Isaac of Ninevah described David as "a man after God's own heart, who because of his virtues was found worthy to generate from his seed the promise of the fathers and to have Christ shine forth from himself for the salvation of all the world," but then noted that David was still punished after committing adultery.[24] Similarly, Irenaeus explained,

> For as God is no respecter of persons, He inflicted a proper punishment on deeds displeasing to Him. As in the case of David, when he suffered persecution from Saul for righteousness' sake, and fled from King Saul, and would not avenge himself of his enemy, he both sung the advent of Christ, and instructed the nations in wisdom, and did everything after the Spirit's guidance, and pleased God. But when his lust prompted him to take Bathsheba, the wife of Uriah, the Scripture said concerning him, Now, the thing which David had done appeared wicked in the eyes of the Lord (2 Samuel 11:27).[25]

While Jerome specifically referred to David's sinfulness as including the murder of Uriah, both Isaac of Ninevah and Irenaeus only mention the adultery with Bathsheba. 2 Sam 12:9–10 quantifies the evil that David did in the sight of the Lord as two things: killing Uriah, and taking Uriah's wife as his own wife.[26]

Thomas O'Loughlin observed that adultery was one of "a trio of capital sins" in early Church discipline in the West, with the other two being murder and apostasy. One who committed these sins could not simply be restored by prayer and penitence, but was excluded for a time from participating in the Eucharist and asked to perform special acts of prayer, fasting, and almsgiving.[27] This interest in adultery could explain why David's adultery gets such attention by the church fathers; however, in many cases, patristic discussion of David's adultery can be organized under the larger caution to beware the wiles of women.[28] Ambrose of Milan explicitly stated that Bathsheba seduced David, describing her as "a person of remarkable beauty, as strong in the charm of her face as her body, and with so much attraction that she seduced him and made him feel the desire to possess her."[29] In Jerome's letter to Eustochium, he includes David as one of many biblical men who are attacked with lust from the devil, including Samson,

Solomon, and Absalom. "In his assaults on men, therefore, the devil's strength is in the loins, in his attacks on women his force is in the navel. Do you wish for proof of my assertions? Take examples. . . . David was a man after God's own heart, and his lips had often sung of the Holy One, the future Christ; and yet as he walked upon his housetop he was fascinated by Bathsheba's nudity, and added murder to adultery. Notice here how, even in his own house, a man cannot use his eyes without danger."[30] In the Pseudo-Clementine letters *Ad Virgines*, the author considers a number of admonitory biblical examples, and has the following to say about David.

> Does not the case of David instruct you, whom God found a man after His heart, one faithful, faultless, pious, true? This same man saw the beauty of a woman—I mean of Bathsheba—when he saw her as she was cleansing herself and washing unclothed. This woman the holy man saw, and was thoroughly captivated with desire by the sight of her. See, then, what evils he committed because of a woman, and how this righteous man sinned, and gave command that the husband of this woman should be killed in battle. You have seen what wicked schemes he laid and executed, and how, because of his passion for a woman, he perpetrated a murder—he, David, who was called the anointed of the Lord. Be admonished, O man: for, if such men as these have been brought to ruin through women, what is your righteousness, or what are you among the holy, that you consort with women and with maidens day and night, with much silliness, without fear of God? Not thus, my brethren, not thus let us conduct ourselves; but let us be mindful of that word which is spoken concerning a woman: Her hands lay snares, and her heart spreads nets; but the just shall escape from her, while the wicked falls into her hands (Ecc 7:26).[31]

Bathsheba bears different levels of responsibility in all of these comments. When Irenaeus asserted that it was David's lust which prompted him to take Bathsheba, he subtly excused David and gave agency to the lust. Both Jerome and Pseudo-Clement assumed that Bathsheba was naked when David saw her, filling in the gap in the story of 2 Sam 11 which says nothing about Bathsheba's state of dress or undress. Jerome, however, blames the devil, while Pseudo-Clement paints Bathsheba with the brush of a proverbial ensnaring woman. Ambrose is the one who most clearly blames Bathsheba for seducing David. In some ways, his position is unsurprising considering that the title of his work is *The Apology of David*. Ambrose—who was a former magistrate, and thus quite familiar with legal arguments—utilizes two steps in his attempt to vindicate David.

Ambrose practices in David's favor the *deprecation*, minimizing the responsibility of the guilty king, whose sin—virtually the only one he committed—was but a momentary lapse in a multitude of good works. He also utilizes the *purgatio,* declaring the royal prophet's transgression happened because of human frailty and the divine plan of salvation, for God sought to show men that they could emulate the perfection of the saints, and Bathsheba "was figuratively wedded to David."[32]

In those two steps and in their subsequent implications, Ambrose includes most of the major interpretive assertions about David and Bathsheba in the Patristic era: David sinned, but overall, he was a good person; his sin and penance was an example for others; and both he and Bathsheba represented something more spiritual.[33] Still, as can be seen in the other interpretations, one can maintain that David sinned and not blame Bathsheba for seducing him.

The gravity of David's sins is lessened somewhat by an explanation from Augustine, who interprets Nathan's parable as making the point that David continued to be a person of virtue. He wrote, "But in [David's] case, this unbridled passion was not a lasting disposition, but only a passing one. For this reason, that illicit passion was called by the prophet, in his accusation, a guest. He did not say that the man had offered the poor man's ewe lamb as a feast to his king, but to his guest.[34] In other words, Augustine has understood the "guest" in Nathan's parable to be David's sinful lust; it was not something that remained in David's life. Augustine's interpretation here is similar to that of Rashi's, even to the level of the language: what Augustine referred to as "the immoderate desire," Rashi called "the evil inclination."[35]

When John Chrysostom discussed David's grief regarding the first child who died, he did not deny that David committed adultery, but softens it somewhat by describing David's emotions towards Bathsheba as follows: "even though his child were born of adultery, yet that blessed man's love of the mother was at its height, and you know that the offspring shares the love of the parents."[36] In Chrysostom's "Homily 50 on Matthew: 14: 23–24," he explained that though a great person of faith can prevail over great challenges, they "suffer evil from the less; as Elias felt toward Jezebel, as Moses toward the Egyptian, as David toward Bathsheba."[37] In those examples, Bathsheba is compared to Jezebel, the archetypal wicked woman in the Old Testament,[38] and she is a source of "evil," though Chrysostom also suggested that she is "less"; a lesser encounter, or of lesser significance in the larger context of David's story.

With the possible exception of Ambrose, none of the church fathers suggested that David did not sin. In Augustine's treatment of Matthew 1:6, he explained that Bathsheba is "the woman with whom [Solomon's] father had sinned. . . . Solomon was born of her with whom David had sinned."[39] Augustine's larger point is that, by alluding to David's sin in the past, Matthew's genealogy emphasizes that Jesus—the ultimate king—has conquered sin.

David As an Exemplar of Penitence

David is often used as a cautionary example of sinfulness, but he is also often appealed to as an exemplar of penitence. Pacian of Barcelona wrote,

> May we by all means be filled with revulsion for sin, but not for repentance. . . . Does David not say, 'Every single night I will bathe my bed, I will drench my couch in my tears'? [Ps 6:6] And again, 'I acknowledge my sin, and my iniquity I have not concealed'? [Ps 32:5] And further, 'I said, "I will reveal against myself my sin to God," and you forgave the wickedness of my heart'? [Ps 32.5] Did not the prophet answer [David] as follows when, after the guilt of murder and adultery for the sake of Bathsheba, he was penitent? 'The Lord has taken away from you your sin.' (2 Sam 12:13)[40]

Pacian's main point was to highlight David's repentance, in particular, as a model for repentance in general with its grief and the subsequent forgiveness from God. Yet in his language, Pacian nudges Bathsheba into David's actions, when he says that David committed murder and adultery "for the sake of Bathsheba." This phrase can imply that David did what he did with regard to Bathsheba, or because of her, and not necessarily that he did these things because she wanted him to do so. In this way, Pacian is less obvious than Pseudo-Clement and Ambrose in placing blame on Bathsheba, but her name is still associated with the guilt of murder and adultery.

Jerome is another church father who praises David for his penitence, exclaiming, "The whole repentance of a sinner is exhibited to us in the fifty-first Psalm written by David after he had gone in unto Bathsheba the wife of Uriah the Hittite, and when, to the rebuke of the prophet Nathan he had replied, I have sinned. Immediately that he [David] confessed his fault he was comforted by the words: the Lord also has put away your sin" (2 Samuel 12:13).[41] Jerome is following the text of 2 Sam 12:13, when Nathan responds to David's confession by saying, "the Lord has put away your sin." And yet, Nathan continues the sentence by telling David that the child born will die. Certainly, Jerome's intent was pastoral, to assure people of God's pardon after repentance. And like many preachers today, Jerome emphasized the part of the text important for his overall message—the immediate assurance after confession—while leaving out what follows, the negative consequences of David's sin.

Isho'dad of Merv extended David's penitence to 1 Kings, explaining that the reason David did not know Abishag was "not because he was by now devoid of concupiscence but because he restrained the movements of concupiscence, fearing that it might be believed that he, who had many women, had asked for that girl out of lust. He paid for his inordinate desire for Bathsheba through his restraint toward this girl and inflicted this punishment on himself: indeed, the sin with Bathsheba remained fixed in his memory until his death."[42] David's penance, for Isho'dad, continues in his practice of restraint regarding Abishag.

Bathsheba As an Example of Holiness

Because David is the primary character, he is given primary attention from the church fathers. Jerome referred to Bathsheba independent of David in his letter to Paulinus, answering Paulinus's question, "Why are the children of believers said to be holy [1 Cor 7:14] apart from baptismal grace?" Jerome quoted Tertullian's explanation, but also presented answers from the Bible: "it is a scriptural usage sometimes to give the name of holy to those who are clean, or who have been purified, or who have made expiation. For instance, it is written of Bathsheba that she was made holy from her uncleanness" (2 Sam 11:4).[43] In Jerome's letter to Eustochium, Bathsheba was one of his examples that women are tools used by the devil against men.[44]

Jerome also commented on Bathsheba's appearance in Matt 1:6 as part of Jesus' genealogy. For Jerome, the Old Testament women mentioned (Tamar, Ruth, and "the wife of Uriah the Hittite") were sinners whose inclusion foreshadowed the role of Jesus as savior of sinful humans.[45] Jerome's divergent uses of Bathsheba—as an example of holiness, a tool of the devil and a sinner—need not (necessarily) demonstrate interpretive inconsistency. Rather, Jerome's discussions of Bathsheba illustrate how the church fathers sought to use scripture for practical, moral teaching. Scripture, for them, was itself so vast and complex that one text (or, one biblical character) could be utilized differently in different situations.[46]

Bathsheba As a Type

Most patristic discussions about Bathsheba identify her as a type, either of the church, or of the law. She is not yet a type of the mother of Christ; that will happen in the medieval period, when Solomon the temple builder is a type of Christ, and as the mother of Solomon, Bathsheba becomes a type of Mary, the mother of Christ.[47] The church fathers tend to emphasize Eve/Mary typology, perhaps because of their lack of focus on texts like 1–2 Sam and 1–2 Kings; more attention was given to Genesis, so more typology was done with the patriarchs than with the characters from the monarchy. Frans van Liere offered as explanation: "The Church Fathers regarded Samuel and Kings with suspicion for their worldly character, and often wondered what salvational significance these verses might have."[48] When Bathsheba was identified, it was often in connection with Psalm 51 because of the superscription to that psalm, which reads: "a psalm of David, when the prophet Nathan came to him after he had gone to Bathsheba."[49] Psalm 51—which has a rich history of interpretation, particularly among Christians—has a thin historical connection to David and Bathsheba.[50]

A Type of the Church

When Cassiodorus explained Psalm 51, he associated David with Christ and spoke about Bathsheba as follows: "Bathsheba manifested a type of the Church or of human flesh . . . ; this is clearly apt at many points. Just as Bathsheba when washing herself unclothed in the brook of Cedron [2 Sam 15:23] delighted David and deserved to attain the royal embraces, and her husband was slain at the prince's command, so too the Church, the assembly of the faithful, once she has cleansed herself of the foulness of sins by the bath of sacred baptism, is known to be joined to Christ the Lord."[51]

Hippolytus did not reference Bathsheba, but in his commentary on Daniel, he explained Susanna bathing as a type of the church. Later, these two bathing characters are connected by similar iconography, and the "bath" will continue to be understood as a type of baptism.[52] Isidore of Seville connected Bathsheba with the church, by doing rather fancy interpretive footwork with the etymology of her name in the Greek texts, where Bathsheba is rendered Beersheba, or "seven wells." In Song of Songs, the bride—whom Isidore understood to be the church—is called a well of living water (Song 4:15), and because the Holy Spirit came to the church on Pentecost on the seventh day of the week, "in the giving of this gift of seven, the Church was established as a brimming well."[53]

Isidore also looked at the etymology of Uriah's name, and came up with another fantastic typological equation. Uriah's theophoric name means, "my light is Yahweh," but Isidore understood "the Hittite" (in the Greek) to mean "cut off,"[54] such that together, the names mean that Uriah was a bearer of light and then cut off, or fallen from grace: Lucifer. Isidore recognized the gravity of the textual David's sin, even going so far as to call David "despicable," but he focused more on typological interpretations of David, Bathsheba, and Uriah: "The most desirable of all men, when he was walking in the solarium, fell in love with the Church, washing the grime of the ages off her body. He took her from her house of clay into a house of spiritual contemplation. Afterwards he killed the devil that had been plaguing her, thus liberating her from an endless marriage."[55]

Augustine presented a very similar etymological explanation of Uriah's name.[56] He also described Bathsheba as a type of the church whose bath is "cleansing herself from the filth of the world and rising above and trampling upon its house of clay by spiritual contemplation."[57] Like Isidore and Augustine, Ambrose assigned types to Uriah and Bathsheba, as follows:

She who had not been united with Christ in any sort of legitimate marriage which had been done by faith, because she had been introduced by an uncommon way to conquer her gratitude outside of the prescriptions of the Law; her nakedness, that of a pure heart, and her unveiled simplicity, thanks to the sacrament of bathing which justifies, had been obligated to seduce the heart of the true David, the eternal king, and provoke his heart to love. It was within his rights that he came to her, and hiding the truth to deceive the other, Uriah—the word meaning "my light" or "enlightenment"—that it is the prince of the world who transforms himself into an angel of light.[58]

For Ambrose, Bathsheba could represent humanity before the coming of Christ, insofar as the poor man in the parable is Uriah—or, the devil—who possesses the ewe lamb before the rich man—Jesus—comes to take her away from the possession of the evil one. Also for Ambrose, Bathsheba is a type of the gentile church, not of the Jewish synagogue.

Ambrose, Isidore, and Augustine each illustrated first, the creativity of some of the typological connections; but, second, how problematic they can be. David, in 2 Sam 12, is not justified for killing Uriah. When David is Christ, and Uriah is the devil, violence is not only permitted, but even celebrated. Typology that is rooted in anti-Judaic statements can justify actual, real violence against Jews. Certainly, this does not happen simplistically as cause-and-effect, as if Christian typology is the reason for Christian violence against Jews. Rather, the rhetoric and actions shape one another in a cyclical manner, as can be seen more clearly with the benefit of hindsight.

Bathsheba As a Type of the Law

The anti-Judaic typologies become salient when Bathsheba is seen by some church fathers as a type of the law. In Eucherius's commentary on Samuel, he referred to Bathsheba as a type of the law of the carnal letter that binds the people, and Uriah as a type of the Jewish people whose knowledge of the law the Messiah (David) attempts to raise to new heights. "When David takes Uriah's wife from him and joins her to himself . . . our redemptor appears in the flesh, and begins to speak the law spiritually, which had previously been held according to the letter. He draws out what is the essential part of the Jewish people and joins it to himself."[59]

So, too, Gregory the Great explained in his *Morals on the Book of Job* that when David "draws Bathsheba to himself," it signifies Christ allegorically joining himself to the formal Law. He writes:

united to a carnal people . . . For 'Beersheba' means 'the seventh well,' assuredly, in that through the knowledge of the Law, with spiritual grace infused, perfect wisdom is ministered unto us. And whom does Uriah denote, but the Jewish people, whose name is interpreted, 'My light from God'? Now because the Jewish people are raised high by receiving the knowledge of the Law, they glory 'in the light of God.' But David took from Uriah his wife, and united her to himself, surely in that the strong-handed One, which is the meaning of 'David,' our Redeemer, showed Himself in the flesh, while He made known that the Law spoke in a spiritual sense concerning Himself.[60]

Thus, Gregory argued that because David married Bathsheba and took her away from Uriah, he proved that the law (Bathsheba) is not legitimately held by the Jewish people (represented by Uriah), but instead, the law must be joined to Christ (or David), who is proclaimed by the law.

If such interpretations of the biblical text seem—at best—counterintuitive, it is because they are.[61] And yet, there is a logic in these hermeneutical moves, explained by Gregory: "What, then, in respect of the fact, is more foul than David? What can be named purer than Uriah? What again in respect of the mystery can be discovered holier than David, what more faithless than Uriah?"[62] Elsewhere Gregory explained, "But such is often the case, that the historical meaning of anything is virtuous whereas the fuller meaning is sinful, just as a historical event that is a reason for condemnation in the writings becomes a cause of virtue by the intervention of prophecy."[63]

As Isidore's interpretation demonstrates, desire is good if it represents Christ falling in love with the church, while if it is David's lust that leads him to rape Bathsheba, that is clearly a fault. Within patristic exegesis there is a tradition where the obvious meaning of the text was taken to be the opposite of the mysterious, or true meaning. This tradition accounts for how and why Gregory, Ambrose, Eucherius, and Isidore can acknowledge that David did something terrible, but at the same time reflect something spiritually wonderful, and Uriah acted honorably, but reflects something contemptible.

Consequences of Such Results

Still, even if these interpretive traditions are contextualized and understood, their consequences cannot be ignored. What does it suggest if the obvious meaning, the plain sense of a text is not understood as the deepest, true meaning of the text? It points toward Gnosticism, implying that the latter is only available to those who are able—by special revelation, or secret knowledge, or even peculiar intellect—to find it. Even Origen, the champion of an allegorical approach to texts, began with the literal sense of the text as primary, and moved to allegory when and where the literal did not make sense.

When evaluating the church fathers' position on women, it is important to avoid anachronism. But even when the language is subtle in its blame of

Bathsheba, it indicates that a woman is at fault for what a man has chosen to do, taking away his responsibility, and often blaming the victim. Such practices are all too common, even today. Less subtle are the anti-Judaic implications in describing Bathsheba as a type of the law, when Christians and Christianity are what is considered true and good, and Jews and Judaism are considered false and bad. Perhaps few Christians would make that claim so boldly now, but this position is pernicious in its subtlety.

Without ignoring the negative consequences of these interpretations, there are still positive things to be seen. Again, by reading the Old Testament allegorically or typologically, the early church could read it as scripture, as sacred texts that taught morals and beliefs that could be pressed into consistency with the New Testament. Marcion's position, though extreme, was not without its sympathizers; and, many in the early church struggled with literal readings of Old Testament texts.

More specifically for the character of Bathsheba, the typological interpretations of her preserve her life in the history of interpretation. As a minor character, she could have been easily overlooked. Although her textual character is interpreted negatively by many of the patristic exegetes (she was naked, she seduced David who committed grievous sins because of her), her typological character is largely positive: she is the church of the gentiles, the spiritual law which guides correct living. Even those details that are mustered as evidence against the textual Bathsheba, such as her nudity, are understood typologically as something positive: her nakedness becomes symbolic of her purity, her washing figures the cleansing waters of baptism. An illustrative contrast can be made with the Reformers, who eschewed typology, so in their interpretations Bathsheba was simply a naked seductress, period.

In the subsequent historical time of the Middle Ages, Bathsheba's nakedness is heightened, as the iconography of that time depicts her bathing nude more frequently, and even more explicitly. She is less a virtue or a symbol of something spiritual, and moves into being an object of desire and an agent of seduction. As the hermeneutic pendulum continues to swing, some of the older interpretations of Bathsheba persist while new ones also develop.

4

Bathsheba in the Bath
in the Medieval Period

Every evening that summer I went up to the roof with my
hand maidens to bathe between the blue-grey evening sky.
Well, it was hot and I wanted cool water on my skin.

Bathsheba's opening monologue from the opera
And David Wept, *by Ezra Laderman*

"So . . . is Bathsheba's name related to the fact that she is seen when she is in the bath?" Whenever I hear that question in my undergraduate introductory Bible class—a not uncommon occurrence—I do a mental eye roll before explaining that though the two words may be connected in English, the Hebrew "*bath*" means "daughter of," and then I silently vow to spend more time with my students discussing issues of translation. The perennial question, however, points to the reader's tendency to focus on the single moment of Bathsheba's bathing despite the complexity of her character and the variety of scenes where she appears. Such a tendency is explicable: though the text is sparse in its information about Bathsheba, it is when she is in the bath that the text describes her as "exceedingly beautiful." And the bathing scene is fraught with sexuality: though 2 Sam 11:2 simply states that David *sees* the bathing woman, his subsequent actions of "taking her" and "lying with her" suggest that he must have desired her enough to follow with those actions. If the clause in verse 5 is about her purification, it may intensify the sexual suggestiveness, as Exum explained: "The intimacy of washing is intensified by the fact that this is a ritual purification after her menstrual period, and this intimacy, along with the suggestion of nakedness, accentuates the body's vulnerability to David's and our shared gaze. A woman is touching herself and a man is watching."[1]

The erotic nature of this image, however, may be less than is so often assumed. In the quote above, Exum noted that Bathsheba's nakedness is a suggestion; the text does not specify that she is undressed.[2] As discussed in chapter 1, it is one of the many gaps that we as readers fill in when we read 2 Sam 11. Perhaps if the text made it clear that Bathsheba's bath consisted of her washing herself under her clothes—a decidedly less sexy image—that scene would not have the adhesive power that it does.

As previously noted, earlier historical eras depicted this scene in varied ways. In the Patristic Era, Bathsheba's bath is a baptism when Bathsheba is a type of the church, or of sinful humanity. In *b. Sanh*, Bathsheba was washing her hair behind a screen, and David only saw her after his arrow knocked over the screen when he was shooting at Satan in bird form. Bathsheba's bath is depicted in a variety of ways in the medieval era, when "depiction" is literal and visual, as this historical time produces iconography of Bathsheba. Certain medieval pictures of Bathsheba explicitly illustrate her nudity, undressing Bathsheba in such a way that lends to interpretations of her as seductive and even culpable in the act of adultery with David.

But this is not the only way she is portrayed: she is also painted "bathing" with her clothes on, often only putting her feet into the water. Elisabeth Kunoth-Liefels includes several of these images in her study of Bathsheba bathing, including Jean Colombe's Book of Hours of Louis of Laval, various iterations of Lukas Cranach's painting of Bathsheba bathing from 1526 and Wolfgang Krodel's 1528 painting.[3] Moreover, some pictures of Bathsheba bathing appear on a folio with multiple scenes of David's life, where an image of her bath is on the same page as an image of David kneeling penitent or David defeating Goliath. Still other visual artifacts include pictures of Bathsheba from other scenes in her own story, such as her petition to Solomon on behalf of Adonijah. All of the varied and varying iconography of Bathsheba's bath in the medieval period demonstrates the multiplicity of interpretive potentials for that single scene, and by extension, the multiplicity of interpretive potentials for her whole story. Some pieces of art depict David in the background where he could not see Bathsheba's nudity, but still present her naked to the viewer. As discussed in chapter 1, Exum observed that such viewers become voyeurs, the ones gazing at a naked woman.[4] Is it our own desire to be voyeuristic that makes this interpretation of Bathsheba so prevalent?[5]

Medieval Exegesis

Medieval exegesis is an immense field, in part because it begins to interpret the Bible through different "senses," including the historical sense, the moral sense, and the allegorical sense.[6] When Bathsheba is interpreted using the literal or historical sense,[7] her nudity makes her vulnerable to accusations of seduction and culpability in the act of adultery with David. But medieval exegesis also continued the patristic practice of interpreting Bathsheba allegorically, where she was understood to be a type of the church or of the law. As was true in the Patristic period, the allegory often made Bathsheba's nakedness into a virtue. For example, a quote attributed to Hildebert of Tours (c. 1055–1133) has him speaking approvingly of Bathsheba as the naked law, unclothed in any allusions. But also similar to the patristic interpretations, these positive allegories of Bathsheba could have negative implications for Judaism, as can be seen in the complete quote: "Bersabee is the law; King David, Christ; Uriah, the Jews. The naked girl pleases the king. The naked law, not clad in allusions, pleases Christ. He takes her from the Jews, and joins her to himself. Her husband is unwilling to enter the house, and the people of Israel do not come into spiritual understanding. Uriah, in his deception, keeps the letter, perishes through the letter. Thus the Jew, too, dies by following the letter."[8]

The layers of meaning evident in Hildebert's interpretation are illustrative of the hermeneutical complexity in the medieval era: while he allegorizes Bathsheba, David, and Christ, the allegory also draws on some of the literary details of the story, in that Uriah's death came about through the letter written by David (2 Sam 11:14–15). But as in the interpretations of the Patristic period, the allegory can only be taken so far; when allegorizing David into Christ it is hard to include that David killed Uriah.

Visual Exegesis

In addition to the varying "senses" of scripture employed in the medieval era, artistic interpretation grew exponentially during this historical time. The particular issue of Bathsheba's being clothed or unclothed while bathing provides a helpful test case to consider the "circular hermeneutic" which comes about when an artist depicts a biblical text. An artist who draws a text must pay attention to the text's descriptions—or lack thereof—including the gaps. At times the artist will fill in a gap that the text leaves open, or will make a concrete choice to visualize something in a single particular way, when the text itself may have a number of potentials.[9] For example, when the text merely says that Bathsheba was bathing (2 Sam 11:2) there is the potential that Bathsheba was bathing naked, in a place where she could be seen. Other potentials include that it was difficult to see her, that she thought she was bathing both at a time and in a place where she could not be seen, that she was bathing mostly covered up and washing herself underneath a loose-fitting garment. Monica Walker Vadillo noted that in the text, "there is no indication of the general situation of Bathsheba. Was she indoors, outdoors, in a pool, in a fountain, in a bathtub, dressed, naked, et. cetera? No information is supplied by the Bible in this respect, so it was the artist's prerogative to create an appropriate setting for her, hence the difference in her visual representations."[10]

The hermeneutical circle becomes complete when, after one of the drawings of a biblical text is seen, its viewer will read the text with the image in mind.[11] Thus those who saw images of Bathsheba bathing naked would hear or read about her bathing, and mentally insert her nakedness into the text. During the time of Iconoclasm, John of Damascus defended the making of images by asserting, "The image is a memorial, just what words are to the listening ears."[12] But Anna Esmeijer explained that in the fourth century the image replaced the word in what she titles "visual exegesis," which is "a kind of exposition of Holy Scripture in which the customary roles of word and image have been reversed, so that the representation or programme provides the Scriptural exegesis in very compressed picture-form, and the text itself is either completely omitted or else limited to explanatory inscriptions, tituli, or very short commentary."[13] Though Esmeijer is describing a formal product—a piece of art that is itself visual exegesis of a biblical text—her description applies in a more informal way to what happens to many who read the story of Bathsheba and David in 2 Sam 11. The image begins to overshadow the words of the text, and the potential of meaning becomes more limited by the experience of seeing a certain image.

Throughout the medieval era, at least eighteen discrete scenes from the story of David and Bathsheba were depicted,[14] but by the late fifteenth century, the majority of manuscripts contain the single scene of Bathsheba bathing.[15] Several practical reasons can explain this shift: manuscripts with multiple scenes were more costly and often not feasible because of space; if a frame was large, other scenes could be included in miniature squares or rondels around a central scene, but that was not an option with small images. And practicality aside, no single piece of art depicting a single scene, or a single biblical character, automatically limits or does violence to the text. As stated above, there are good reasons to depict a dramatic scene in a given account. It becomes problematic when visual exegesis replaces the text and the entirety of the story is not available to those consuming the art. The problem is compounded by artists later in the medieval period who continued the previous iconographic trends of Bathsheba bathing naked, perhaps by copying previous images without ever consulting the text. The hermeneutical circle thereby became a vicious cycle.

Illustrations of Bathsheba were found mainly in three genres in the medieval era.[16] First, the medieval era produced entire illustrated bibles (or illustrated individual biblical books), in which illustrations were inserted to accompany the text. The second genre is the Book of Hours, a devotional resource that included an abbreviated form of the liturgical prayers to be prayed at different hours, as was practiced in the monasteries. But these Books of Hours were private, for lay people. They included the seven Penitential Psalms, if not the entire Psalter.[17] Books of Hours were often the only form of art owned by the middle class, which accounts for the popularity of the images found within. Many owners of these Books of Hours were female. Roger Wieck explained that at the time, male clerical advisors thought that "women . . . needed the pictures to help them in their piety. The images were, literally, visual aids."[18]

The third type of biblical illustration was found in what was known as Moralizing Bibles, which tended to emphasize the connections between the Old and the New Testament, often through interpreting the Old Testament characters, stories, and events figurally, as types that prefigured Christ. Another kind of Bible, the *Biblia Pauperum* or "Bible of the Poor" extended that typology even further, providing a more mystical interpretation on the life of Christ, where the Moralizing Bibles unsurprisingly placed more emphasis on a moral or practical understanding of the text.[19] In addition to casting Bathsheba as a type of the church, or the bride of Christ, when David was interpreted as Christ, the *Biblia Pauperum* understood Bathsheba to be a type of Mary, the mother of the anointed one, when Solomon was a type of Christ. Again, the medieval era continued the interpretive practice of typology that was done in the Patristic period, but in these documents, the typology was done through illustrations.

Most of the iconography of Bathsheba in the medieval era can be attributed to the emphasis on the book of Psalms during that historical period. Francis Wormald explained, "With the possible exception of the Gospels, the most popular book of the Bible in the middle ages was unquestionably the Psalter. . . . This pre-eminence is hardly surprising in view of the fact that it formed the basis of the canonical Hours of the Church, being recited in full during the course of one week. The Psalter was also the basis of much private devotion."[20]

Bathsheba only appears in the superscription to Psalm 51 which introduces it as "a psalm of David, when Nathan the prophet came to him after he went to Bathsheba." But if Bathsheba's connection to the psalms is textually thin, it is traditionally robust: it was during the medieval period that the Davidic authorship of the entire book of Psalms became emphasized through what are known as "rood" legends. These rood legends told the purported history of the wood of the cross by positing that the cross was made from a holy tree.[21] One common theme in the legend was that David sat under the tree (whose wood became the wood for the cross), and did penance there for the sins he committed with Bathsheba and Uriah. As part of his penance, he composed first Psalm 51, and then composed the rest of the Psalter—the implication being that once he repented through Psalm 51 then it was simple to write the rest of the psalms. "The implication is that once David had repented in Psalm 50 [Latin] it was a simple task for him to come up with the remaining psalms."[22] Not only was the book of Psalms increasingly important during the medieval period, but Michael Kuczynski has argued that because of the emphasis on penitence in this time period, Psalm

51 (or, Psalm 50 in the LXX and Vulgate) was considered the most important psalm.[23] Thus not only did the number of images of Bathsheba increase during this period with its emphasis on the psalm, but the nature of those images may have been influenced by medieval understandings of penance. In particular, erotic images of Bathsheba related to the penitence of David.

But as mentioned above, Bathsheba was illustrated in medieval art in other ways than as naked and seductive. This chapter will pay attention to the visual interpretations of her, focusing on two things: first, is Bathsheba illustrated as naked or not? And second, is the image of Bathsheba bathing the only image of her in a given manuscript, or are there other images of her or David? The images included in this chapter are by no means exhaustive, but are representative, and include some not published in other anthologies of Bathsheba bathing.[24]

Bathsheba in Art
Bathsheba Bathing in Sacra Parallela 923

One of the earliest visual images[25] of Bathsheba in the medieval period is found in the *Sacra Parallela* manuscript Parisinus Graecus 923, which can be dated to the year 862.[26] There are 1,658 illustrations, most of which are portraits, done in a Byzantine style with a predominance of gold.[27] The text includes a collection of "quotes from the Bible and patristic texts for ethical, moral, and ascetic edification."[28] In fol. 282v of this manuscript, Bathsheba is depicted bathing nude while David is watching her. According to Mati Meyer, this is "the first known image of her bath in art history,"[29] and Walker Vadillo explained, "the iconography of David watching Bathsheba bathing in the *Sacra Parallela* marks a starting point for the development of this type of representation."[30] Thus, Bathsheba is bathing naked in this image, but the manuscript also includes other imagery of Bathsheba, including pictures from the text of 1 Kgs, with Nathan speaking to her, and her speaking to both David and Solomon. Moreover, Bathsheba is not the only naked bather in the *Sacra Parallela;* David and Susanna are also depicted in similar ways. In the image that accompanies the text of 2 Sam 12:20, when David washes himself after the death of the first child, David bathes naked in the same posture as Bathsheba with a comb in his hand (fol. 203r). Meyer explained, "Were we to surmise that this image is not an artistic error but an intentional and meaningful part of the manuscript's program, intriguing vistas of interpretation unfold before us."[31]

Kurt Weitzmann noted the similarity in the *Sacra Parallela's* depictions of Bathsheba and Susanna (fol. 373v), including that both seem to be combing their hair.[32] Meyer, however, noted the differences, including that Susanna's posture is the opposite of Bathsheba's; she is facing in a different direction. And while Bathsheba has an attendant, no one is touching her, but one of the old men

"The bath of Bathsheba," *Sacra Parallela*. Paris, Bibliothèque nationale de France, gr. 923, fol. 282v. © BnF Paris

"The bath of David," *Sacra Parallela*. Paris, Bibliothèque nationale de France, gr. 923, fol. 203r. © BnF Paris

"Susanna spied upon by the Elders; the bath of Susanna," *Sacra Parallela*. Paris, Bibliothèque nationale de France, gr. 923, fol. 373v. © BnF Paris

seizes Susanna's arm; "she turns her head and glares at them with an expression of dismay or fear."[33] The comparisons and contrasts with Susanna are done in other forms of art, including other medieval iconography where Susanna may be depicted similarly to Bathsheba, though she usually has a halo to emphasize her sanctity; Bathsheba never appears with a halo.[34]

In the Patristic era, Hippolytus allegorized Susanna's bath as a type of the church being washed clean, which was similar to how Bathsheba's bath was interpreted. Their stories are told quite differently in the text: though both include accounts of women bathing, the text about Susanna makes clear that she is careful to bathe in her garden behind shut doors (Sus 17) and the elders are only able to see her because they are hiding (Sus 10–11, 18–20). Susanna also responds to the elders' demand that she lie with them by saying, "I am completely trapped. For if I do this, it will mean death for me; if I do not, I cannot escape your hands. I choose not to do it; I will fall into your hands rather than sin in the sight of the Lord" (Sus 22–23). By contrast, 2 Sam 11 does not record Bathsheba refusing David. It could be that she did refuse his demand, but that is another gap in the story. Bathsheba could be like Susanna, who is known to be spied upon, virtuous and endangered. Or, Bathsheba could be unlike her. The varying ways that the stories of Susanna and Bathsheba allude to one another do offer other interpretive potentials for their characterization.[35]

"Bathsheba Bathing,"
Vatican Psalter.
Rome, Vatican
Museum, gr. 752,
fol. 162v. © Biblioteca
Apostolica Vaticana

Bathsheba Bathing in Vatican Psalter gr. 752

Another early image of Bathsheba bathing is found in the Vatican Psalter gr. 752, dated to the middle of the 11th century. It is a Byzantine psalter, produced during the time when the capital of the Roman Empire was transferred to Byzantium, and characterized by an aesthetic that favored symbolism over more naturalistic representation of figures.[36] In fol. 162v Bathsheba is depicted bathing naked in a golden tub with an attendant on either side, one of whom pours water over her head. In this stylized iconography, her nudity is not explicit—in fact, it appears that her hair is strategically placed over her breasts. This bath image appears at the beginning of the catena to Psalm 50 (51), and is followed immediately by Theodoret's preface to the psalm which includes the comment, "blessed are those whose sins and evil doings can be purified by just taking once the grace of baptism."[37] It is therefore not coincidental that the tub in which Bathsheba is immersed resembles a baptismal font, and that Bathsheba's bath is indicative of the cleansing of baptism. Theodoret was an important interpreter of the so-called Antiochene school in the Patristic period, so the inclusion of his words here—with a medieval work of illustration—is a salient example of the overlap between these historical eras. One cannot completely separate one historical era and its interpretations from another.

David is not present in Bathsheba's bathing scene, which is the only image of Bathsheba in Vatican Psalter gr. 752. There are a number of other images of David, though, including him sending Uriah to war (fol. 163 r), kneeling penitent before Nathan (fol. 163 v), and images from other parts of his story (fighting Goliath, marrying Michal, with the sons of Korah, and so on). David is also depicted at least twenty times with Christ, and in half of these scenes he lacks his customary halo and is kneeling before Christ in a position of penitence.[38] Ioli Kalavrezou, Nicolette Trahoulia, and Shalom Sabar argue that this Psalter especially emphasizes David's sinfulness and consequent restoration as a way of critiquing the emperor at the time this Psalter was produced, who himself was known for his adultery.[39] But as Kalavrezou, Trahoulia, and Sabar describe the single depiction of Bathsheba bathing, "although David is not shown watching her, as the narrative requires, the element of sin cannot be eliminated from this scene. A conscious choice was made to depict the bath, the event precipitating David's sin of adultery."[40]

While these authors have carefully researched the historical context of the production of this Psalter, it seems as if their assessment of Bathsheba has been flattened to fit their overall argument, especially given the nature of the image of Bathsheba bathing in this Psalter. The artist's choice to depict Bathsheba bathing in a tub that resembles a baptismal font suggests that Bathsheba is not only a temptress, but a type of the church. In this allegorical interpretation, as in the Patristic period, Bathsheba's bathing naked was not a seductive act that led to adultery, but it was a positive indication of the sacrament of baptism. Walker Vadillo explained, "In the Moralizing Bibles Bathsheba appears nude, but her nudity is closer to the Christian concept *nuditas virtualis,* a symbol of purity and innocence, than to *nuditas criminalis,* symbolic of lust, vanity and self-indulgent sin. When Bathsheba appeared bathing it was taken as a sign of the Church cleansing itself from the worldly stains so that it could become the bride of Christ. . . . In this context Bathsheba has a definite positive meaning: an object to be desired because she is the representation of the Church."[41]

Understanding Bathsheba's bath as a figure of baptism opens up a larger vista with which to view the iconography presented in this manuscript, and also has broad implications for understanding her. Though Vat. Gr. 752 does indeed emphasize David's sinfulness and restoration, it does so without depicting Bathsheba as an agent of temptation. Rather, she is a reminder of the sacraments that the church held important in the process of restoration. Seeing Bathsheba in this manner—positively, as a figure of baptism—may prevent the all too easy collapse of David's sin with the assumption that Bathsheba also sinned.[42]

"Miserere," *Copenhagen Psalter.* The Royal Library, Copenhagen, Manuscript Thott 143 2°, fol. 68r.

Bathsheba not Bathing in the Copenhagen Psalter Thott 143 2°

The Copenhagen Psalter Thott 143 2° includes not only the Psalms, but also a calendar and a prayer of consecration. Erik Petersen has argued that it should be dated to the end of the thirteenth century; though the illustrations, the saints in its calendar, and its litany all suggest an English context, two other additions to the manuscript link it to Medieval Jutland (Southern Denmark and Northern Germany).[43] In addition to full-page illustrations of scenes from the life of Christ—his birth, crucifixion, and resurrection—it also includes a considerable number of illustrated initials. Bathsheba appears on one of those illustrated initials; the initial M found at the beginning of Psalm 50 (51), "Miserere" (fol. 68r). This is the only image of Bathsheba in the Psalter, but she is not depicted in her bath. Instead, she is with David, slightly behind him with her head resting on his shoulder while Nathan confronts both of them. Behind Bathsheba, David, and Nathan is an image of Uriah being stoned by a man on a wall.

Obviously, this image takes liberty with the biblical text: there is no word as to whether or not Bathsheba is present when Nathan confronts David in 2

Sam 12, and in 2 Sam 11, Uriah dies when the archers shoot arrows from the wall
(2 Sam 11:24), not by being stoned. The stoning mentioned in 2 Sam 11 is part
of Joab's coded message to David when he alludes to the death of Abimelech
(2 Sam 11:20–21), not how Uriah dies. And, as Joab's message indicates, Abimelech is killed after a woman drops a millstone on his head (Judg 9:53), but in the
image, it is clearly a man with a beard who is dropping stones on Uriah. What
the Copenhagen Psalter lacks in textual fidelity, it makes up for in its reminder
that David and Bathsheba—together—bear responsibility for Uriah's death. One
need not depict Bathsheba naked to censure her for her role in the murder of
her husband.

Bathsheba Bathing and More in the Morgan Picture Bible and the Queen Mary Psalter

Unlike the Copenhagen Psalter, which has only a single image of Bathsheba, the
Morgan Picture Bible and the Queen Mary Psalter each depict Bathsheba in a
number of scenes. The Morgan Picture Bible (also known as the Crusader Bible,
the Maciejowski Bible, and the Shah 'Abbas Bible) was made in Paris, probably
for Louis the IX, in the thirteenth century[44] and is a stunning example of French
Gothic Illumination. As the titles indicate, it is an illustrated bible, and contains
images from some 340 episodes from Genesis, Exodus, Joshua, Judges, Ruth,
and Samuel.[45] The images in this Bible are accompanied by inscriptions in three
languages: Latin, Persian and Judeo-Persian.[46]

Bathsheba appears in fol. 41v, where in the upper right of the image, she is
bathing naked, easily in view of David who points at her from across the way.[47]
In the bottom left of the page there is an image of the act of intercourse. Bathsheba is still naked in this image, though David's hands are placed strategically
over her breasts so her nudity is less explicit than in other iconography. By placing these two images—of Bathsheba bathing and having sex with David—on the
same page, the Morgan Picture Bible is explicitly connecting Bathsheba's naked
bath with sex. It is illustrative to compare the imagery of David and Bathsheba
in the Morgan Picture Bible with the scene of Amnon and Tamar, because while
the bodies are in similar positions, Amnon seizes Tamar's wrist. Diane Wolfthal
explained that such a gesture is often employed in medieval art as a sign of
sexual attack, or at least a sign of force.[48]

As mentioned above, the images of bathing and adultery are not the only
ones in the Morgan Picture Bible, and Bathsheba appears in all four quadrants
of fol. 42v, clothed in each scene. In the image on the top left, Bathsheba is informed by a messenger about Uriah's death. She and a member of her household
express their grief in their facial expressions, presumably an interpretation of 2
Sam 11:26. The image on the top right is of David marrying Bathsheba,[49] while

"David and Bathsheba,"
Queen Mary Psalter.
The British Library,
Manuscript Royal 2 B
VII, fol. 56v.

in the third image on the bottom left of the folio, Bathsheba is lying in bed after giving birth to her son. She is directing a servant who stands above her bed, while another woman rocks the newborn child in his cradle. The fourth image of Bathsheba on the bottom right is of her seated, holding the child on her lap while Nathan confronts David. By including images of Bathsheba in those other scenes from 2 Sam, the Morgan Picture Bible points to more of her story than just the bathing scene.

The image of Bathsheba in bed with David in the Queen Mary Psalter—which originated in England between 1310 and 1320—is similar to that found in the Morgan Bible. Unlike the Morgan Bible, however, the Queen Mary Psalter does not depict Bathsheba in the bath, and therefore does not depict her naked. Instead, their first encounter is illustrated with her clothed in a tower across the way from David in his palace (fol. 56v). And the Queen Mary Psalter also includes more images from later in Bathsheba's story. While the Morgan Picture Bible stopped with 2 Sam, the Queen Mary Psalter has an image of Bathsheba from 1 Kgs in which she is appealing to David.

Bathsheba Bathing in Books of Hours

Most of the medieval Books of Hours contained the seven Penitential Psalms, and while not every Book of Hours included images of Bathsheba, it was in these manuscripts where the theme of Bathsheba bathing flourished.[50] There are variations on the theme of her in the bath: in some, David alone is looking at Bathsheba, while in others, additional men are with David observing her bathe. Bathsheba is bathing unattended in certain Books of Hours, while in others, she is attended by maidservants wearing headdresses; she either has a bare head or more simple ornamentation on her head than her attendants. Bathsheba some-times is outside in what looks like a pond, while in other illustrations she is in a semi-enclosed place. Clare Costley King'oo explained that the most common design in France and England in the sixteenth century is of Bathsheba standing in an elaborate fountain while David watches, sometimes accompanied by ladies in waiting who are giving her symbolic objects.[51]

One of the most overtly seductive images of Bathsheba is found in the Book of Hours of Louis XII (Ms 79r), where the court painter has depicted her in a de-liberately provocative manner. She is explicitly and graphically naked—even to the level that details of her genitals are visible underwater. Thomas Kren wrote: "while Bathsheba is immersed in her bath at the hips, her body below that point is still visible through the cool, blue water. Indeed her genitalia are precisely rendered, showing the labia, and originally they must have seemed even more strongly a focus of the miniature than today, because Bourdichon used silver paint, now tarnished, to convey the shimmer of light across the surface of the water."[52]

She is in full view of David, who occupies the upper left of the painting, and she coyly watches him watching her. Walker Vadillo also noted that Bourdichon hinted at women of ill reputation by painting the face of a cat for the spout of the fountain in which Bathsheba is bathing, because the French *chat* was a symbol for prostitutes.[53] Kren admits, "In relation to the biblical narrative, this depiction takes liberties," and he noted that Bathsheba is "displaying her charms for [David] as well as the viewer, indeed even more brazenly for the latter."[54] A similar image—though less overtly seductive—is found in a Book of Hours from Rouen France (fol. 057r), in which Bathsheba's hand is very close to her genitals, and other men besides David are watching her. A different Book of Hours (MS Harley 2969, fol. 91), also has an image of Bathsheba bathing naked at the begin-ning of the Penitential Psalms, but in this depiction she is less naked because of a towel draped over her lower half. Based on the expression on her face, this Bathsheba seems less aware of David's presence than in Bourdichon's painting, and at the same time she is bathing, she is also receiving a letter from a mes-senger presumably summoning her to David.[55]

"Bathsheba Bathing," *Book of Hours of Louis XII* by Jean Bourdichon, Ms 79r. J. Paul Getty Museum. Image courtesy of the Getty's Open Content Program.

As discussed above, the primary focus of these Books of Hours was the penitent David. Other Books of Hours do have Bathsheba bathing, but the image is smaller and marginal, while the largest part of the page shows David kneeling penitent before God. This is the case in the Hours of Admiral Prigent de Coëtivy, dated between 1443–1450 (CBL W 082 f.77).[56] Bathsheba is bathing naked wearing a headdress, but the wooden tub in which she is bathing hides her lower half. A servant is pouring water into the tub, while David is depicted above and to the right, looking down on bathing Bathsheba. These images are less than half the size of the image of David kneeling and looking up to God. The image of David in the Book of Hours from Paris, circa 1420–1425 (Ms M. 1004, fol. 78r) also has him kneeling penitent before God, with Bathsheba in a wooden bathtub slightly below and to the right. She is observed by the king and another man, but her bathtub is in a tent, which could suggest some attempt at privacy even as David and the other man can view her. Again, the image of her is a fraction of the size of the image of penitent David. This page also includes the image of David killing Goliath on the bottom of the page.[57] Another Book of Hours from slightly later in the century, circa 1465 (Ms. M. 1003, fol. 113r), has the familiar image of David kneeling in prayer, but Bathsheba is not depicted

"Bathsheba Bathing," Book of Hours from Rouen, France. The Pierpont Morgan Library Manuscript H.1, fol. 057r. The Morgan Library & Museum. MS H.1. Gift of the Heineman Foundation, 1977.

"Bathsheba," Book of Hours, Use of Rome. The British Library, Manuscript Harley 2969, fol. 91.

"David Penitent," *The Coëtivy Book of Hours*. Chester Beatty Library, Manuscript W 082, fol.77.

"David communicating with God." Pierpont Morgan Library, Manuscript M. 1004, fol 78r. The Morgan Library & Museum. Ms M. 1004. Purchased on the Fellows Fund with the special assistance of Mrs. Vincent Astor, Mrs. Charles W. Engelhard, Mr. Haliburton Fales, 2nd, Miss Alice Tully, and Miss Julia P. Wightman, 1979.

"David: in Prayer." Pierpont Morgan Library, Manuscript M. 1003, fol 113r. The Morgan Library & Museum. MS M. 1003. Gift of Mr. and Mrs. Landon K. Thorne, Jr., 1979.

bathing. Instead, she is sitting with David, who has his arms around her, in a roundel to the right of the page. The roundels above and below are of Uriah, first receiving the message from David, and then being killed in battle.

The Bedford Book of Hours—produced in May 1423 for the wedding of John, Duke of Bedford to Anne of Burgundy—includes the familiar image of David penitent (MS 18850 f. 96r), but it is neither the largest nor the only image in the scenes. In an arch, the artist has depicted Bathsheba and Uriah standing together inside a house, while David peers in at them with his harp in hand. Slightly above and to the left in the arch, David gives Uriah a letter, and the top of the arch has David kneeling before God. The arch is surrounded by miniatures that include St. Paul falling from his horse as well as various virtues and vices. In the Dunois Hours, produced circa 1439–1450 (Yates Thompson 3, f. 172v), is a personification of Lust, as a woman riding a white goat while carrying arrows and a mirror. Immediately behind her is David watching Bathsheba bathing naked in the bath. Other Books of Hours depict Bathsheba "bathing," but the bath is more of a foot wash, for Bathsheba is clothed with her dress pulled up to her thighs. This is the case for the image of Bathsheba from the Book of Hours from Troyes from 1480 to 1490 (The Hague, KB, 76 G 8, fol. 93r).

"Miniature of David and Bathsheba, with miniatures of St Paul and the virtues and vices," *Bedford Book of Hours, Bedford Master.* US Public domain, via Wikimedia Commons, BL Add MS 18850, fol. 96r.

"Lust," *Dunois Hours.* The British Library, Manuscript Yates Thompson 3, fol. 172v.

"David sees Bathsheba bathing from a window of his palace," *The Book of Hours from Troyes*. Den Haag, Koninklijke Bibliotheek, Manuscript 76 G 8, fol. 93r.

"David and Bathsheba; David Slaying Goliath," Master of Cardinal Bourbon, Ms. 109, fol. 14. J. Paul Getty Museum, image courtesy of the Getty's Open Content Program.

"David and Bathsheba: Bath-sheba Bathing," *Hours of Claude Molé*. Pierpont Morgan Library, Manuscript M. 356, fol. 30v. The Morgan Library & Museum. MS. M. 356. Purchased by J. Pierpont Morgan (1837–1913) in 1908.

Certain Books of Hours included Bathsheba bathing naked, but that was not the only image on the page. For example, the Book of Hours produced by the Master of Cardinal Bourbon has an image of Bathsheba bathing naked above an image of David killing Goliath (Ms. 109, fol. 14).[58] In the Hours of Claude Molé, Bathsheba is shown typically bathing naked with David and a male attendant watching, but the image includes David and Bathsheba in bed in the upper left, as well as Uriah's death in the lower left (Ms. 356, fol. 30v). King'oo makes the point that the indirect nature of David's homicide made it more difficult to represent the sin in a single dramatic illustration, which may be why there were more images of David watching Bathsheba bathing, but she also wrote, "by focusing on adultery rather than murder, the favored images (of David and Bathsheba) made illicit sex representative of all sin."[59]

As noted earlier, many artists place the viewers in the position of voyeurs of Bathsheba's naked body, even when David is not able to see it.[60] Hans Mem-ling's interpretation of Bathsheba from 1485, just over a decade before the Book of Hours of Louis XII, has David barely able to see anything of Bathsheba at all, and she seems wholly unaware that he is looking at her, but her naked body is fully exposed to the viewers. Memling's image draws attention to Bathsheba's nudity, and we ought not gaze without reflection. In contrast with Memling's depiction of Bathsheba, a German woodcut from the early sixteenth century has

(left) "Bathsheba" by Hans Memling, 1485. US Public domain, via Wikimedia Commons. *(right)* "Bathsheba Bathing, from Women's Wile (Weiberlisten)" by Hans Burgkmair. Metropolitan Museum of Art, Gift of Felix M. Warburg, 1920. Open Access for Scholarly Content, via Internet Archive.

Bathsheba bathing with her back to the viewers. She is facing David, so possibly aware that he can see her, but she has a cloth covering her front, so her nudity is only a suggestion.

Because certain Books of Hours, as well as other images in the medieval period, clothe Bathsheba and include scenes from her story in addition to the bathing one, we know that the nude Bathsheba is not the only potential for meaning, and that a deliberate choice is made to depict her bathing naked.[61] Erasmus wondered, "Why is it necessary to depict in the churches . . . David looking from a window at Bathsheba and luring her into adultery? . . . These subjects, it is true, are taken from Scripture, but when it comes to the depiction of females how much naughtiness is there admixed by the artists?"[62]

Some offer reasons for this: John Harthan has stated that the depictions of the temptation of David allowed manuscript illuminators to "safely give their patrons a mild erotic *frisson* by portraying nudity."[63] Wieck suggested that

"Coronation of the Virgin." The British Library, Manuscript King's 5, fol. 28.

illustrations of the naked Bathsheba in these Psalms associated with penitence intended to be literally provocative, as they "seem to offer less of an admonition against sin than an occasion for it."[64] King'oo saw a connection between the focus on sexual transgression as that the sin that occasions the Penitential Psalms and Michel Foucault's hypothesis that sexuality became the central focus of the rite of confession, "transforming sex into a 'privileged theme' in the disclosure of sin."[65] She noted that Foucault's hypothesis is contested, especially by Thomas Tentler who cautions against overemphasizing the medieval church's preoccupation with sex. But Tentler still agrees "while it is true that the medieval church could excoriate all kinds of vices and all kinds of sins, it was inordinately concerned with the sexual."[66] King'oo warns against overemphasizing the sexual nature of the interaction between David and Bathsheba, especially given that the story and imagery finds its way into primers for children, for example.[67] King'oo's point demonstrates how a singular image can be interpreted in more than one way over time. The same is certainly true for Bathsheba's character.

Bathsheba Crowned in Biblia Pauperum

In the Patristic period, Bathsheba was often interpreted as a type of the church, or of the law. In the medieval period, another typological identity gets added: that of Mary, mother of Christ. *Biblia Pauperum* (*Bibles of the Poor*) were made in Northern Europe during the late medieval period, and they consisted of images from Jesus' life accompanied by two slightly smaller pictures of Old Testament images that prefigured the central one. The image of "the Coronation of the Virgin" is flanked by a picture of Solomon with Bathsheba on the left, and Esther and Ahasuerus on the right (King's 5, f. 28). Not only is there visual similarity between Bathsheba and Mary, but the explanatory text which accompanies the image makes it clear that the two are related: "We read in the Third Book of Kings, chapter 2, that when Solomon's mother Bethsabee had come to him at the palace, King Solomon ordered that his mother's throne be placed next to his throne. Bethsabee signifies the glorious Virgin whose throne was placed next to the throne of the true Solomon, Jesus Christ."[68]

These images demonstrate some of the values of typological interpretation, including its ability to make connections between the Old and New Testaments. Not only is Bathsheba's throne placed by Solomon's, but another typological link between Bathsheba and Mary is that Bathsheba had a request for Solomon in a way similar to how Mary asks Jesus to do things. Similar is obviously not the same, especially given that Solomon refused Bathsheba's request. Additionally, there is no official coronation of Mary in the gospels; she is extolled as the bride and queen of her son in the Apocryphal Assumption of Mary as well as in liturgies and popular devotions. Canonical biblical references for identifying Mary as the Queen of Heaven come from Rev 12:1–6, itself a very non-literal text. Typology, however, enjoys a certain amount of fluidity, and the connections need not be exhaustive to be present.

When Wayne Craven discussed the carvings on the façade of the Cathedral of Auxerre (dated circa 1260), he described a scene of David and Bathsheba sitting together on the throne as king and queen, in a niche adjacent to one that depicts their marriage.[69] Craven wrote, "The image of David and Bathsheba seated together on a throne is not a common one in mediaeval art, and one is struck by the similarity it bears to the Coronation of the Virgin: a male and female figure—each probably crowned, originally—seated on a throne and turned toward one another. This typological prefiguration is the key to the specific iconographic significance of the six scenes of the David and Bathsheba cycle at Auxerre."[70]

In other words, Bathsheba represents the Virgin Mary while David represents Christ. Again, the typology is fluid; in Craven's explanation, David can represent Christ and Bathsheba his wife—the church—or his mother, Mary. Elsewhere, it is Solomon, the son of David, who prefigures Jesus, the true son of David; and Bathsheba, Solomon's mother, is a type for Mary. The Cathedral at Auxerre includes an image of Bathsheba bathing naked, but with the more allegorical connotations of the other images of her from that site, it may be that her bath is also viewed more allegorically than in Books of Hours which might represent her bath as an occasion for sexual sin. In addition to differences of art form—the Cathedral at Auxerre has stone carvings, where Books of Hours are illustrated images—the Cathedral of Auxerre was a massively funded public project, viewed by more people than those who set eyes on a Book of Hours.

Bathsheba Blamed in Medieval Commentaries

Art was not the only way Bathsheba was received in the medieval period, but she fares better in Christian medieval commentary when she is allegorized; when she is understood to be a historical or literal person, she is often blamed for the adultery and murder.[71] For example, in the *Catena Aurea,* a commentary on the four gospels, Remigius wrote concerning Matt 1:5: "Let us enquire why Matthew does not mention Bathsheba by name as he does the other women. Because the others, though deserving of much blame, were yet commendable for many virtues. But Bathsheba was not only consenting in the adultery, but in the murder of her husband, hence her name is not introduced in the Lord's genealogy."[72]

Rabanus Maurus reads Matthew's genealogy similarly, writing, "this woman, after adultery and homicide were committed at the same time, bore to King David a son in a marriage so criminal that it would seem not worthy to be named in the genealogy of our Savior. But the name of her husband, that is, of Uriah, as if listed of the proper man, so that the magnitude of the crime is recalled even because of this man, while he is called back into memory after he was killed for the sake of his wife."[73] Not only do these interpreters explicitly claim that the adultery was consensual, but they give Bathsheba a good deal of responsibility for Uriah's death. The interpreters in the Enlightenment will assume that Bathsheba is complicit in the sexual act, but place less blame on her for Uriah's death than these medieval interpreters do.

When Christian interpreters in the medieval period interpret Bathsheba allegorically, she may fare better, but their interpretations have egregious anti-Judaic consequences. For example, St. Bruno, the founder of the Carthusian order, understands David's command to Uriah to go to his house and wash his feet (2 Sam 11:8) as Christ's invitation to the Jewish people (represented in Uriah) to be baptized into the church. According to St. Bruno, Uriah's rejection of the invitation brought about his downfall in the same way that the Jewish rejection of Christ and Christianity brought about theirs.[74] Early twelfth-century poet and hymnist Adam of St. Victor summarizes the idea succinctly: "Uriah the husband of Bersabee was slain in war against the sons of Ammon, and Bersabee then married King David herself, and was made queen (2 Kings 11). Thus the Synagogue, identified in Uriah, was destroyed and has died out. But the Church, signified by Bersabee, has been joined by a pact of marriage to Christ, King eternal."[75]

Rabinus Maurus allegorized Uriah not as the Synagogue, but as the Devil, explaining, "But mystically interpreted, David stands for Christ . . . but Uriah, who is labeled as 'my light of God,' stands for the Devil, who changes himself into the Angel of Light (Lucifer), who dares to say to God: 'My light of God' and 'I will be like the Most High.' All, whom the grace of God sets free, had been assigned to the worst marriage of this one, so that the church 'without stain and wrinkle' might be united as spouse to her true Savior."[76]

While such a dual identity for Uriah seems to strain against logical understanding, if not typological ones, the implied connection between Jews and the Devil illustrates the flagrant attitude of anti-Judaism in the interpretation of the story of David and Bathsheba.

Bathsheba also gets brought up in the Anchorene Wisse, a guide for anchoresses from about 1225 to 1250 in England, as an example of how women should not show themselves to men. Anne Savage and Nicholas Watson noted the emphasis on penitence and ascetics in the anchoritic life,[77] and also commented on the fact that the explicit assumption in this document is that any sexual incident is always the woman's fault. They wrote that such an assumption

> may anger some modern readers, who see this as typical of medieval male misogyny. Perhaps it is so. But the anchoresses are only meant to be concerned with their own guilt, not that of those they unwittingly tempt into sin, so that the question of male responsibility is mostly irrelevant here—though it is dealt with satirically in the next paragraph. Furthermore, one of the author's major concerns is not with sin, but with the physical danger an anchoress may be in if she should seem in any way sexually attainable.[78]

After castigating Dinah for going out to look at the women in the land (Gen 34:1),[79] the Anchorene Wisse explained, "In the same way Bathsheba, by uncovering herself in David's sight, caused him to sin with her, a holy king though he was, and God's prophet (2 Samuel 11:2–5)."[80] Though David is the one who commits "immeasurably serious and mortal sins," these sins and evil "all came about not because the women looked foolishly on men, but because they uncovered themselves in the sight of men, and did things through which they had to fall into sin."[81] In this interpretation, Bathsheba is the one who causes David to sin.

Obviously, there is more to Bathsheba's story in the medieval period than the single scene of her bath, which itself gets depicted in varying ways. She does not always uncover herself in David's sight; or, to be more precise, the artists do not always uncover her. In this historical era, Bathsheba plays many roles. She is not only the Queen Mother and a type of Mary Queen of Heaven, but she is also a seductress, and one who bears some responsibility for Uriah's death. When Bathsheba is culpable—in adultery, in murder—she is less positive, but she also has agency in the story. Her agency is something that will get eroded in the historical era and theological commentaries of the Reformation.

5

Bathsheba Reformed
in the Reformation

It is well for us to understand that the Reformers' exegesis of Scripture
could not remain detached research and scholarly interpretation of the
Bible. We can observe everywhere their direct participation in the life
and suffering of the church, the seriousness and urgency with which
they comfort and exhort, the way they debate and instruct.

Hans-Joachim Kraus, "Calvin's Exegetical Principles"

A seismic shift in religion and culture happened with the Protestant Reformation. The rallying principle of *Sola Scriptura* placed a renewed emphasis
on the authority of the written and preached word. But the phrase "scripture
alone" threatens to become a misnomer; for the reformers, it still meant that
scripture required interpretation. As John Thompson explained, "*sola Scriptura*
was not *nuda Scriptura.* Rather, the Scriptures were seen as the book given to
the church, gathered and guided by the Holy Spirit."[1] In fact, the elevation of
scripture as authoritative for doctrine meant that it needed to be taught and
explained, as it was in countless sermons, commentaries and systematic theolo-
gies produced during the time of the Reformation. Moreover, *Sola Scriptura* is
not *Totus Scriptura.* The center of the Protestant biblical canon was thoroughly
Pauline, filtered by Augustine's reading of Romans. The Old Testament was not
exhaustively represented, but was culled to support doctrine, particularly the
doctrine of soteriology.

Salvation, sin, and grace were of paramount interest in this time period, and
therefore it might seem that Bathsheba—the woman associated with David's
sins—would also be of interest. In fact, finding information about Bathsheba in
the Reformation is like finding a needle in the haystack of doctrine. For example,
with reference to the superscription of Ps 51, Martin Luther does not discuss
Bathsheba at all, and John Calvin only touches on her name before making the
larger theological point about God's grace to David.[2] In contrast with other

historical periods, in the Reformation there is much less focus on Bathsheba as a full character, and more focus on her as the object with which David sinned. When Bathsheba was depicted in medieval art as a seductress bathing naked to tempt David, her character had agency, but in the Reformation she is not only objectified as a woman, but flattened so far as to become an object. When Bathsheba represented a type of the church or the law in the interpretations of the church fathers, her character became more than a literary character. During the Reformation, Bathsheba is not a reprobate in need of reform; there is not even that level of interest in her.

This shift in the way Bathsheba was understood is connected with a shift in the interpretation of David. During the Patristic and medieval periods, David was understood as a figure or analog of Christ. In this anagogical interpretation, when David was Christ, Bathsheba was the bride of Christ; that is, she was the church. David—as Christ—was a figure of righteousness, who married Bathsheba as the church, and in some interpretations, as the church representing the gentiles, to save her from her sinfulness. But in the Reformation, with its focus on salvation, sin, and grace, David was not primarily a representative of Christ,[3] but instead was a representation of sinful humanity. Therefore, interpreters did not need to engage in fancy hermeneutical footwork to explain away the plain sense of the text where David sinned by committing adultery and murder, because if David is Christ, then those actions of David must be accounted for. Rather, in the Reformation David's sins become a significant illustration that even one "after God's own heart" (1 Sam 13:14), one chosen and beloved by God, can—and did—commit awful sins. When Calvin told his congregation that the story of David and Bathsheba "should make our hair stand straight up on edge," he went on to explain that the reason for such a hair-raising response was "that a servant of God as excellent as David should fall into such a serious and enormous sin that he could be judged as the most morally lax and promiscuous person in the world."[4] The power of David's story in the Reformation was that after these sins, David repented and was forgiven. In such an account, Bathsheba as a character doesn't matter. She could have been an object stolen by David.

Though Bathsheba is more functionary and less a full character in the time of the Reformation, she still appears in Reformation interpretations. John Wesley and Ulrich Zwingli make passing references to her: Zwingli referred to Bathsheba as "the dear wife of the godly Uriah,"[5] and Wesley described the moment that David saw Bathsheba by explaining, "'He was walking upon the roof of his house,' (2 Sam. 11:2) probably praising the God whom his soul loved, when he looked down, and saw Bathsheba."[6] Martin Luther and John Calvin refer to Bathsheba in sermons and lectures. For Calvin, in particular, Bathsheba is an example—like David—of a sinner who repents and receives grace. Bathsheba is also present in marginal notes of English Bibles produced during this historical period, and is discussed by a Venetian nun who was one of Bathsheba's first female interpreters. Previous interpretations of Bathsheba did get reformed and remade during the Reformation, and even though the interpretations of her are less robust than in other historical times, she continues to survive.

Martin Luther

While it is hard to synthesize Luther's complex approach to the Bible, it is easy to say that Scripture was of utmost importance to him. Luther was first and foremost a biblical scholar and teacher who produced a wealth of exegetical material, much of which is still available.[7] Luther was confident in the clarity of Scripture, and it was in the context of this belief that Luther asserted the hermeneutical principle, "Scripture is its own interpreter."[8] Luther also sought to balance the belief that Scripture was not simply an ancient document addressed to God's people in the past; it was to be applied to people's lives in that day.[9] But such application was not to be indiscriminate; in his sermons on Exodus, *How Christians Should Regard Moses,* he encouraged people to "look and see to whom it has been spoken, whether it fits us."[10] In this way, Luther anticipated a concern of modern hermeneutics; attention to the context of a given text.

As with many of the other interpreters, Luther focused on David's sin. In reference to the works of the flesh (Gal 5:19), Luther explained that David "fell horribly into adultery," as Peter also fell when he denied Christ. However, these sins were committed out of weakness, and when the two men—David and Peter—realized their sin, they repented. Luther concludes, "No person is free from temptations."[11] In fact, as Luther commented on the Bible, he often made the biblical patriarchs and matriarchs into "mirrors of contemporary German life."[12] In this way, Luther's hermeneutic is similar to the Midrash, with the belief that the text is eminently relatable to the contemporary world.

Luther also connected David with the ancient Greek hero Hercules, and in that interpretation referred to Bathsheba as follows: "The heathen say of Hercules, who was their David, that he finally let the women make a fool of him. One put a veil on him, another placed a distaff and spindle in his hand, and on account of his great love he had to spin. Well, perhaps it is credible that such great princes become fools in their love for women, as David did with Bathsheba."[13]

Luther went on to use even more colorful language, including the metaphor that "adulation is a kitten that licks David."[14] Indeed, Luther's language regarding David and Bathsheba is noteworthy in two places: first, Luther—like many before and after him—used the language of "love," not lust, for David's feelings about Bathsheba. Second, to use the word "fool" to describe David is a gentler way to talk about David's sins.[15]

While the medieval period heightened the sexual aspect of the story by its portrayal of Bathsheba bathing naked as symbolic of all sin and penance, the Reformation tends to downplay the sex. For example, in Luther's lectures on Genesis 16, he wrote, "Because of its modesty the Hebrew manner of speech is very pleasant. 'Go in to Hagar,' says Sarah. In like manner Scripture says of David (Ps 51): 'He went in to Bathsheba.'"[16] Calvin similarly noted the Hebrew expression "he slept with her" in 2 Sam 11:4, and commented that Scripture uses this language "in order to hide what is wicked."[17] Luther did not lay out what it means for a man to "go in to" a woman, but draws on the phrase to comment on the meaning of Bathsheba's name, "daughter of quiet." Luther used this etymology to explain that times of peace produce vices, and a "daughter of quiet" is symbolic of luxury, which leads to temptations and desires.[18]

Luther's explanation of Bathsheba's name appears in his commentary on Psalms 85–150. Surprisingly, Luther did not comment on David and Bathsheba in reference to Psalm 51, but he did bring her up when he discussed three other Psalms: Ps 85; Ps 101:5 as the reference to Hercules, above; and also in reference to Ps 15:14. In the latter, Luther defined bloodguiltiness, and explained that David—the purported author of Ps 15—is referring "especially to the sin committed with Bathsheba and against Uriah."[19]

Luther was also interested in Bathsheba's role as Solomon's mother. In reference to 2 Sam 7, he cautioned against reading the description of the offspring from David's body, raised up after David's death (2 Sam 7:12) as referring to Solomon; instead, for Luther, the Davidic offspring mentioned in that chapter was Christ. Luther explained: "For although Solomon was not yet born at this time, indeed the adultery with his mother Bathsheba had not yet even been committed, he is nonetheless not the seed of David born after David's death. . . . For Solomon was born during David's lifetime. It would be foolish, yes, ridiculous, to say that the term 'raised up' here means that Solomon should be raised up after David's death to become king or to build the house."[20]

In this brief reference to Bathsheba as Solomon's mother, we can see—again—that Bathsheba is not the main point; she is a parenthetical comment in a larger conversation about David, Solomon, and Christ. Luther also referenced Bathsheba as he connected her to Tamar, and to the other women mentioned in Jesus's genealogy in Matt 1. Luther assumed that the four women were all gentiles, and therefore explained that in Christ, gentiles and Jews are related by blood. "For according to the line of Abraham, [Jesus] is the brother and cousin of all the sons of Israel. According to his mother, he is a brother and also a cousin, on the father's as well as the mother's side, of all Egyptians, Canaanites, and Amorites; for he was born from Tamar, from Ruth, and from Bathsheba, the wife of Uriah."[21]

Ultimately, for Luther—as with the church fathers and Christian medieval tradition—the entire Bible was understood to be Christological. In 1525 Luther asked Erasmus, "Take Christ out of the Scriptures and what will you find left in them?"[22] He told his students in 1532, "Christ is the central point of the circle around which everything else in the Bible revolves."[23] Another analogy he used was that the Scripture, and in particular the Old Testament, was the swaddling clothes in which Christ was to be found.[24] Luther's singular focus on the Christological testimony of the entire Bible is one reason for his egregious anti-Judaic attitude and words. This is less evident in his interpretations of Bathsheba, but palpable in many other places.[25] Though Luther was committed to the applicability of the Old Testament in ways similar to the rabbis, he also wrote such violent treatises against Jews that the history of consequences of his interpretations cannot be ignored.[26]

John Calvin

If Luther was the catalyst leader in the Magisterial Reformation, Calvin is known as the systematizer, especially as can be seen in his *Institutes*. For all of Calvin's systematizing, however, he was less than systematic about his descriptions of Bathsheba. On the one hand, Calvin described David as abusing, violating, and ravishing Bathsheba, "acting like a sheer brute."[27] But Bathsheba also "consented" and "willingly agreed." Though she did not want the marriage,[28] she gains from it. This lack of systematic thought regarding Bathsheba is likely because she appears not in Calvin's writings of dogmatic theology but in his sermons.[29] Calvin is a good preacher, making declarative claims about 2 Sam 11–12. He makes similarly decisive claims about Bathsheba, but those claims ultimately contradict. Such contradictions, however, may be less apparent to the person in the pew listening to the sermons than they are to one who is combing through the written copies of his sermons to find details about Bathsheba. Perhaps the principle is that Bathsheba is mysterious and paradoxical, and her character is not easily systematized.

Calvin preached on 2 Sam 11–12 over nine days in August, 1562,[30] so he had a good amount to say about Bathsheba. Relative to the other topics and characters, though, she is mentioned very seldom. Uriah is the topic of an entire sermon, and gets praised or noted in all the other sermons. Bathsheba gets scattered throughout the sermons, but is not mentioned in certain places that might seem obvious, such as when Calvin talks about the death of the child. Although the biblical text refers to the child as the one born by "the wife of Uriah the Hittite" (2 Sam 12:15), Calvin says "David's/his child." Bathsheba is a footnote to the larger conversation about David, and about human sin and divine mercy.

In these sermons, Calvin sought to close the gaps in the text, often preaching phrases to the effect that something is "absolutely clear," "a small child could get this, "no need to discuss this further," and so on. Calvin also uses strong language to refer to what David did to Bathsheba: "he abused her," "ravished her," "violated her." Yet with this strong language, Calvin did not use the language of rape; it is always adultery.[31] Bathsheba is the adulteress, not the victim. What this allowed Calvin to do was to include Bathsheba with David as a recipient of God's grace. He described her as a sinner like David, so that like David, she would be a recipient of mercy and be an example to us of repentance. If Calvin were to paint Bathsheba as a victim of David's assault, it would be a different story, for God does not rescue her. By depicting her as culpable, Calvin brought her forward as a model for sinful humans. This tendency—to blame and castigate David, but also to see wrong in Bathsheba—continues even more strongly, across interpreters, in the Enlightenment.

Calvin's both/and description of Bathsheba begins with his preaching about her bathing. He first explained that Bathsheba is not to be condemned because she bathed, and invokes Susanna as a comparative example. Calvin went on to say, "But she should have exercised discretion, so as not to be seen. For a chaste and upright woman will not show herself in such a way as to allure men, nor be like a net of the devil to 'start a fire.' Bathsheba, therefore, was immodest in that regard."[32]

Calvin, like Frymer-Kensky and Leneman, understood the bath in 2 Sam 11:4—"and she was purifying herself from her uncleanness"—as a second cleansing. He asserted, "There is no doubt that this was meant to be understood of the sprinkling which was done after someone had been soiled by some sin which they had committed."[33] However, Calvin continued by asking in what sense was Bathsheba's purification real, explaining, "It was nothing but a shadow, full of hypocrisy. The very fact that she felt that she was guilty before God was in itself a good beginning. But she did not continue, she remained in mid-stream. She thought that she had been properly absolved when she sprinkled herself as required by the Law, but she only considered the external appearance. Well, from all that, we must remember that when we have offended God, we are to begin examining ourselves, and feel that we are really polluted before both him and his angels, and hence we are to seek to purify ourselves—but not in a hypocritical fashion."[34]

Bathsheba is, therefore, only of limited value as a model of faith, particularly when she is acting hypocritically. Calvin similarly viewed Bathsheba's mourning in 2 Sam 11:26 as "hypocritically going through another farce, just as she had done when she cleansed herself from her uncleanness."[35] He allowed that she may have been touched by Uriah's death, "For she would surely have had to be utterly insensitive not to show some love to a man whom she had married, who indeed was so virtuous, as we have seen," but because Bathsheba became David's wife it demonstrates that she only feigned affection when she mourned for Uriah.[36] Calvin explained that it would have been better for Bathsheba to remain hidden away at home instead of "going around brazen-faced, and giving herself a good time with her adulterous partner."[37] In this particular sermon, Calvin assumed that Bathsheba forgot about Uriah, and referred to Bathsheba as "an adulteress, who was the cause of the death of her husband."[38]

Nonetheless, Bathsheba—like David—is a model of how God shows mercy to sinners. For example, Calvin castigated David's servants for allowing him to use them "as pimps," explaining that they should have resisted him because they drew Bathsheba "into such perdition that she would have been finally lost if God had not ultimately had mercy on her."[39] In reference to 2 Sam 12:24, when David "comforts" Bathsheba, Calvin understood "comfort" as teaching repentance. Calvin preached, "Because both of them had grievously sinned, he undoubtedly exhorted her to repentance, so that there was a mutual accord between them. . . . David received the message sent to him by Nathan as meaning that it was not only for him, but at the same time for his wife Bathsheba, so that they rejoiced in the grace that God bestowed on them—not only, indeed, for having buried the great offence that they had committed, but also for blessing their marriage."[40]

Therefore, Calvin concluded that what we see in both David and Bathsheba shows us that the promises of God are not useless. If the two of them, to whom Calvin referred as "two poor creatures more miserable than anything else,"[41] can receive God's grace, then those who are listening to Calvin's sermon ought to be encouraged that such promises are true in their own lives.[42] Bathsheba is an example of God's mercy, and for Calvin, that cannot happen without understanding that she sinned. If she was a victim, God is less merciful, for where was God when she was being victimized? But if Bathsheba participates in sin, she can also participate with David in receiving grace.

It is important for Calvin that Bathsheba is Solomon's mother, as it is another example of God's grace. But as Calvin commented on this, the force of his thought was more about David. Calvin wrote, "Surely, David had earned for one crime eternal destruction for himself and for his descendants, and as much as the fault was in him, the way of God's blessing had been closed off, so that he would not derive anything from Bathsheba other than the seed of vipers. But indeed, so foul a crime of his in the death of Uriah moved toward the opposite outcome by the marvelous plan of God, since from that ill-starred marriage, full of treachery and polluted at length with many stains, Solomon was born."[43] As happens so many times with the Reformers, Bathsheba may be mentioned, but the point has to do with God and David.

Bibles: Geneva and Tyndale

Bathsheba also appears in marginal comments in Bibles produced during the Reformation. The sixteenth-century Geneva Bible is one of the earliest complete translations of the Old and New Testaments into English, predating the King James version by some fifty years.[44] This English translation also included a number of annotations in the margins which were strongly Calvinist and Puritan, and therefore were disliked by the Anglicans of the Church of England. Bathsheba is mentioned not only in reference to 2 Samuel, but also in the marginal notes on 1 Kings and Proverbs. In marginal notes on 1 Kgs 2:13, the Geneva Bible explains that when Adonijah (the eldest living son of David when Solomon takes the throne) came to Bathsheba to request Abishag's hand in marriage, Bathsheba "feared lest he would worke treason against the king."[45] Another marginal annotation explains that Solomon bowed to Bathsheba his mother when she approached him, "In token of his reverence, and that others by his example might have her in greater honour."[46] Bathsheba is also identified as the mother of King Lemuel mentioned in Proverbs 31.[47] Prov 31:1 reads, "the prophecie which his mother taught him," but the annotation in the Geneva Bible comments, "the doctrine, which his mother Bathsheba taught him."[48]

Bathsheba is present in the marginal notes in the Tyndale Bible, or perhaps more precisely, the "Matthew-Tyndale Bible." William Tyndale's translation, notes, and commentary were considered heretical by the Catholic Church and the Church of England, and after Tyndale was burned at the stake in 1536, his friend John Rogers operated under a pseudonym to publish the Matthew-Tyndale Bible in 1537. Not much is said about Bathsheba in 2 Sam 11–12, but further explanation is given when Bathsheba says to David in 1 Kgs 1:21 that she and Solomon will be considered "sinners." The Tyndale marginal note reads, "That is, shall seem to have offended and sinned against them, when we be deprived from the kingdom."[49] The "them" is referring to Israel, and Bathsheba is appealing to David with a more national perspective than a personal concern for her own well-being and that of Solomon.

Arcangela Tarabotti

There may have been female interpreters of Bathsheba before the Reformation, but Arcangela Tarabotti is one of the first identified. She was a Venetian nun who was forced to enter a convent in 1617 when she was thirteen years old because her marriage prospects seemed slim; she had inherited a physical deformity from her father.[50] While Tarabotti was in the cloister, she wrote at least six literary works. One of the earliest, titled *Paternal Tyranny*, was a scathing commentary against the patriarchal systems of the time, and in particular, the customs and practices concerning adultery.[51] In part, Tarabotti was responding to Giuseppe Passi's diatribe against women titled *The Defects of Women* (*Dei donneschi difetti*).[52] Passi had argued that an adulterous married woman deserved more punishment than the man, but Tarabotti used the story of David and Bathsheba to refute Passi. Because God spoke through Nathan to David and not to Bathsheba in 2 Sam 12:1–15, Tarabotti explained, "God's reproof of adulterous King David is ample testimony that men deserve greater punishment than women in violating the marriage bed. He said nothing to Bathsheba."[53] Tarabotti also asserted that Bathsheba did not know about David's plan to have Uriah killed.[54]

Tarabotti was bothered by the appeal to the story of Bathsheba and Dinah (Gen 34) to support the view that a woman needed to be kept in enclosed places. She wrote:

> You preach a sheltered life for women, digging up evidence from the tale of Bathsheba: while bathing in an open place she made even King David lie— that holy prophet whose heart was in tune with God's. Ask yourselves, witless ones, who was the true cause of her fall, and then deny it if you can. It was nothing else but the king's lust. Uriah's wife was at home, minding her own affairs bathing—whether for enjoyment or necessity, it matters little—but David eyed her too. Her beauty inflamed him, and his eyes were the gateway to his heart; by various ruses he obtained the satisfaction his sensuality demanded. What blame can one possibly attribute to that innocent woman, overwhelmed by the splendor of the king's majesty? She is more worthy of pardon than the royal harp player: she allowed herself to be overcome by a force from on high, as it were; he succumbed to the pull of flesh doomed soon to rot and darts from two eyes that pierce only those wanting to be wounded.[55]

To those who describe Uriah's murder as committed "out of love for Bathsheba," Tarabotti wrote, "it was not her fault, but David's savage nature, his overweening ambition."[56] She points out that David was neither the first nor the last man to commit adultery, and exclaims, "If only King David were imitated for his repentance as much as for his adulteries!"[57]

Adultery was a serious crime during the time of the Reformation; the punishments could include the death penalty, although Joy Schroeder noted that capital punishment was not often imposed.[58] Some sixteenth-century commentators, such as Lutheran reformer Johannes Brenz, argued that "the adulterous concubine" in Judges 19 deserved the death sentence.[59] Schroeder also demonstrates how the story of Potiphar's wife was used generally in the Reformation to warn against the seductive charms of an adulteress.[60] Though there are certainly some who warn against Bathsheba as an adulteress, it is notable that she is largely not specifically discussed in this role, perhaps because David's culpability is so clear.

But again, Bathsheba is largely not specifically discussed during the Reformation. The same woman referred to in the Geneva Bible as teaching Solomon doctrine gets ignored by other Reformers in their pursuit of doctrine. A general metaphor for the way that the Old Testament gets used during the Reformation is as an organ donor for doctrine, with the Reformers as medics harvesting the bits that can be donated to enliven their faith, and leaving the carved up carcass of the whole body of the Old Testament. The entire thing cannot be transplanted; whole stories in their literary context will not fit into doctrinal logic. Yet, as with organ donation, the heart continues to beat inside a new chest; the eyes enable a new recipient to see. In the same way that the Patristic use and appropriation of the Old Testament enabled it to survive in that historical context, the Reformation use of these texts meant that they lived on. Even if Bathsheba's existence in the Reformation was less robust than in previous or later interpretations, she continued to survive.

6

Bathsheba Enlightened
in the Enlightenment

"Have courage to use your own reason!"—that is the motto of enlightenment.

Immanuel Kant, An Answer to the Question: What Is Enlightenment?

But in the time in which our translation was made, Biblical criticism
was in its infancy, if indeed it did exist; and we may rather wonder
that we find things so well, than be surprised that they are no better.

Adam Clarke, Commentary on 2 Samuel

Bathsheba Contextualized, Commented and Criticized

In the historical period of the Enlightenment, Bathsheba is received in new
ways, as is fitting with new views of and approaches to the Bible. The title
of Michael Legaspi's *The Death of Scripture and the Rise of Biblical Studies* describes the shift that happened in the centuries after the Reformation when the
Bible was no longer only an inspired, authoritative source of divine revelation.
Instead, the written text was to be studied using evidence-based methods, particularly historical approaches.[1] Frank Kermode, following Hans Frei, explained
that in the eighteenth century, interest in biblical stories as factual superseded
a consideration of them as story, saying "'scientific' scholarship began to treat
narrative as a mere veil over historical occurrence."[2] These tools included philology, literature, geography, and anthropology.

Jonathan Sheehan argued that the myriad ways for studying the Bible
in the eighteenth century compensates for it losing its hold as a definitive center
of religious meaning. He asserted that "the difference and alienness of the Bible
would bind together Christians in a community of scholarship and perpetual
labor over the text of the Bible."[3] Stephen Moore and Yvonne Sherwood located
the disjunction in biblical criticism between earlier eras and the Enlightenment
around the issue of morality, in Kantian terms of moral faith and moral unbelief.[4]

Bathsheba's reception in the Enlightenment is distinct from earlier historical periods in three ways. First, there is an attempt to place Bathsheba in the context of the Middle East, such as when her bath is described as "in accordance with general Eastern custom."[5] Second, because the commentary becomes the primary expression of Enlightenment biblical scholarship, the totality of Bathsheba's story—from both 2 Samuel and 1 Kings—is represented. And third, Bathsheba is criticized, particularly in reference to the clause in 2 Sam 11:4 which says, "and she came to him." Enlightenment authors, like so many in previous historical eras, are clear that David is in the wrong. But there is a unique emphasis that Bathsheba could also be culpable in the act of adultery.[6] Obviously, the text does not plainly depict Bathsheba as a victim, and there are gaps as to her motives and feelings. Still, one meaning potential is that Bathsheba was victimized, and that potential is not actualized at all in this historical time.

Enlightenment: Translation and Scholarship

Sheehan defines the Enlightenment as "the new constellation of practices and institutions . . . that the eighteenth century used to address the host of religious, historical, and philosophical questions inherited from the Renaissance, the Reformation, and the Scientific Revolution."[7] One such question that still remained was that of translation of biblical texts. During the sixteenth century, multiple translations of the Bible into the vernacular shifted authority away from the Vulgate. Those many translations, however, gave way to two predominant ones: the King James Bible in English and the Luther Bible in German. Sheehan described this as "the big crunch" after "the big bang" in translations, and explained, "With the big crunch came consequences: texts were fixed, liturgies solidified, catechisms hardened into rigid forms."[8] In Germany and England during the eighteenth century, there was a resurgence of multiple translations, but these were produced for scholarship, not primarily for faith and worship.

"Translation," broadly speaking, also included translating the ancient culture and language of the Old Testament into something more palatable and relatable to modern Christian Protestants. This singular goal was accomplished in different ways by different Enlightenment scholars: English minister Edward Harwood sought to make the Bible more pedagogical, suitable for teaching morality, while Benjamin Kennicott was more philological, producing a text that was free from the Masoretic points in an attempt to correct the "very many and very material mistakes first introduc'd by the Jews."[9] S. R. Driver's *Notes on the Hebrew Text of the Books of Samuel* and C. F. Burney's corresponding *Notes on the Hebrew Text of 1 Kings* attempt to establish the best text by comparing the different versions, and though they have little to say about Bathsheba's character, Driver includes the variation on her name from the Greek LXX.

Though historical approaches came to be the dominant mode in biblical studies, literary and cultural approaches were also valued in the Enlightenment. For example, Robert Lowth's 1741 "Lectures on the Sacred Poetry of the Hebrews" introduced the concept of parallelism to the academic world, but also argued that what had been understood as simplistic writing was in reality something much more literarily sophisticated.[10] And in the 1760s, Carsten Niebuhr led a Danish scientific expedition to study the history, geography, and culture of the Near East in order to gain a deeper understanding of the Old Testament.[11] The expedition was tragic, with only one of its six members surviving, but its discoveries reverberated into Old Testament studies in subsequent years. Not only is Bathsheba's bath compared with Near Eastern customs, but when Henry P. Smith referred to the purification mentioned in 2 Sam 11:4, he explained, "That such a time was favorable to conception was known to the Arabs at an early day."[12] Adam Clarke referred to "Friar Bacon's Method of restoring and strengthening the Natural Heat" in his comment on Abishag's appointment to warm David (1 Kgs 1:2) as proof that David's physicians were scientifically sound.[13] And A. F. Kirkpatrick wrote, regarding David's command to Uriah to go wash his feet (2 Sam 11:8), that such action is "An indispensable refreshment after a journey in the East, where sandals only were worn. Cp. Gen. xviii.4, xliii.24; Luke vii.44."[14] Kirkpatrick's comment demonstrates how the idea—and ideal—of knowledge of cultural customs might mean missing other textual literary details, such as the euphemism in the phrase "wash your feet." In fact, another characteristic of this historical era is that the text is often read at face value. When it says that Bathsheba came to David (2 Sam 11:4), the interpreters understand her to have volition. When Bathsheba tells Adonijah, "Good, I will speak to the king concerning you," (1 Kgs 2:18), they do not sense any political subterfuge in her statement. Because so many of the interpretations of Bathsheba from the Enlightenment come from commentaries, this chapter will describe the various interpretations of her following the plot of the story, starting with her bath.

Bengal Women and Bathing Bathsheba

Many of the commentaries attempt to contextualize Bathsheba's bathing—and David's rooftop—in the architecture and customs of that historical period, often by analogy to other Near Eastern cultures. For example, in John Lange's 1877 commentary, he explains that she was bathing "in the uncovered court of her house, where, in accordance with general Eastern custom, there was a well."[15] Joseph Benson, in his 1841 *Critical and Explanatory Notes* on 2 Samuel explained that Bathsheba's bath took place in her garden, and David's rest in the heat of the day was "as the manner was in those countries," while his walk upon his roof was possible "for the roofs of the house in that country were flat for this purpose."[16] Simon Patrick, Bishop of Ely, in his 1703 commentary also mentioned that Bathsheba could have been bathing in her garden, but another possibility was that she was bathing in her chambers, with the "casements" open. He offers various motivations for her bath, including purification, pleasure, or to cool herself off on a hot day; but, regardless of the reason for Bathsheba's bath, Patrick compares her to "Proserpina washing herself, and exposing her whole body to [Jupiter's] view, which inflamed his lust after her."[17]

Adam Clarke explained that David's repose on his roof was "to enjoy the breeze, as the noon-day was too hot for the performance of business. This is still a constant custom on the flat roofed houses in the east." But then Clarke queried, "How could any woman of delicacy expose herself where she could be so fully and openly viewed? Did she not know that she was at least in view of the king's terrace? Was there no *design* in all this? . . . In a Bengal town pools of water are to be seen everywhere, and women *may be seen* morning and evening *bathing* in them, and carrying water home. Thus David might have seen Bath-sheba, and no blame attach to her."[18] This seeming non sequitur is an apparent attempt at softening the blame on a woman who apparently did still have some delicacy in her. Later in his commentary, however, Clarke asserted, "*Bath-sheba* was probably *first* in the transgression by a too public display of her charms."[19]

Other commentators have been more circumspect about Bathsheba's knowledge about David seeing her. Kirkpatrick, in his 1880 commentary, wrote that David's house was in a location where he could see down into Uriah's house, "which must have been in the lower courtyard of the palace, where the bodyguard were lodged, or near at hand in the Lower city."[20] Lange, after offering the possibility that she was bathing in the uncovered court of her house, asserted, "In either case, the place was private, visible only from a neighboring roof; and in the East people refrain from looking down from a roof into neighbors' courts . . . so that it is on this ground an unfounded suggestion that Bathsheba was purposely bathing in an exposed place in order to attract the king's gaze."[21]

None of these commentators described Bathsheba's bath as an intentionally seductive act. Patrick's comparison with Proserpina comes the closest, though he made that comparison to explain the clause about Bathsheba's beauty, and did not criticize Bathsheba for taking her bath. They might wonder about where and how Bathsheba bathed, but they did not go so far as the medieval artists did when painting a naked and seductive Bathsheba.

Cannot Be Acquitted of Blame

However, as mentioned above, Enlightenment interpreters insisted on Bathsheba's culpability, even if David is clearly in the wrong. As Kirkpatrick put it,

"Bath-sheba can not be acquitted from blame, for it does not appear that she offered any resistance. Vanity and ambition prevailed over the voice of conscience."[22] Carl Friedrich Keil and F. Delitzsch's censure of Bathsheba is based on 2 Sam 11:4. They explained, "In the expression, 'he took her, and she came to him,' there is no intimation whatever that David brought Bathsheba into his palace through craft or violence, but rather that she came at his request without any hesitation, and offered no resistance to his desires. Consequently Bathsheba is not to be regarded as free of blame."[23]

Lange read 2 Sam 11:4 in a similar manner, though he again asserted that her *bathing* was not seductive. He wrote, "The narrative leads us to infer that Bathsheba came and submitted herself to David without opposition. This undoubtedly proves her participation in the guilt, though we are not to assume that her bathing was "purposed" in order to be seen."[24] Joseph Hall has suggested, "Had Bathsheba been mindful of her matrimonial fidelity, perhaps David had been soon checked in his inordinate desire; her facility furthers the sin."[25]

One interpreter who is slightly more sympathetic to Bathsheba is Joseph Benson, who referred multiple times to her feelings. In Benson's description, Bathsheba is "oppressed with terror, no doubt, for she had committed a sin for which the law condemned her to be stoned. . . . Alas for poor Bathsheba! Her confusion and distress were doubtless unutterable."[26]

In reference to 2 Sam 12:24–25 where David "comforted" Bathsheba, Benson explained that said comfort was necessary for her who "no doubt, was deeply afflicted for the loss of her child, and dejected for her sin." Then Benson observed that Bathsheba is never directly spoken to about her guilt or her punishment, and he concludes, "She was punished in the calamities that befell David; who enticed her, and not she him, to commit the foul sin of adultery, and was innocent in the murder of Uriah."[27] Thus, although Benson does not shy away from asserting that Bathsheba committed a sin, his language suggests that there is something unfair about her shared punishment with David.

Matthew Henry has also been less critical of Bathsheba than others, perhaps because he has been so systematic in his discussion of David's wrongs. Henry listed the occasions for David's sin which include his neglect of business, love of ease, and a wandering eye, and then described the steps of the sin. In terms of Bathsheba's culpability, Henry explained Bathsheba was "too easily consenting, because he was a great man, and famed for his goodness too; surely thinks she that can be no sin, which such a man as David is the mover of." Henry also described Bathsheba as "a lady of good reputation" who "no doubt, had preserved her purity" until David had drawn her into sin.[28] But Henry concluded, "David has sinned, and Bath-sheba has sinned, and both against [Uriah], and therefore he must die; David determines he must."[29]

Even if these interpreters place (more) blame on David, as Henry does in ascribing Uriah's death to David, they see Bathsheba as a participant in their sexual encounter. Largely based on the words in 2 Sam 11:4, that "she came to him," they understand Bathsheba as complicit, not as a woman who was unable to refuse the king. They rightly note that any resistance from Bathsheba is not discussed in the text; it is a gap. But consistently, they fill the gap about her desire or motivation by reading Bathsheba and David's sexual interaction as adultery and not rape, concluding that she is in some way to blame for what happened. Because of my own social context, it is painful to observe these interpreters' lack of attention to the power differentials between Bathsheba and King David, perhaps especially given all the education and training they have about the text. In contrast, a 21st century actress playing Bathsheba—discussed in the next chapter—points out that a woman would have to obey the king, no matter what he would say. Though such questions of power were not part of the Enlightenment approach to biblical studies, the consequences of their reading Bathsheba's complicity become more evident when contrasted with the way she is understood in different eras.

A Hypocritical Veil

Nearly every Enlightenment commentator described Bathsheba's mourning for Uriah in 2 Sam 11:26 as a pretense, despite the text's lack of censure of her and the threefold repetition of their spousal relationship. In *The Royal Sin: Or Adultery Rebuk'd in a Great King*, published in 1738, Joseph Trapp described the events in 2 Sam 11:26 as "the mock-solemnity of mourning,"[30] while Kirkpatrick wrote, "There is no indication that Bath-sheba's mourning was more than a formal ceremony."[31] Henry similarly explained, "She submitted to the ceremony of mourning for her husband, as little time as custom would admit."[32] Clarke asserted, "The whole of [Bathsheba's] conduct indicates that she observed the *form* without feeling the *power of sorrow*. She lost a *captain* and got a *king* for her spouse; this must have been deep affliction indeed: and therefore . . . "She shed reluctant tears, and forced out groans from a joyful heart.""[33] Even Elizabeth Cady Stanton in *The Women's Bible* of 1895, who allows that Bathsheba suffered loss, cast aspersions on Bathsheba's motivation when she commented, "to be transferred from the cottage of a poor soldier to the palace of a king was a sufficient compensation for the loss of the love of a true and faithful man."[34]

In *An Exposition of I & II Samuel,* Henry, John Pink, and Arthur Gill responded to 2 Sam 11:26 by commenting, "What vile mockery! Only God knows how often the outward 'mourning' over the departed is but a hypocritical veil to cover satisfaction of heart for being rid of their presence. Even where that be not the case, the speedy re-marriage of weeping widows and widowers indicates how shallow was their grief."[35] Smith, however, has no problems with the timing of David's marriage to Bathsheba, explaining, "Marriage very soon after the death of a consort is common in the East, so that this haste did not violate the conventions."[36]

This aversion to what is seen pejoratively as "ritual" is a particularly Protestant problem, heightened during this historical time. The interpreters assume that if Bathsheba is observing a form, it must be empty of true emotion. Or, as in the case of Henry, Pink, and Gill, they understand the remarriage as indicative of the shallowness of grief, not considering that there could be other, practical reasons why a woman would remarry. While these Enlightenment interpreters seek to be objective about the text and to understand it in its historical and cultural context, there are cultural blinders they wear because of their own context and presuppositions.

Tokens of God's Displeasure and Reconciliation

Though these Enlightenment interpreters blame Bathsheba for adultery, they also make clear that David did wrong. In *The Royal Sin,* Trapp explained that Nathan's parable shows David "the evil of the sin he had been guilty of, in defiling Bath-sheba." Trapp's language becomes even more pointed as he explained that when David realized he was "the man" (2 Sam 12:7), David must have seen "it was impossible for him to restore purity and chastity to the wife whom he had polluted with adultery; or to restore life to the husband whom he had made an inhumane sacrifice to his lust."[37] Clarke had commented, perhaps pointing forward to the tragic succession narrative, that David's "extraordinary attachment to this beautiful woman was the cause of all his misfortunes."[38] Henry, however, is more positive about this verse, explaining, "Though David's marrying Bath-sheba had displeased the Lord, yet he was not therefore commanded to divorce her; so far from this, that God gave him that son by her, on whom the covenant of royalty should be entailed. Bath-sheba, no doubt, was greatly afflicted with the sense of her sin and the tokens of God's displeasure. But God having restored to David the joys of his salvation, he comforted her with the same comforts with which he himself was comforted of God, v.24. *He comforted Bath-sheba.* And both he and she had reason to be comforted in the tokens of God's reconciliation to them."[39]

Henry's inclusion of Bathsheba as receiving comfort from God along with David is similar to the move that Calvin made when Calvin explained that like David, she was the recipient of grace.[40] Calvin, however, did not go so far as the Enlightenment interpreters in blaming Bathsheba for coming to David as a sign of her complicity in the act of adultery.

The Elevation of Ahithophel's Granddaughter

Few specifically refer to the relationship between Bathsheba and her grandfather Ahithophel, but Kirkpatrick is careful to explain that "Ahithophel's adherence to Absalom (xv. 12) as an act of revenge for the seduction of his granddaughter and the murder of her husband . . . must be regarded as very doubtful." Kirkpatrick gives two reasons for his doubts; first, that it cannot be proved that Eliam son of Ahithophel (2 Sam 23:34) is the same Eliam as the father of Bathsheba (2 Sam 11:3), and second, "even if the relationship is granted, an ambitious and unscrupulous man such as Ahithophel would be more likely to regard the elevation of his granddaughter to the position of the king's favorite as an honour, than to feel aggrieved at the circumstances by which it was effected."[41] Kirkpatrick's explanation demonstrates his desire to fill in the gap about Ahithophel's motivations, a desire he shares with other interpreters throughout history. But his appeal to proof is typical of Enlightenment methodologies.[42] Ahithophel gets more attention in the novels of the twentieth and twenty-first centuries.

A Sovereign Influence over the King

As mentioned above, the genre of the commentary means that more of Bathsheba's story is told, in contrast to when she is included in medieval Books of Hours only in reference to the Penitential Psalms. Earlier Jewish interpretations emphasized Bathsheba's role as Queen Mother in 1 Kings, and that role is also discussed in the Enlightenment as interpreters note how she would be motivated to act on Solomon's behalf. Those who weigh in on David's purported oath that Solomon would be king (1 Kgs 1:13, 17) assume that it happened. And only Kirkpatrick hints at Bathsheba's role in Adonijah's death, explaining, "Adonijah died for presuming to appear as the rival of Bath-sheba's son."[43] The other interpreters do not think Bathsheba had any idea what would happen to Adonijah after he requested Abishag's hand in marriage; instead, they describe her "womanly interest in [Adonijah's] love-affair"[44] and her "simplicity."[45] Bathsheba is not seen as conniving towards Adonijah, the potential rival of her son. If the interpretations of her are patronizing, overall they are optimistic.

Adam Clarke explicitly stated that the oath David made regarding Solomon's succession "is nowhere else mentioned," but still said, "It is very likely that David made such an oath, and that it was known only to Bath-sheba and Nathan."[46] Clarke also offered the reason for Nathan's use of Bathsheba as follows, "[Nathan] knew that this woman had a sovereign influence over the king. If Bath-sheba was a source of pleasure to David, must she not also have been a source of pain to him? For could he ever forget the guilty manner in which he acquired her?"[47]

Benson, who described Bathsheba in 2 Sam sympathetically, clarified why Nathan chose to talk to Bathsheba. Though she was "private and retired in her apartment, was ignorant of what was done abroad,"[48] Bathsheba was still "likely to be most zealous in the cause, and most prevalent with David."[49] Benson also seems to have assumed that the oath was made, as he explained Bathsheba's wish in 1 Kings 1:31 that David would live forever as follows, "Though I desire thy oath may be kept, and the right of succession confirmed to my son, yet I am far from thirsting after thy death, and should rather rejoice, if it were possible, for thee to live and enjoy thy crown for ever. There could be no higher expression of love and thankfulness, than to desire never to see Solomon on the throne, if it were possible for David to always enjoy it."[50]

Again, there is no seeming cynicism in these interpreters' understanding of Bathsheba, nor any irony in what she says. J. Rawson Lumby's description of the oath is quite similar to Clarke's. He wrote, "We have no record of the oath to which Bath-sheba alludes, but we may be sure that the king had imparted to her the promise which God had made to him that Solomon should be his successor in the kingdom."[51] Like Clarke, Lumby gives no explanation as to how or why we may be sure that this oath was made, but he is positive that it happened.

Matthew Henry explained that Nathan appealed to Bathsheba "as one that had the greatest concern for Solomon, and could have the freest access to David."[52] Cady Stanton described Bathsheba's concern for Solomon by asserting, "Bath-sheba's ambition for her son was so all absorbing that she cared but little for the attentions of the king."[53] Henry goes on to give a thorough description of Bathsheba's interaction with David, as follows:

> Bath-sheba, according to [Nathan's] advice and direction, loses no time, but immediately makes her application to the king, on the same errand that Esther came to call king Ahasuerus, to intercede for her life. She needed not wait for a call, as Esther did, she knew she should be welcome at any time; but it is remarked that when she visited the king, Abishag was ministering to him, (v. 15) and Bath-sheba took no displeasure either at him or her for it. Also that she *bowed, and did obeisance to the king,* (v. 16) in token of her respect to him, both as her prince and her husband; such a genuine daughter was she of Sarah, who obeyed Abraham, calling him lord. They that would find favour with superiors, must shew them reverence, and be dutiful to those whom they expect to be kind to them. Her address to the king, on this occasion, is very discreet.[54]

For Henry, Bathsheba's actions were exemplary of how respect should be given to superiors, but Matilda Joslyn Gage in *The Woman's Bible* responded differently to their interaction. She wrote,

In Bath-sheba's interview with David one feature impresses me unfavorably, that she stood before the king instead of being seated during the conference. In the older apostolic churches the elder women and widows were provided with seats—only the young women stood; but in the instance which we are considering the faithful wife of many years, the mother of wise Solomon, stood before her husband. Then David, with the fear of death before his eyes and the warning words of the prophet ringing in his ears, remembered his oath to Bath-sheba. Bath-sheba, the wife of whom no moral wrong is spoken, except her obedience to David in the affairs of her first husband, bowed with her face to the earth and did reverence to the king. This was entirely wrong: David should have arisen from his bed and done reverence to this woman, his wife, bowing his face to the earth. Yet we find this Bible teaching the subservience of woman to man, of the wife to the husband, of the queen to the king, ruling the world to-day.[55]

Gage went on to critique the Czar for having his wife kneel before him when he placed the crown on her head. Obviously, Gage was less interested than others of the Enlightenment in contextualizing the social interactions; for her, the comparative social interactions were "older apostolic churches" instead of other Middle Eastern practices. Gage did not limit her criticism to David; she also critiqued Solomon for the way he treats "that mother to whom he was indebted not only for his throne, but also for life itself." Gage explained that when Solomon received his mother, he showed her proper reverence and request, but when Bathsheba requested that Abishag be given to Adonijah, Solomon did not keep his word. Gage wrote, "No indeed, for was she not a woman, a being to whom it was customary to make promises for the apparent purpose of breaking them?"[56] Gage did note that Adonijah's death is a consequence of the interaction between Bathsheba and Solomon, but her larger concern was that men are not legally held accountable when they break promises to women.[57]

Did Not Detect the Artifice

One of the gaps regarding Bathsheba is why she agrees to ask Solomon to give Abishag to Adonijah (1 Kgs 2:18). None of the Enlightenment interpreters thought she suspected that Adonijah's request was an attempt to make a bid for the throne, or that she realized that the request would end in his death. James Montgomery described Bathsheba as "figuring unwittingly in the death of the crown prince."[58] More than one author picks up on Bathsheba's question to Adonijah in 1 Kgs 2:13, "Do you come in peace?" Lumby commented, "There was the same sort of alarm in Bath-sheba's mind as was in those of the people of Bethlehem when Samuel came to visit Jesse before David was anointed

(I Sam. xvi. 4), when the elders of the town trembled. She expected no good from any scheme of Adonijah's, and her question refers more to the national welfare than to her personal concerns."[59]

Benson explained that Bathsheba might suspect Adonijah of "some evil design against her or her son . . . knowing his ambition and envy at Solomon, and his hatred against her, as the chief cause of his being cast down from his aspiring views and high hopes."[60] Keil also has Bathsheba suspecting "an evil intention" from Adonijah when he first approaches her, but explained that because Adonijah knew how to skillfully hide any dangerous implications in his words, "Bathsheba did not detect the artifice."[61]

A number of interpreters have explained that the reason Bathsheba described Adonijah's request to Solomon as "small" (1 Kgs 2:20) is because she did not realize it was, in fact, a big deal. Lumby wrote that she esteemed it to be small "because she did not perceive Adonijah's design in it, nor the circumstances connected with it."[62] According to Keil, it was "her womanly simplicity" which caused her to regard the request as small,[63] and Lumby similarly wrote that Adonijah perhaps used Bathsheba for "this simplicity of hers . . . and thought that his petition, coming to Solomon through her, might appear less dangerous."[64] These descriptions of Bathsheba are less egregious than the one given by contemporary scholar Roger Norman Whybray, who described Bathsheba as "a good natured rather stupid woman who was a natural prey both to more passionate and to cleverer men,"[65] but "rather stupid" is only a few degrees away from simple. Montgomery was perhaps slightly less patronizing when he described Bathsheba's "womanly interest in [Adonijah's] love-affair, to which she finds no objection. . . ."[66] However flat the Enlightenment reading is of Bathsheba—in that they do not assume irony or motivations underneath a plain reading of the text—the reading is not innocent; the interpretations of Bathsheba reveal some of the systematic misogyny that is evident in this era.

When S. R. Driver commented on Bathsheba's name in his *Notes on the Hebrew Text of the Books of Samuel,* he referred to the Greek translation βηρσαβεε "Bersabee" as "the strange corruption."[67] Different LXX manuscripts call Bathsheba different names: the Alexandrian text refers to her as Βεεθβησα [Beethbēsa], while Vaticanus and Lucianic have variations on βηρσαβεε [Bērsabee] and Driver's attention to these differences is fitting with the scholarly interest in the Enlightenment. If someone is referred to by different names, however, that can indicate some of the complexity of that person. Margaret Thatcher is called "The Iron Lady" by some and "Maggie" by others. The complex ways in which interpreters in a single historical era receive Bathsheba point to the different possibilities for her character, which are expanded in the twentieth and twenty-first centuries.

7

Bathsheba Told, Sung, Acted, and Politicized in the Contemporary World

Pop-culture loves the Bible.

Kevin Harvey, All You Want to Know about the Bible

The most challenging part about playing Bathsheba was to be able to switch off the part of your brain that tells you that as a twenty-first century woman, you're allowed to say no.

Melia Kreiling, www.crossmap.com

Bathsheba's character survives in the twentieth and twenty-first centuries as she gets interpreted and received in new forms. She is sung in operas and in rock music. She is filmed in movies, miniseries, and animated cartoons. She becomes the main character in novels in the genre of "Christian Historical Fiction" and a comparison for female characters in books loosely based on the story of 2 Sam 11. She is even referenced in political discussions in Israel and the United States. Unsurprisingly, the varying genres of song, film, and written word engage in different types of interpretation. In Christian fiction, Bathsheba is characterized as a woman of deep personal faith, while the alternative band "The Pixies" described her as a "crazy baby" in their song, "Dead." She can be plotted on all points on the spectrum from victim (as in the 2013 miniseries, *The Bible*), to sexual aggressor (as in Joseph Heller's 1984 novel, *God Knows*). Some of the specific emphases in more ancient interpretations get repeated in contemporary expressions. For example, in the *VeggieTales* animated retelling of the story, "King George and the Ducky," Bathsheba is a yellow rubber duck coveted by the cucumber King David. The focus in that version is on the King's misdeed, and she is an inanimate toy, similar to how the Reformers focused on the sins of David to such an extent that Bathsheba—the object of David's sins—was objectified.

One broad characteristic of this historical time is that the interpretations are no longer only faith-based, but more popular. As Yvonne Sherwood observed in regard to popular interpretations of Jonah, some of them "look like intentionally cartooning, lampooning, secularizing pastiches of the biblical."[1] However, Sherwood went on to confess her personal suspicion that there has been an overemphasis on the piety and seriousness of past interpreters, and explained, "The reductive (modern?) sense that a writer/artist will interpret a biblical text with either straight-faced piety or a desire to satirically debunk it, is too simplistic, and excludes all kinds of ironic, mixed modes of relations between text and reader."[2]

While those contemporary interpretations of Bathsheba that are faith-based —such as those in the genre of Christian Historical Fiction—are devout and concerned with the sacred authority of the biblical text,[3] many of the popular interpretations of her can be classified as "mixed." For example, Heller's *God Knows* pulls David down from any pedestal and retells other biblical stories in a crude and crass way. But amidst the irreverence, *God Knows* raises a serious theological question about God's killing of David and Bathsheba's first child.

Another shift in the interpretations of this time period is the way that the biblical text is read or not read. Timothy Beal observed that today, even people who read biblical texts devotionally do not read the entire chapter, or book, or surrounding context. When apps send "a daily reading" to someone's phone, or people read on a screen instead of a bound book,[4] the surrounding context is often missed.[5] Unless someone is trained—as in seminary or a Ph.D. program in biblical studies—to pay close and careful attention to the contexts of biblical text, there will be varying levels of attention to those contexts. Popular interpretations, in particular, seem to utilize images and general themes from the Bible without worrying about the accuracy of every detail. For example, when Leonard Cohen conflates the story of David and Bathsheba and Samson and Delilah, it could be that he did not carefully read Judges and 2 Samuel, or it could be an intentional juxtaposition of those "dangerous" women.[6]

Despite the varying genres, what all these contemporary interpretations have in common is a desire to make Bathsheba's story and situation connect in some way to the time and culture of the twentieth and twenty-first centuries. That same impulse motivated rabbinic interpreters to make the ancient laws applicable to their own time and situation. Though current interpretations make Bathsheba's story relate in different ways—such as by turning it into a romance, or a political thriller—the desire is still the same. As Bathsheba's story gets adapted, the character of Bathsheba gets adapted and survives. This chapter will review how Bathsheba is adapted and interpreted in story, in song, on screen, and in politics.

Bathsheba in Story

The form of the novel allows for much more character development and nuance than can be found in the biblical text. In fact, those things are inevitable when the story that only occupies seventy-six verses in the biblical text gets extended into hundreds of pages. There are three broad categories of Bathsheba in story: Christian fiction, novels set in the contemporary world with the plot based on the biblical text, and retellings that are set in the ancient world but written in the contemporary one; but all of these might be explained as a sort of "fanfiction."[7] In the same way that fans of an original work—such as J. K. Rowlings's *Harry Potter* series, or Stephanie Meyers's *Twilight* series[8]—are creating fiction about the characters or settings from that work, these authors of works about David and Bathsheba are writing scenes to explain what a character is thinking or feeling during a scene in the original work.

Bathsheba in Christian Fiction

Both Francine Rivers's 2001 *Unspoken: Bathsheba* and Jill Eileen Smith's 2011 *Bathsheba: A Novel* are set in the ancient world and provide a sort of midrash on biblical Bathsheba, the title character.[9] Both authors are writing as Christians,[10] published by Christian publishing houses. There are, of course, differences between the two books, but four similarities are striking. First, in neither book is David depicted as a sexual aggressor or a rapist, because the romantic overtones would fall flat if he were characterized in such a way. Instead, he is sympathetic. In Rivers's words, when David learns who Bathsheba is—"married to one of his best and most reliable friends, daughter of a man he trusted and who trusted him"—his initial response is to feel his stomach drop, and think, "Could anything be worse?"[11] In the same scene, however, after David's advisor tells him that he is the king, and whatever he wants is his, Rivers wrote: "David lowered his hand and raised his head. He was the king. . . . His heart began to pound. What if he did summon Bathsheba to his private chambers? What if they did find pleasure in one another's arms? What harm could one night do? Who would ever know? His desire for Bathsheba burned hotter."[12]

Smith's description of David is similarly conflicted. She wrote: "David looked away, feeling a sudden death blow to his plans. Bathsheba. He knew that name. They had met before, and he had dismissed her beauty because she belonged to one of his mighty men. . . . Irritation spiked within his breast, the earlier restlessness . . . but the desire to have her would not flee."[13]

Smith set the encounter between David and Bathsheba soon after Abigail died in childbirth, explaining that his grief over her death is why David decides not to go to war, against the counsel of Ahithophel.[14] She described David as "lonely," with "empty longings, that no woman seemed to fulfill."[15]

Second, neither novel depicts Bathsheba as a victim. Undoubtedly this is related to the authors' choices for David's characterization; because he is not a rapist, she is not the victim. He is the one who initiates their encounter, but she is not unwilling. In Rivers' version, Bathsheba is eight years old when she declares that she loves David and wants to marry him. Her marriage to Uriah is arranged, and though she has affection and respect for Uriah, she has always loved David. After Uriah's death, Bathsheba tells David, "I loved Uriah . . . But not as I've loved you. You were always the man of my dreams."[16] Rivers also wrote, "David knew Bathsheba would come to him. She had been extending him an invitation when she had so boldly met his eyes during her bath. If she regretted her impulse, he would take pleasure in swaying her."[17] Rivers narrowly avoids characterizing Bathsheba as a seductress and David as an aggressor when she makes it clear that Bathsheba chooses to be "swayed" by David,[18] and by presenting Bathsheba as "in love" with David and deeply conflicted after their night together.

In Smith's account, Bathsheba loves Uriah, and is lonely and afraid for him when he is away at war. Smith's Bathsheba is more conflicted and confused about her feelings for David from the start,[19] and remains conflicted during their sexual encounter. Smith wrote, "She should not be here. But she could not stop the longing, the desperate need to give herself to him, to know him as she was fully known. 'I will stay,' she whispered beneath the gentle pressure of his lips on hers. Emotion throbbed between them like a living, breathing thing. His kiss deepened, heating her blood, until desire won over reason."[20] Like Rivers, Smith also presented Bathsheba as feeling guilty for sleeping with David, but in Smith's account Bathsheba does not wish to leave David or his bed.[21]

Third, as is evident in their writing, both Rivers and Smith characterize Bathsheba with complicated emotions. None of these are in the biblical text, but are only present in the gaps. It is almost as if the bricks of the biblical story become disproportionate to the mortar of emotions and feelings that Smith and Rivers give to Bathsheba. Again, they are able to do so because of the space and time the genre affords to character development.

Fourth, in both of these novels, Bathsheba's story continues beyond 2 Sam 12. Smith used two full pages to describe Bathsheba's grief at the death of her first child, and also explained that Ahithophel advises Absalom's revolution because he is angry at Bathsheba. Rivers had Bathsheba unaware of what Adonijah's request for Abishag will mean, but presented Bathsheba as a woman of deep personal faith, with David telling her, "Of all my wives and concubines, only you have wholeheartedly sought the Lord."[22] Smith also described Bathsheba's faith in terms of her interest in following the law, and worshipping God with David, but overall, Smith's Bathsheba is a protagonist in a romance novel. For Rivers, Bathsheba's story is ultimately about sin and grace. Bathsheba is the model of what David was for the Reformers: an example of someone who makes mistakes and receives God's forgiveness and grace.

Bathsheba in Fiction Set in the Contemporary World

While there are passing references to Bathsheba in Matthew Quick's 2015 novel *Love May Fail* and in Julius Lester's 2005 *The Autobiography of God*,[23] Bathsheba is reincarnated in fuller form in Madeleine L'Engle's 1993 *Certain Women* and in Jack Englehard's 2007 *The Bathsheba Deadline*. Neither of these books retell the biblical story, but reimagine it by setting it in contemporary world. Lest the reader miss the connection, both explicitly refer to the biblical text.

L'Engle's book is based on the life of David, but is about a dying actor—named David Wheaton—as he remembers his life with his eight wives and eleven children. One of the characters in the novel, Nik, is writing a play about biblical David, which allows the others to constantly muse about how their own lives are similar to and different from the lives of the family of biblical David, saying things like, "Alice is no Abishag,"[24] "Wesley Bowman looked like the prophet Samuel,"[25] and "It was like and it was not like . . . If it followed the story, it would have been Chantal, wouldn't it? Chantal would have been Tamar's equivalent. Not Emma."[26]

Bathsheba's analog is Sophie, who is described as loving and affectionate, with "childlike trust" of her husband.[27] Sophie proclaims, "Love and lust don't have to be two separate things."[28] She meets David Wheaton while acting in a scene in which he walks in on her in a bubble bath, and musing about the biblical Bathsheba, Sophie says, "She was no dummy . . . She must have known that she would be visible from the palace roof. She probably wanted her David as much as I did mine."[29] In a conversation about the death of the firstborn child, Sophie gets upset and asks, "You don't believe God would kill a baby, do you?"[30] She is the one who leaves her husband because she "can't stand" his depression,[31] and at the end of the novel is described as composed and more in control of her emotions than she was earlier.[32]

Engelhard's *The Bathsheba Deadline* is set in a newsroom in Manhattan, with three journalists caught in a love triangle that is meant to resemble that between David, Bathsheba, and Uriah. Journalist Jay Garfield gets involved with book critic Lyla, whose husband Phil is a pro- Palestinian recent convert to Islam. Englehard has acknowledged that Lyla's name is "a Hebrew word for night"[33] and described her as having "killer legs," and being "a dangerous flirt."[34] Lyla tells Jay that she loves him, but he talks about lust, "I took her, right there, upon my desk. 'Oh!' she cried out at the start as if it had all been so totally unexpected."[35] After they have sex, Lyla confesses to Jay that she had planned it and had written poems about him. She reveals that she had asked her husband for a divorce, but he refused because of his conversion to Islam. Jay—and Lyla—then plot and send Phil to the Middle East as a combat journalist, where he gets killed.

Jay himself makes the connections with the biblical text, helped by the fact that when he is in a hotel room, the Bible there lies open to the story of David and Bathsheba.[36] Jay muses about how David knew that it was wrong to give into temptation regarding Bathsheba, but concludes "the sin was not the fling but the murder, by proxy, that followed . . . it was the murder of Uriah the Hittite, Bathsheba's husband, that got David to confessing and atoning 'I have sinned against the Lord.'"[37] Thus, Jay's moral quandary is not that he slept with Lyla, but that he had Phil killed.

Both L'Engle and Englehard present the biblical David as a character whose story can be appropriated. A character in *Certain Women* explains, "Maybe we have to sin, to know ourselves human, faulty, and flawed, before there is any possibility of greatness. . . . David did become great only after he'd lost everything."[38] In *The Bathsheba Deadline,* Jay reflects on David in 1 Kings, realizing that he loves David "for his poetry, his faith, his strength, his weakness."[39] In commentaries from the Medieval era and the Reformation, David was a model for penance specifically, whereas in these novels he is more broadly a model for human frailty. He is still meant to be someone with whom to relate.

Bathsheba in Contemporary Fiction Set In the Ancient World

The third broad category of novels is written in the contemporary world, but set in the ancient past. *David the King* was written in 1946 by Gladys Schmitt; in 1973 Stefan Heym wrote *The King David Report,* Joseph Heller wrote *God Knows* in 1984, and Allan Massie wrote *King David* in 1995.[40] Heller's use of language is somewhat more anachronistic to the setting; for example, he wrote that Bathsheba "designed the caftan and the miniskirt, along with her bloomers."[41] The other three are written in a style that mimics older novels, and closely resemble one another in tone, with some distinctive emphases.

Schmitt's *David the King* is distinct in its emphasis on the romance between David and Jonathan, perhaps especially notable given its publication date in 1946. Though Jonathan is David's first love, Bathsheba is the first woman to whom he says "I love you."[42] In *David the King,* Bathsheba comes to David willingly, telling him, "I have loved my lord the King since the hour when I first beheld him."[43] That hour, in Schmitt's novel, was when David was dancing before the ark as it proceeded to Jerusalem; Bathsheba was one of the women scattering flowers on the hillside, and her basket brushed against David's arm so that he took notice of her.[44] *The Bible* miniseries, discussed below, also set David's first encounter with Bathsheba when he was bringing the ark to Jerusalem. Schmitt's novel includes the material from 1 Kings, but at that time in their story,

Schmitt has David no longer loving Bathsheba. "He had learned to say 'I loved her once; and there was a time when I loved her, but it was long ago.'"[45]

Aside from the romance between David and Jonathan, Massie's novel is very similar to Schmitt's. The themes they have in common include that David did love Bathsheba, but no longer does. For Schmitt, the rift began when Solomon was born and Bathsheba turned her affection toward her son. In Massie's account, Bathsheba was unable to forgive David for having Uriah killed because their child died as a punishment; the rift widens when David allows Absalom to return to after the wise woman of Tekoa persuades him (cf. 2 Sam 14) because Bathsheba is afraid that Absalom might want to hurt Solomon. When David is on his deathbed in Massie's novel, he explains that he will make Solomon king "because I am old and cannot oppose his mother Bathsheba, whom I once loved more than any of my wives, except Michal, Saul's daughter, who turned against me, as I have turned against Bathsheba now, though too weary and feeble to oppose her will."[46]

Heym is a dissident German author, and in his *The King David Report* it is not difficult to see the political allegory and satire on truth-telling in a totalitarian state. The framework for Heym's novel is Solomon's commission of "Ethan the Scribe" to write the official history of King David. Because of Solomon's connection to Bathsheba, Ethan admits his dread of having to write about her, particularly when Nathan talks about "the story of that heart-warming, tender love of King David and the lady Bath-sheba, that sweet and blessed union."[47] Heym's Bathsheba is not as fully fleshed out as she is in other novels, but she has a level of complexity. She is described as genuinely grieved over Uriah's death, but also scheming in the plan to have Solomon take the throne. When Ethan sees Bathsheba, he says, "butter would not melt in her mouth, but the tip of her tongue carried death."[48] There have been a number of articles on how Heym's work is based on his experience in the Eastern Block during the cold war, but Heym's theological observations and implications are also significant. In particular, Vladimir Tumanov has argued that Heym undermines "traditional" views of spirituality and power by critiquing what happens when they are conflated, as in the theocracy of David and Solomon.[49]

Heller's tone, as mentioned above, is quite different from the rest. His language is cruder than the others, with David saying, "I wanted to fuck her" and commanding Uriah to "go home and fuck your wife."[50] Heller's Bathsheba is unambiguously a seductress. She knew that David was watching her bathe, and those nights when they cannot have sex, they arrange that she will bathe on the roof as lasciviously as possible in David's view.[51] Amidst the crass descriptions, Heller—as L'Engle did—raises the theological question of how God can kill the firstborn child. L'Engle touched on it more gently, but Heller has David raging against God, specifically evoking Job 38–41 when he says that he wanted to hear from God why the child died, but instead received silence: "I would have welcomed his roar. I wanted to hear him thunder majestically at me out of the whirlwind, I hungered to let me see Him react, I challenged and goaded Him to let me hear, instead of that vast and impenetrable silence."[52] Heller's David says, "I lost God and my infant in the same instant. Until he lifted my sin from me and placed it on my baby, God and I were as friendly as anyone I could imagine."[53]

All of these novels have Bathsheba deeply involved in the politics of making Solomon king. Schmitt wrote, "Bath-sheba was forever about the affairs of Judah and Israel. No tablet of clay went forth from the palace before it had passed through her hands; no matter of state was hidden from her clear, keen eyes";[54] and Heller's Bathsheba incessantly nags David to make Solomon king. For Schmitt and Massie, Nathan is being controlled by Bathsheba. None of these stories imagines Bathsheba as a pawn in Nathan's political machinations to place Solomon on the throne.

Bathsheba in Song

The genre of the song provides a particular challenge and opportunity for interpretation in two ways. First, a song involves both music and lyrics, and meaning can be found in either separately as well as in the combination. The musician Sting explained that lyrics and music "have always been mutually dependent, in much the same way as a mannequin and a set of clothes are dependent on each other";[55] he wonders if lyrics on their own are poetry, or something else.[56] Helen Leneman's interdisciplinary studies of the Bible and music pay close attention to the librettos as well as the compositions, noting how each can communicate a message.[57] In what follows, I note the lyrics, but I also pay attention to how the musical details characterize Bathsheba.

The second challenge and opportunity in a song comes with the amount of play between the author (or songwriter) and the reader (or listener). More often than not, a popular songwriter is reluctant to overdetermine—or even explain—the meaning of a song.[58] The ability for a listener to derive whatever meaning she or he wants out of that song, seems to be particularly true for popular music.[59] The songs that have been chosen are popular ones that either reference the text with Bathsheba's name, or particular aspects of the story, or, according to the songwriter, were influenced by 2 Sam 11. Because Leneman does such a thorough analysis of how Bathsheba appears in oratorios and operas, I do not attempt to include those musical compositions.

Sting, "Mad About You"

With Sting's song "Mad About You" from his 1991 album *The Soul Cages*, we have authorial intent, as Sting explained that it was inspired by the story of David and Bathsheba.[60] The subject walks "a stone's throw from Jerusalem" in the spring, or, "the April moon," and resigns himself to the potential harm to his kingship, "and though you hold the keys to ruin of everything I see . . . / though all my kingdoms turn to sand and fall into the sea / I'm mad about you." Reviewers, however, have missed the connection; for example, J. D. Considine wrote for *The Baltimore Sun*, "the album's only love song, 'Mad About You,' describes romantic passion in terms of desperate insanity."[61] Whenever Sting discusses the story in 2 Sam 11, his chronology of the fabula is wrong: he referred to David making love to Bathsheba after Uriah's death.[62] But Sting's (albeit incorrect) retelling of the story's events makes certain aspects of the text more clear. If the events were to have happened as Sting narrated them, it would indicate David's intentional planning of Uriah's death in order to sleep with Bathsheba. As it is in the text, David takes her and then tries to cover it up. In Sting's version, David is so "mad about" Bathsheba that he will go to extreme ends to be with her, but he waits until Uriah is dispatched before he takes her. In doing so, Sting is capturing something about David's abuse of power, highlighting the murder and subsuming the adultery into passionate love that is consummated after Bathsheba has become a widow.

In terms of the music, Sting explained that he decided to use the musical instrument known as the bouzouki, because "I needed to do something to sound Eastern Mediterranean because the subject of the song was from that area, around Palestine or whatever."[63] The music is fittingly dramatic with short—and intensive—violin strokes, and plaintive saxophone lines that do not melodically resolve. The lack of resolution in the music illustrates the lack of resolution in the narrative of 2 Sam 11.

The Pixies, "Dead"

The Pixies are an American alternative rock band who refer to Bathsheba and Uriah by name in their song "Dead" in their 1989 album *Dolittle*.[64] In the song, Bathsheba is described as a "crazy baby," who is "suffocating / you need a good shed." Later in the song, the singer proclaims, "you're lovely / tanned belly is starting to grow." The singer's own desire is expressed through the words, "I wancha (sic)." If this is David, there is no pretense of refinement; his desire is expressed in a crude manner. That crudeness fits with this band and its style; perhaps the crudeness also fits the text of 2 Sam 11. The singer also admits, "I'm tired of living . . . so gimme . . . my blood is working but my, my heart is dead."

The word "dead" is not sung as part of the melody, but is just yelled out. Uriah's death is highlighted in the repeated lyric at the end, "Uriah hit the crapper," followed by more shouts, "Dead!"

There are two noteworthy lines in the second verse of the song. It begins with "we're apin' rapin' tapin' catharsis." As discussed in chapter 1 of this book, a key interpretive enigma regarding Bathsheba is whether or not she was raped. This song explicitly uses the term, even though it might be subsumed as part of "catharsis." The sexual overtones continue in the second line of the second verse, "you get torn down and I get erected," but in addition to the innuendo, such a statement does describe what happens to Bathsheba's character as she—and her son Solomon—ascend in 1 Kings.

Leonard Cohen, "Hallelujah"

Articles and an entire book have been written about Leonard Cohen's song "Hallelujah," and a conference was held in 2007 at the Experience Music Project museum about the song. It originally appeared on Cohen's 1984 album *Various Positions* when it was greeted with very little fanfare,[65] but the song experienced its own afterlife when it was covered by Jeff Buckley on his 1994 album *Grace*.[66] The lyrics that refer to Bathsheba begin with the words, "your faith was strong but you needed proof / you saw her bathing on the roof." The same verse immediately references Delilah, "she tied you to a kitchen chair / and she broke your throne and she cut your hair." Delilah is the one who binds Samson (though, obviously, not "to a kitchen chair"), and cut his hair, but Bathsheba is the beautiful one who is seen bathing (she is not on the roof, but Cohen is not alone in placing her there). The conflation—or back-and-forth—of the two women might imply that Bathsheba is more intentional about entrapping David than the biblical text specifies. The line about "needing proof" has some resonance with the midrash about how David asked God to test him. And the line "she broke your throne" certainly can be supported in the tragic succession narrative, where David's house fractures and splinters.

Cohen was reluctant to determine the meaning of the song, saying (only) "This world is full of conflicts and full of things that cannot be reconciled. But there are moments when we can . . . reconcile and embrace the whole mess, and that's what I mean by 'Hallelujah.'"[67] Musically, it has similar complexity, with the lyrics describing the exact harmonic progression of the verse, "It goes like this: the fourth, the fifth / the minor fall, the major lift." Most popular songs start with the root chord, or the "one" chord, then move up three steps to the "four," then to the "five" before resolving back to the "one," and the minor key is known to be the "sad" key, while a major key sounds "happy."[68] Alan Light described "Hallelujah" as "Joyous and despondent, a celebration and a lament, a juxtaposition of dark Old Testament imagery with an irresistibly uplifting chorus . . . an open-ended meditation on love and faith."[69]

What is fascinating about "Hallelujah" is how it takes on different associations because it has been played in so many different venues by so many different people. It was the song played during "sad" scenes in TV shows like "The O.C.," "The West Wing," and "E.R." when someone is dying, or there is an accident.[70] It also gets played, every Saturday night, on the Israeli Defense Forces' radio network.[71] Moreover, different artists who cover "Hallelujah" change the lyrics from Cohen's original which gives the piece more flexibility in meaning.[72] Light wrote, "as the song has penetrated deeper and deeper into public consciousness, the personal baggage it gathers, the associations and affiliations, all have an impact on the way it is received."[73] He could easily have been writing about Bathsheba's character.

Bathsheba on Screen

Bathsheba's characterization in the 1951 film *David and Bathsheba* and in the 1985 *King David* was thoroughly discussed by J. Cheryl Exum,[74] so I instead focus on Bathsheba in three more recent cinematic receptions: the *VeggieTales* 2000 animated short, "King George and the Ducky"; the 2009 movie *A Serious Man;* and the 2013 television miniseries, *The Bible.*

Bathsheba the Duck

The express aim of *VeggieTales* is to combine "Sunday morning values, Saturday morning fun"[75] by using cartoons to teach moral lessons from the Bible. In "King George and the Ducky," they use 2 Sam 11–12 to teach about selfishness and contentment. King George (Larry the Cucumber) loves to bathe. He admits in a song that he would much rather relax in his bath than go to war, as a king should. He sings that while some kings love things like leading their troops into battle, he finds that "yucky / I'd much rather stay in my tub with my ducky!" King George has a cupboard full of rubber ducks, but one day after his own bath, he looks down and sees one of his servants (Junior Asparagus) also taking a bath with a single rubber duck.

Obviously, King George is David, his servant Junior is Uriah, and the single duck is Bathsheba. There's a clear difference between the two vegetables in their age, size, height and status. The cucumber king sends the asparagus off to war so he can take his duck. Because the war consists of throwing pies at one another, the asparagus doesn't die—that would probably be too traumatic for children's cartoon—but he is wounded when he gets hit by a pie. After a prophet comes and confronts the king about his selfishness, the king apologizes and learns to be content with what he has.

While the creators of *VeggieTales* are not unique in reducing the story of David and Bathsheba into a moral, what is more distinct is the way they reduce the scandal of the story. Obviously, that is because of its intended audience: children.[76] Also, for children who love their toys and stuffed animals, it is likely not as incongruous that the king would say, "I love my duck." But for adults who watch this, it is hard to miss that Bathsheba—the rubber duck—is an inanimate object.

Bathsheba in The Bible *Miniseries*

The first thing a viewer sees on the screen are these words: "This program is an adaptation of biblical stories that changed our world. It endeavors to stay true to the spirit of The Book." By capitalizing "The Book," the producers are affirming reading the Bible as a single book instead of a library of texts, assuming an aesthetic, if not a theological unity as indicated by the language of "the spirit." By saying that it is something to stay true to, they are making a normative claim. And when the miniseries was produced, it was accompanied by a number of study guides and resources intended to be used by faith based groups.[77] Still, they are clearly not intending to reproduce the text in their adaptation.

David's entire story is told in one forty-five-minute episode, titled, "Kingdom," and his interaction with Bathsheba takes up at least one third of it. The producers conflate some of the stories, such as when David first meets Bathsheba as he is bringing the ark into Jerusalem (2 Sam 5).[78] In this production, David is not dancing naked, but he is shirtless, and dancing with every woman whom he meets in his procession. David notices Bathsheba with Uriah and tells him that she is far too pretty for him. David then pulls her away from Uriah to dance, asking Uriah, "You don't mind, do you?" It is Bathsheba who says, "I mind," but both David and Bathsheba laughingly spin around before David moves on. More textual conflation happens when David is playing with a model of the temple he intends to build; that is when he looks over some gates and then looks over to see Bathsheba bathing. There's no indication that she knows, or can see him. Nathan comes and tells him that he's not supposed to build the temple, his son is, after which David returns to peeping (2 Sam 7 and 11). When David has Bathsheba brought to him, it is clear that she is not interested. She says, "I am loyal to my husband," and "This is wrong," but David is persistent. He is not violent, but his actions and facial expressions are disturbing. The scenes with Uriah are compressed until David writes—in Hebrew—the orders for Joab. When Nathan confronts David, David somewhat petulantly says, "But I was anointed. God blessed me."

After their child dies, Bathsheba comes to David and tells him that she thinks they are cursed, but the final scene is of David, Bathsheba, and toddler

Solomon, who is playing with the model of the temple. Bathsheba says, "Be careful, Solomon." David says, "Let him play. It's the house of the Lord. One day he'll have to build it." The narrator's voice ends the episode with the comment, "Solomon will build God's temple. But, like his father, he will find it impossible to obey God's commandments."

In fact, one of the overarching themes of the entire series is human inability to follow God's commandments, something that David and Solomon exemplify.[79] David has been interpreted as an example of human sinfulness since the second century, so that particular meaning of his story is not new. What does stand out is the unsympathetic way that David is portrayed in "The Bible," as arrogant, power hungry, and frankly creepy. Melia Kreiling, the actress who plays Bathsheba, gave an interview in which she characterized Bathsheba as a lovely and quiet woman "who has to endure some terrible things, and she finds a way to remain dignified and to deal with all of it without complaining."[80] Kreiling also described Bathsheba as the object of David's lust, saying,

> It's not her fault; she can't do anything about it. . . . The most challenging part about playing Bathsheba was to be able to switch off the part of your brain that tells you that as a twenty-first century woman, you're allowed to say no. And Bathsheba didn't have that power against her king. He does what he wants, and she has to find a way to deal with it, so she has to succumb, and that was a little hard at first, to switch into that and not ask, "Why?" So it was about channeling this lovely, quiet woman who will find strength in a different place and not in her fight against him.[81]

Kreiling's comments confirm that the script of *The Bible* did not set out to portray Bathsheba as a seductress, but instead chose to demonstrate the king's power over her and others. Kreiling says, "She focuses her attention on being a devoted mother instead of falling apart, and I really like that about her."[82]

Bathsheba in A Serious Man

When filmmakers Joel and Ethan Coen—known as the Coen Brothers—retell the story of Job in the 2009 *A Serious Man*, Bathsheba appears as the character Mrs. Vivienne Samsky. She is the new next-door neighbor to the main character, Larry Gopnik. He first sees her sunbathing in her backyard when he climbs up on the roof of his own house to fix his television antenna. Initially, Larry can only see her face because her body is hidden by her house's fence; it is only when he walks closer on his roof that he sees she is naked. There is no indication that she knows he can see her. Larry then gets dizzy—from temptation?—and the next scene is of him lying on a bed with a cold washcloth on his head. Later in the film, he goes to her house to offer any help she might need around the house, saying, "I notice that Mr. Samsky isn't around." She responds tersely, "He travels."

When she hears that he's in the doghouse with his wife, she asks, "Do you take advantage of your new freedoms?" and then offers him a joint, which he accepts. He has a dream in which they are having sex. She is on top of him, wearing a bra so that she is not naked, and he is clearly enjoying it more than she; she is smoking a cigarette and looking away. When she breathes smoke into his face, the dream switches to him lying in a coffin with boards being nailed into place over him before he wakes up.[83] The negative connections of sexual failure and death are not hard to make, though the sex between them is left in the realm of dreams and innuendo. Aside from some of the more obvious con-nections—such as that he is on the roof, she is (sun)bathing—the way that Mrs. Samsky most closely resembles biblical Bathsheba is that she, too, is a minor character whose motives are unclear, whose thoughts and feelings are gapped.

Bathsheba in Politics

In December 1994, Bathsheba was evoked in a debate in the Israeli Parliament between Shimon Peres and other members of the Knesset from religious and right-wing parties. Peres, who in that year had been awarded the Nobel Peace Prize jointly with Yitzhak Rabin and Yasser Arafat, said to Knesset member Shaul Gutman, from the right-wing Moledet party, "Your Judaism is not accept-able to me. Judaism is 'for you were strangers in the land of Egypt.' Judaism is for 'love your neighbor as yourself.' What kind of Judaism are you preaching to me? Of hatred, of domination, or facism. This is Judaism? It's not mine. Take it. . . . I recognize the Torah of Moses our teacher and not the Torah of David our patriarch."[84] Peres then continued to not only criticize David for his excessive militarism, but also for his adultery with Bathsheba, saying, "I want to tell the great Torah scholar, Mr. Gutman, that not everything King David did, on land, on the roofs, appears to me to be Judaism, or finds favor in my eyes." Knesset member Rabbi Yosef BaGad of Moledet said that Peres should be ashamed about what he said about King David, to which Peres responded, "I am happy to hear that you are also proud of Bathsheba, no?'"[85] That Bathsheba's name was specifi-cally evoked in this debate, as well as the reference to what king David did "on the roofs" signals that there is still a certain level of unease about what David did with and to her.

A year earlier, in 1993, an article was published in the *Journal of Business Ethics* titled, "The Bathsheba Syndrome: The Ethical Failure of Successful Lead-ers." The piece argues that ethical violations are the by-product of success, particularly when the following four things happen: first, that leaders become complacent and lose focus after they are successful; second, the leader has privileged access to information, people, or objects; third, there is increasingly unrestrained control of resources; and fourth, the leader's belief in her or his personal ability to manipulate outcomes is inflated. Authors Dean Ludwig and Clinton Longenecker explained, "We label the inability to cope with and respond to the by-products of success 'the Bathsheba Syndrome,' based on the account of the good King David. . . . The good, bright, successful, popular, visionary king, David, was nearly destroyed because he could not control his desire to have something that he knew it was wrong for him to have—Bathsheba."[86]

Ludwig and Longenecker's article became part of the assigned curriculum for ethics courses at the U.S. Naval War College. In May 2012, a conference was held there to discuss the syndrome as it was seen in military settings. After the resignation of General David Petraeus in November 2012, a number of journalists used "The Bathsheba Syndrome" to explain Petraeus's extramarital affair with his biographer Paula Broadwell. One article posited a connection between the syndrome and many other military officers who have been fired in the past ten years.[87] The story of David and Bathsheba became a way to explain General Petraus's actions; he was David, and Paula Broadwell was his Bathsheba. Mackubin Thomas Owens explained, "Not all Davids who fall prey to the Bathsheba syndrome have an actual Bathsheba, but Petraeus did."[88]

A number of self-identified Christian feminist bloggers protested the name, "the Bathsheba syndrome," arguing instead that it should be referred to as "the David Syndrome."[89] Notwithstanding that there is a rare medical condition known as "the David Syndrome," there is enough to David's story to make it less clear which aspect is being referenced by the "syndrome." Bathsheba's name makes it clearer which event in David's story is being evoked. It also points to how, despite Bathsheba being more than just an occasion for scandal, she is predominantly associated with the sex, pregnancy, and Uriah's murder in 2 Sam 11.

Bathsheba occasionally appears in other newspapers in the United States, mostly when guest preachers are commenting on biblical texts.[90] In 2014, she was appealed to in three publications from the global south. In the "Tide Newspaper," a Nigerian daily published by Rivers State Newspaper Corporation, author Tagwana John wrote "Still On Immodest Dress Code," and asked, "Looking at the mode of dressing in our society today especially among girls, the question that arises in any decent mind is: do women realize the power and influence they exercise over the thinking and actions of men by way of sexual attraction? Surely, this is beautifully expressed or answered by the story of king David and his tempter, Bathsheba. What was the reasons for her displaying herself immodestly within the view of king David?"[91]

In the article "How I Stole Him Away" from the *Jamaican Observer* on February 23, 2015, the "All Woman" section posted, "Jamaicans would know the story in 2nd Samuel 11 of how King David sent Uriah to the front of the battlefield to be killed so he could have Uriah's wife Bathsheba. Today, while people may not be sending their rivals to war, the actions undertaken by some in order to gain the full attention and affection of someone else's lover could be considered just as devious."[92] The article goes on to give examples from two women and two men about their strategies for stealing lovers.

Bienhome Muivah wrote, in the *E Pao* online journal an essay on Faith and Spirituality, about the power and impact Bathsheba had on Solomon and future Israelite kings.[93] Bathsheba's appearance in all these varying genres across geographical distances further illustrates the flexibility of interpretive possibilities for her character.

Conclusion

Bathsheba Unfinalized

Russian literary scholar Mikhail Bakhtin—a master of neologisms—referred to Fyodor Dostoevsky's heroes as "unfinalizable,"[1] explaining that Dostoevsky understood human souls to be free, indeterminate, and indefinite.[2] Gary Saul Morson and Caryl Emerson point out that Bakhtin not only applies the term to characters, but uses it in many different contexts. "Bakhtin advances the term *unfinalizability* (*nezavershennost'*) as an all-purpose carrier of his conviction that the world is not only a messy place, but is also an open place. . . . It designates a complex of values central to his thinking: innovation, 'surprisingness,' the genuinely new, openness, potentiality, freedom and creativity—terms that he also uses frequently."[3]

Reception history of Bathsheba's character demonstrates how she resists any single, simplistic or "finalized" characterization. She comes up in surprising and "genuinely new" ways, such as in the "British lifestyle brand" named after Bathsheba, which was described as drawing "clear inspiration from the humbling effervescence of her legend," and debuted with a beachwear line.[4] Her story demonstrates meaning potentials that have been actualized over years.

The open nature of Bathsheba's unfinalizability is undoubtedly rooted in the biblical text. The artful narration with enough gaps regarding motivations and actions invites the reader to fill in those gaps and participate in making meaning of Bathsheba. Did Bathsheba know what would happen when David sent messengers to take her? What was her relationship like with her husband, Uriah; her father, Eliam; or her grandfather, Ahithophel? Was she aware of what would happen to Adonijah when she asked Solomon to give Abishag to Adonijah?

Bathsheba's reception in the Midrash and Talmud provides an example of how textual gaps are filled in varying ways. Bathsheba is described as bathing modestly behind a screen (*b. Sanh.* 107a), as not legally married to Uriah when David sent for and slept with her (*b. Meṭ.* 58b, *b. Ketub.* 9b and *b. Šabb.* 56a), and as abstaining from and initiating sex with David at varying times after Uriah died and before Solomon was born.[5] The rabbis also expanded Bathsheba's character beyond the events narrated in 2 Sam and 1 Kgs; by identifying Solomon with King Lemuel mentioned in Prov 31, they identified Bathsheba as the mother who is responsible for the wisdom contained in that chapter.[6] Bathsheba is the wise teacher of her proverbial wise son, acting to reprove and admonish him when needed.[7]

When the church fathers received Bathsheba, they—unlike the rabbis—placed varying levels of blame on her for seducing David. But she is also an example of holiness.[8] Moreover, in the church fathers' allegorical interpretations, Bathsheba transcends identity as a human woman to become a type of the church or the law. In those interpretations, Bathsheba's nakedness is something positive; her bath becomes a type of baptismal purification which marks relational life with God.

Bathsheba's bath was the subject of much attention in the medieval period, though it, too, is received in different ways over different genres. Certain artists illustrated Bathsheba in Books of Hours as bathing naked in explicit and seductive poses, emphasizing the interest in sexual sin in this era. Other artists, however, presented Bathsheba modestly washing her feet while clothed, and still others continued the allegorical association of her bath with a baptism. In typological bibles such as *The Bible of the Poor,* Bathsheba's role as Solomon's mother is compared to Mary's role as the mother of Jesus Christ.

During the Reformation, Bathsheba was primarily received as the object of David's sin, with surprisingly little attention paid to her. In John Calvin's sermons she participates with David in the sin of adultery, but she also participates in receiving God's mercy and grace. Venetian nun Arcangela Tarabotti received Bathsheba in a different manner than Calvin when she emphasized that it is not Bathsheba who should be faulted for the act of adultery, but David.

The fault—or blame—was shared between David and Bathsheba during the Enlightenment reception of Bathsheba, because of the clause in 2 Sam 11:4, "and she came to him." David was still understood as doing wrong, but Enlightenment commentators were quick to include Bathsheba as also culpable. By contrast, Bathsheba was not considered as culpable or conniving in any "plot" to place Solomon on the throne or to dispatch Adonijah as his rival.

It is during contemporary receptions of Bathsheba that she has been viewed as a victim, or as a conniving and scheming seductress whose aim is to get her son on the throne.[9] Bathsheba has been plotted in novels; shot in films, animations, and television miniseries; and sung about on popular songs. By all accounts, her story will continue to inspire various receptions.

This study will likely not be the final(ized) one of Bathsheba. That ought not to be a surprise; we are always in the middle of the stream of history. Though it flows from the past, it continues to flow into the future. In the third-wave feminist book *ManifestA,* authors Jennifer Baumgardner and Amy Richards wrote,

"The real power of speaking out is that women achieve the strength and clarity necessary to be neither victims nor victimizers but proud survivors."[10] The minor, enigmatic biblical character Bathsheba has survived through time by those who have received her and spoken out about her in varying ways. Though she fades out of the scene in the biblical text, she refuses to fade from thought and study. Bathsheba will continue to survive in the centuries to come.

NOTES

Introduction

1. Sternberg, *Poetics of Biblical Narrative*, 191. In particular, the verse which recounts the actual act of adultery is shockingly spare. The way in which the external actions are described, in rapid sequence of verbs: "he sent, he took, she came, he lay, and she returned," gives rise to what Sternberg called a "clash between matter and manner in the discourse." Ibid., 197. Andreas Kunz also observed the sparseness of Bathsheba's presentation as he explained, "Die Erzähler skizziert sie in wenigen Strichen als handelnde Frau" [The narrator sketched her as an acting woman using a few strokes.] Kunz, *Die Frauen und der König David*, 348.

2. Many other biblical characters also fade out of the story without a report of their death, such as Ishmael and Hagar, Dinah, many of Jacob's sons, and so on. These characters—like Bathsheba—may even play a significant role in the biblical narrative for some time, but they are not the focus of the larger story.

3. Brueggemann, *David's Truth*, 13.

4. Rimmon-Kenan, *Narrative Fiction*, 130.

5. Ibid., 128–29. Rimmon-Kenan identified different kinds of gaps, the most common of which is the hermeneutic, or information gap, which can range from very trivial to very important. Moreover, gaps can be temporary—filled in later in the text—or permanent. Sternberg differentiated between a gap, which he described as relevant and "omitted for the sake of interest" and a blank, which is irrelevant and "omitted for lack of interest." Sternberg, *Poetics of Biblical Narrative*, 236.

6. Iser, "The Reading Process," 285. Elsewhere, Iser explained that "every literary text invites some participation on the part of the reader. A text which lays things out before the reader in such a way that he can either accept or reject them will lessen the degree of participation as it allows him nothing but a yes or no. Texts with such minimal indeterminacy tend to be tedious, for it is only when the reader is given the chance to participate actively that he will regard the text, whose intention he himself has helped to compose, as real. For we generally tend to regard things that we have made ourselves as being real. And so it can be said that indeterminacy is the fundamental precondition for reader participation." Iser, "Indeterminacy," 13–14.

7. Auerbach, *Mimesis*, 9.

8. Ibid., 11. Auerbach went on to explain that the reason the biblical narrator—whom he identifies as the Elohist—wrote in such a manner is because he believed in the objective truth of the story of Abraham's near sacrifice, and that the biblical texts overall claim absolute religious authority, as it gets expressed in doctrine. Ibid., 11–12.

9. Witek, "Anatomy of a Dance Hit: Why We Love to Boogie with Pharrell," *NPR. com,* June 2, 2014, http://www.npr.org/blogs/health/2014/05/30/317019212/anatomy-of-a -dance-hit-why-we-love-to-boogie-with-pharrell [Accessed Jan. 18, 2015]. Also see Witek, Clarke, Wallentin, Kringelbach, and Vuust, "Syncopation, Body-Movement and Pleasure in Groove Music," *PLoS One,* April 16, 2014. doi:10.1371/journal.pone.0094446.

10. Ismael Beah described the storyteller as only a shepherd who can guide the story, but once the story has been told, it no longer belongs to the storyteller but to those who want to take it in new directions. Beah, *Radiance of Tomorrow,* ix.

11. While Adele Berlin does not go so far as to suggest that Bathsheba is not worth noting, Berlin does describe Bathsheba in 2 Samuel as "a complete non-person . . . simply part of the plot." Berlin has argued that it is not until 1 Kings that Bathsheba will become a character in the events to help her son Solomon succeed David on the throne. Berlin, "Characterization in Biblical Narrative," 224. The Reformers, discussed in chapter 4, take a similar approach to Bathsheba. Instead of focusing on her actions as a character, she is more functionary: the object of David's sin.

12. Holub, *Reception Theory,* x.

13. Jauss was greatly influenced by Hans-Georg Gadamer's ideas that interpretation comes from a fusion of two horizons: the horizon of the work which was contextualized in the past, and the horizon of the interpreter in her own subjective context. Gadamer, *Truth and Method,* 302–307. Gadamer also developed his principle of *Wirkungsgeschichte,* which is usually translated as "history of effects," but the German roots of these terms is where we find both distinction and overlap. The German *Rezeption* is different from *Wirkung,* the latter often translated as "response" or "effect." But both terms have to do with the impact of a literary work. Roland Boer explained, that for Gadamer, "Rezeption-sgeschichte marks the active task of interpreting, appropriating, and applying a biblical text, whether in scholarly work, religious observance and sermons, conscious cultural re-readings in literature or film or art and so on. By contrast, Wirkungsgeschichte desig-nates a more passive and unwitting effect of the text on society and culture, especially in the way the Bible shapes law, art, politics, social values, prejudices, and preconceptions. Often the two are blended, if not confused, so that 'reception' becomes the blanket term." Boer, "Against 'Reception History,'" http://www.bibleinterp.com/opeds/boe358008.shtml [Accessed Dec. 12, 2014].

14. Jim West, "Reception History: A Simple Definition," http://zwingliusredivivus .wordpress.com/2011/07/15/reception-history-a-simple-definition [Accessed Jan. 18, 2015]. An example of this could be when reception history focuses on homilies without looking at the text preached on.

15. Beal, "Reception History and Beyond," 366.

16. Gary Martin demonstrates how other fields struggle with finding "the original," offering the examples of Shakespeare's *King Lear* and Handel's *Messiah.* Martin, *Multiple Originals,* 24–25.

17. Beal, "Reception History and Beyond," 371. Such a shift—from "reception" to "pro-duction" would certainly address the concern with the passivity of "reception."

18. Ibid.

19. Fernando Segovia explained that cultural criticism does pay attention to actual flesh-and-blood readers instead of ideal ones. Moreover, Segovia understands cultural studies to pay attention to the ideological dimensions of these texts and their interpretations, but he is loath to advance a simple equation of cultural studies and ideological criticism. Segovia also seeks to ask about the end of cultural criticism, and draws on Elisabeth Schüssler-Fiorenza's rhetorical-emancipatory paradigm. A cultural critic ought not remain withdrawn, but ought to add her own voice to the struggle. Segovia, "Cultural Criticism," 322–36.

20. Breed, "Nomadology of the Bible," 308.

21. Ibid., 309. Matei Călinescu also used the metaphor of "haunting" as he explained, "It is not only the case that historically earlier texts haunt later ones, but also that later texts haunt earlier ones." Călinescu, *Rereading*, xi.

22. In this analogy, there are also some limits to what can actually happen: the bear will not get up, put on a tutu and begin to pirouette. Correspondingly, a text's virtual potentials are also limited: Bathsheba is not a witch who brews a love potion to make David desire her, nor does she represent Christ.

23. Where some might want to oppose the virtual and the real, Deleuze argued that those are not in opposition in the same way that the virtual and the actual are. "The virtual is fully real in so far as it is virtual." But neither is "virtual" the same as "possible" because the virtual becomes actualized. Deleuze, *Difference and Repetition*, 208–211.

24. Breed also draws on Deleuze's work in *The Fold*, in which Deleuze notes how problematic it is to conflate the essence of something (what it is) with its description (what it does). For example, instead of saying "the tree is green," it would be more accurate to say, "the tree greens." Deleuze, *The Fold*, 53. Breed explained that if we think of the potential of biblical texts, we are better able to consider their different manifestations, instead of thinking of them singularly. Breed, *Nomadic Text*, 117.

25. Breed, "Nomadology of the Bible," 309.

26. Though Beal was concerned about the overemphasis on the original text, Breed was concerned that Beal's call to cultural criticism might focus on a singular meaning in a specific cultural context. Breed wrote, "cultural history presupposes that a biblical text means something particular in each time and place and that there is a specific social construction of the text in each context. Thus the cultural historian allows that there are multiple meanings to a text, but that in each context there is still a limitation of meaning, that is, the biblical text is a (singular) discursive object in each context." Breed, "Nomadology of the Bible," 309.

27. "Original context" has meant, for many, that the text has a singular "right" meaning, which is the author's intent within the author's historical context. Other contemporary scholars who note the overemphasis on this include Roland Boer and Dale Allison.

28. Breed asserted, "The truth is that texts always leave their contexts, especially their putative original contexts, and contexts never seem to do anything to stop them. Actually, the situation is even worse: original contexts simply disappear into the mists of time while the texts romp around in the present." Breed, *Nomadic Text*, 93.

29. Junior, "Re/Use of Texts," http://www.atthispoint.net/editor-notes/reuse-of-texts/ 265/ [Accessed July 29, 2015].

30. In January 2004, when the 16-year-old chimpanzee "Gracie" escaped for the fourth time from her enclosure at the Los Angeles Zoo, the *LA Times* published an article titled, "Gracie Acts More Like Hairy Houdini," http://articles.latimes.com/2004/ jan/22/local/me-zoo22 [Accessed Jan. 16, 2015]. In April 2014, Brian Burnes wrote in the *Kansas City Star*, "It wasn't careless zookeepers that were responsible for the escape of seven chimpanzees from their Kansas City Zoo enclosure on Thursday afternoon. It was clever chimpanzees." *Kansas City Star*, http://www.kansascity.com/news/local/ article344810/Seven-chimpanzees-use-ingenuity-to-escape-their-enclosure-at-the-Kansas -City-Zoo.html [Accessed Jan. 16, 2015].

31. Junior, "Re/Use of Texts," http://www.atthispoint.net/editor-notes/reuse-of-texts/ 265/ [Accessed July 29, 2015].

32. Seow, *Job 1–21*, 184–85.

33. Nicholls, *Walking on Water*, 190. The analogy of a scrapbook does not preclude the existence of some sort of scheme of organization, selectivity, and editing, but even if one has heavily edited her pictures from her cruise around the Mediterranean, her scrapbook tends to be largely sentimental for *her*, or those whose pictures were included (hence the line, "you had to be there"). The "scrapbooker" always runs the risk of having left someone off the page, but those long dead interpreters cannot see if their works made the collection.

34. Charles H. Cosgrove has urged interpreters to acknowledge the criteria they use—which are often "extra-exegetical"—when choosing between different interpretations of a given text, in order for them to take responsibility for their interpretations and their ethical implications. Cosgrove, "Toward a Postmodern Hermeneutica Sacra," 43. In general, feminist biblical interpretation maintains a lack of pretense of "objectivity," encouraging an interpreter to state her or his situatedness.

35. Hankins, "The Book of Job's Past, Present, and Future Consequences," http:// marginalia.lareviewofbooks.org/the-book-of-jobs-past-present-and-future-consequences -by-davis-hankins/ [Accessed Jan. 25, 2015].

36. Again, one of Beal's concerns about the way reception history had been practiced was its overemphasis on the text, instead of its interpretation.

37. Breed, *Nomadic Text*, 117. Such a question will move its asker—and answerer— away from the idea of meaning as something inherent in the text, something that A. K. M. Adam referred to as "the myth of subsistent meaning," the idea that "meaning" is an immanent property of a text. Adam, *Faithful Interpretation*, 3–5.

38. However, this diachronic study is not exhaustive; see below.

39. Repphun, Galbraith, Sweetman, and Harding, "Beyond Christianity," 7.

40. Steussy, *David*, 92.

41. Exum, *Plotted, Shot, and Painted*.

42. Khaleel Mohammed's *David in the Muslim Tradition* (2014), provides a helpful description of the varying ways that Islamic interpreters have understood the Qur'anic verses that seem to refer to David's adultery. Mohammed, *David in the Muslim Tradition*.

43. Kunz, *Die Frauen und der König David*, 206.

44. Ibid.

45. Häusl, *Abischag und Batscheba.*

46. Kunoth-Liefels, *Über die Darstellungen der "Bathsheba im Bade."*

47. Besançon, *"L'affaire" de David et Bethsabee.*

48. The latter reference considers the debates between Finkelstein, Silberman, and Thompson; and between Lemche and Davis regarding the dates of the narratives. Lemaire, "David, Bethsabée et la Maison de David," 41–53.

1 — Bathsheba in the Bible

1. I have written previously and at greater length on the gaps in the narrative concerning Bathsheba; what follows is an abbreviated version of that, paying particular attention to the gaps that are filled throughout reception history. Koenig, *Isn't This Bathsheba?* Two other notable studies that treat the gaps in these texts are first, Meir Sternberg's chapter on 2 Sam 11, "Gaps, Ambiguity, and the Reading Process" in *Poetics,* 186–229, and second, Keith Bodner's *David Observed: A King in the Eyes of His Court.* Sternberg focuses on the different possibilities in the biblical chapter for David, Uriah, and Joab, with less attention specifically on Bathsheba; and, Bodner considers more of David's story than just 2 Sam 11–12.

2. Garsiel, "The Story of David and Bathsheba," 249.

3. There is a *Kethib/Qere* in this verse which signifies between what is written, "*kethib,*" and what is supposed to be read, "*qere.*" "The messengers," הַמַּלְאָכִים, is what is written, but "the kings," המלכים, is to be read. The Greek Septuagint (LXX), the Aramaic Targums, the Latin Vulgate, and multiple MSS confirm this reading. Yet, "messengers" do play an important role in the story. They appear in verse 4 when David sends them to get Bathsheba, and a single messenger (המלאך) gets sent to tell David the news of the battle in 2 Sam 11:19, 22, 23, and 25.

4. Wenzel, *Fasciculus Morum,* 661.

5. H. Hirsch Cohen reasoned that it must have been a particularly hot day and that David must have been unable to get up from his bed until evening because it was too hot. Cohen went on to explain that the heat heightened David's susceptibility to sexual temptation, writing, "a sirocco-type heat wave must have imprisoned David in his room that entire afternoon and greatly weakened his self-control." Cohen, "David and Bathsheba," 144. Nineteenth-century interpreters such as Adam Clarke explain that the resting during the hot noon hour is "still a constant custom on the flat roofed houses in the east."

6. Bailey, *David in Love and War,* 86.

7. For example, Jill Eileen Smith's novel sets the meeting between David and Bathsheba shortly after Abigail's death. Bathsheba first sees David from afar at the funeral, where she observes how much he loved Abigail and how grief stricken he is by her death. Smith, *Bathsheba,* 41.

8. J. Cheryl Exum, "Bathsheba Plotted, Shot, and Painted," 47–73, and *Plotted, Shot, and Painted: Cultural Representations of Biblical Women.* David Gunn similarly examined Bathsheba's characterization in visual and cinematic forms in his 1996 article "Bathsheba Goes Bathing in Hollywood: Words, Images, and Social Locations."

9. Mulvey, "Visual Pleasure and Narrative Cinema," 6–18.

10. Exum, "Bathsheba Plotted, Shot, and Painted," 71. The viewer's voyeurism of Bathsheba is discussed further in chapter 4, "Bathsheba in the Bath in the Medieval Period."

11. Exum notes that in the 1985 movie, both Bathsheba and her attendant are washing Bathsheba's breasts, "rather thoroughly, I would say. Indeed, there are suggestions of homo-eroticism and nymphomania—certainly not innocent washing—in the way Bathsheba enjoys her bath." *Plotted, Shot, and Painted,* 67.

12. For example, Stephen L. McKenzie explained that Bathsheba's bath was done to purify her from her menstrual discharge, as Lev 15 commands. *King David,* 157. Lest I cast stones, I must admit I also explained Bathsheba's bath in that way in my *Isn't This Bathsheba?,* 37. Frank Kermode was more circumspect about the type of bath when he wrote, "perhaps the bath is mentioned not solely to explain the arousal of David's desire at seeing Bathsheba naked, but also to indicate that he was at least not guilty of ritual impurity . . . This seems unlikely, but such are the questions raised by gaps." Kermode, "New Ways with Biblical Stories," 126.

13. Frymer-Kensky, *Reading,* 147.

14. Leneman, *Love, Lust, and Lunacy,* 275.

15. Steussy, *David,* 62.

16. Sternberg, *Poetics,* 236. Frank Kermode wrote, "I think myself that Sternberg is a little too confident that he can invariably tell a blank from a gap, but that there is a difference is undoubted." Kermode, "New Ways," 125.

17. In Smith's novel, not only does Bathsheba observe David grieving at Abigail's funeral, but she also attends a celebration of a festival at the palace with her grandfather, Ahithophel.

18. Auerbach, *Mimesis,* 9.

19. Cf. Yee, "'Fraught with Background,'" 240–53.

20. Rachel Adelman points out that such a question might be overly polarized, as if it is entirely one or the other. She wrote, "A grey area lies between the binary of 'active' and 'passive' subject, which disrupts the categorical reading of their intercourse as either seduction or rape. In coming into the king's private domain, she is the means of a divine trial, which, like the Trojan Horse, bodes terrible consequences for David, as a 'gift' which is both bidden yet forbidden." Adelman, *Female Ruse,* 180. David T. Lamb has argued that Bathsheba was raped by David. He explained, "While the text never states explicitly that David forced her to have sex, the fact that the text places all of the blame for what happened on him and none of it on her, and that the crime warranted a death sentence for him, makes a highly compelling argument that he raped her. I'd call it a power rape." Lamb, *Prostitutes and Polygamists,* 134. Brent Emery specifically has argued against Lamb because of the verbs used in the text. Emery, "Comparing Texts in Hebrew Scripture Helps Clarify Claims of Rape," http://www.thenewstribune.com/news/local/community/gateway/g-living/article44756976.html [Accessed Nov. 14, 2015].

21. Sandie Gravett, "Reading 'Rape,'" 279. Anne Létourneau has argued, however, for referring to the act as rape, particularly when doing a contextual reading. In a paper presented at the annual SBL conference in 2015, she pointed out how problematic—and even dangerous—it is to equate the absence of protest with consent. Létourneau, "Bathing Beauty."

22. Neither is there the word שׁגל (cf. Isa 13:16, Zech 14:2), nor the niphal of חמם (cf. Jer 13:22), nor even the verbal root פתה (cf. Jer 20.7). Gravett has argued that some of the verbs commonly used to describe sexual intercourse (שׁכב, "to lay," or ידע, "to know") can be used to depict sexually violent acts of rape, but only when combined with other words such as the piel of ענה, or חזק, "strength, force." *Ibid.,* 281. Matthias Augustin noted the connection that exists between David's taking of Bathsheba in 2 Sam 11 and Pharaoh's taking of Sarai in Gen 12:10–20. Augustin, "Die Inbesitznahme der schönen Frau," 145–54.

23. Gray does argue for a connection, however, particularly when he uses the language of "intensification" in the sexual encounters. He wrote, "whereas David 'takes' (לקח) Bathsheba (2 Sam 11.4), Amnon 'seizes' (חזק) Tamar. This sense of intensification as we move from David's seduction of Bathsheba to Amnon's rape of Tamar is also apparent in the terms by which, in each case, the moment of consummation is described. With regard to David, we are told, וישׁכב עמה[and he lay with her] but concerning Amnon, וישׁכב אתה [and he lay her](v. 14).

David sleeps with Bathsheba in some sort of relational configuration which, once, admittedly basely, started, persists until the end of his life, whereas Amnon, as is quite literally reflected in the syntax, 'lays' Tamar and then with instantaneous callousness, boots her out." Gray, "Amnon," 48. Another difference between the stories of David and Bathsheba and Amnon and Tamar is that 2 Sam 13 does include Amnon's feelings for Tamar; he loves her, and then hates her, while no such corresponding feelings are ascribed to David in 2 Sam 11. Cf. Leneman, "Portrayals of Power," 147, discussed below.

24. Freedman, "Dinah and Shechem," 60; Yamada, *Configurations of Rape,* 136.

25. The text says, "because he found her in the open country, and though the betrothed young woman cried out for help there was no one to save her" (Deut 22:27). Location is also important in other ancient Near Eastern laws (ANET, 181, 196). Cf. Pressler, *View of Women,* 32.

26. Steussy, *David,* 78. Steussy has argued that David's action might be called "sexual harassment," in the modern sense of that term, especially because his action involves his abuse of power, though she acknowledges that the text's approach to such issues does not mirror the kind of responses we might have today.

27. In *b. Yoma* 22b, R. Huna observed how four of David's children experience tragedy and/or death: Tamar, Amnon, Absalom, Adonijah. Joel Rosenberg referred to the number and the saying from the Talmud in his "Meanings, Morals and Mysteries," 67.

28. de Vaux, *Ancient Israel,* 160.

29. Daniel Bodi examined David's behavior in light of ancient Near Eastern texts from Mari and Mesopotamia in *The Demise of the Warlord.* Bodi noted that the "warlord" was supposed to do two things: focus on war, not dally with women; and, take care of the "resident alien" (Akkadian *ubāru*). Strikingly, David's failure in both of these areas did not prevent the prominence of David's descendants, leading Bodi to suggest, "The novelty of the Hebrew narrative is the deconstruction of the traditional warlord ideology." Bodi, *Demise,* 227.

30. In Prov 6:25, the verb refers to seduction done by women, "Do not let her [the adulteress] take you with her eyelids" (אל־תקחך בעפעפיה). The legal code of the Bible does not use the word לקח, "to take," to refer to adultery or rape.

31. For this reason, Horst Seebass explained that David's wrong was an "abuse of power." Seebass, "Nathan und David," 205–206.

32. Gunn, "David and the Gift," 20.

33. For example, A. F. Kirkpatrick wrote, "Bath-sheba can not be acquitted from blame, for it does not appear that she offered any resistance," Kirkpatrick, *Second Book,* 327; and Keil and Delitzsch explain, "Bathsheba is not to be regarded as free of blame." Keil and Delitzsch, *Biblical Commentary,* 383.

34. Benson, *Critical and Explanatory Notes Vol 1,* 893.

35. *Josephus' Antiquities,* 7.131.

36. Leneman, "Portrayals of Power," 147.

37. Sun acknowledges her experience as a Chinese woman, explaining, "for a long while I still conformed to the traditional stereotypes of a Chinese woman: passive, submissive, and hidden behind the scene. There were several incidents in my life when I should have spoken up for myself but I did not." Sun, "Bathsheba Transformed," 30. Sun described Bathsheba's action in sending someone to speak as "the first step toward the journey of voice." Ibid., 35.

38. A literal translation of 2 Sam 11:5 is "And the woman conceived, and she sent and she told to David, and she said, 'I am pregnant.'" Mieke Bal notes that the one who "sends" in a narrative is in a position of power. Bal is drawing on the work of A. J. Greimas who uses the French terms *destinateur* and *destinataire* ("sender" and "receiver") to distinguish between actors in a narrative. Bal uses the terms "power," and "receiver." Bal, *Narratology,* 198. David's power is evident in that he "sends," שלח, a number of times in 2 Sam 11; in vv. 1, 3, 4, 6, 14, and 27. Joab also "sends" to David, in 2 Sam 11:18.

39. Chrysostom, "Homilies on Colossians," 299.

40. The word רגלים, "feet," is a biblical euphemism for genitals (cf. Exod 4:25, Isa 6:2, 7:20, Ruth 3:4, 8, 14); instead of simply commanding, "Go home and sleep with your wife," David uses this euphemism to hold open the meaning. Uriah himself later fills this gap in 2 Sam 11:11 when he vows that he will not go home and "lie with my wife."

41. The 1951 film *David and Bathsheba* includes a speech wherein David explains "I said nothing to you until you told me that there is no love in your marriage. Yes, you told me that, and so did Uriah." The 1985 film *King David* portrays Uriah as an abusive husband. Exum, *Plotted, Shot, and Painted,* 23–24. Exum also has argued for a naïve Uriah in her *Tragedy and Biblical Narrative,* 176.

42. Sternberg, *Poetics,* 221.

43. Fokkelman, *Narrative Art and Poetry,* 69.

44. Bal, *Lethal Love,* 34.

45. Clarke went on to characterize Joab using the following terms: "He was a *ruffian,* not a *soldier;* base and barbarous beyond example, in his calling; a pander to the vices of his monarch, while he was aware that he was outraging every law of religion, piety, honour, and arms!" Clarke, *The Old Testament: Volume II,* 336.

46. The text first reports that some of the men in David's army fell, and then says,

"and also Uriah the Hittite died" (2 Sam 11:7). Joab's messenger presents the news to David in the same order in 2 Sam. 11:24, with the additional adjective that Uriah is "your" (that is, David's) servant. Though David's primary command was that Uriah be killed, his death is mentioned secondarily, after the death of the others.

47. Cf. Polzin, *David and the Deuteronomist,* 74; Jobling, *1 Samuel,* 43–77; Bodner, *David Observed,* 109.

48. For example, Bodner wrote, "arguably, Joab's actions are virtually indispensible for David retaining his hold on power." Bodner, *David Observed,* 98. Those actions were occasionally reprehensible, such as when Joab killed Abner (2 Sam 3), Absalom (2 Sam 18), and Amasa (2 Sam 20). But also, through the woman of Tekoa, Joab brokered Absalom's return to Jerusalem (2 Sam 14:1–23); and, it was Joab whose speech to David, while David was mourning for Absalom, resulted in David returning to his throne (2 Sam. 19:5–7).

49. Joab is in the first verse of 2 Sam 11, and appears at the end of 2 Sam 12, enveloping the events that take place in these texts. In 2 Sam 12:26, it is Joab who captures Rabbah, the capital of Ammon, but in 2 Sam 12:27 he invites David—apparently absent from the fighting for all that time—to come and claim the city. Daniel Bodi referred to the warning, "lest it be called by my name" (2 Sam. 12:28) as "ironic," explaining, "Joab seems concerned with David's military fame as a warlord, especially if his misconduct with the wife of one of his elite officers was going to be part of his other, unfavorable reputation. The formulaic expression does not denote ownership of the city. Rather, the victory in battle confers fame on the warlord and increases the honor of the conqueror of a particular city." Bodi, *Demise,* 98.

50. Calvin, *Sermons on 2 Samuel,* 516.

51. Henry, Gill, and Pink, *Exposition of I & II Samuel,* 402.

52. Jill Eileen Smith devotes two pages to describing Bathsheba's grief at Uriah's death.

53. The word ספד can be translated as "to wail" or "to lament." While it is a verb—Bathsheba mourns—it is interesting that in a chapter devoid of emotions, it gets read as an action instead of a feeling.

54. Two words in the verse get used for husband, איש, and בעל. Several English translations only use the word "husband" once, which avoids repetition but also misses the threefold emphasis on their relationship. One could translate בעל as "master" instead of "husband," which might be where some get the idea of a domineering Uriah.

55. Kirk-Duggan, "Slingshots, Ships, and Personal Psychosis," 56.

56. Even though Bathsheba was married to David at the end of 2 Sam 11, the first place where she is referred to as David's wife—not Uriah's—is in 2 Sam 12:24 where David comforts her. In the Matthean genealogy, Bathsheba is referred to not by her personal name but as "the wife of Uriah the Hittite," the same way she was described throughout 2 Sam 11–12.

57. Niu Zhixiong has surveyed the varying ways that David's action in 2 Sam 12:16–23 have been received, including that David is mourning for the dead, performing penitential rites in the hopes that God might change God's mind, or engaging in a cycle of mourning and rejoicing. Zhixiong, *The King Lifted,* 135–51.

58. Cady Stanton, Elizabeth. *Women's Bible*, 57.

59. Rivers, *Unspoken*, 124–25.

60. L'Engle, *Certain Women*, 259.

61. Cf. Leonhard Rost, *Succession*, and the following critiques: Thornton, "Solomonic Apologetic"; Bailey, *David in Love and War;* Lawlor, "Theology and Art"; Miller and Roberts, *Hand of the Lord;* Keys, *Wages of Sin;* and Römer and de Pury, "Deuteronomistic Historiography." Adelman notes the role that women play in determining the succession in chapter 5 of her *Female Ruse.*

62. Tod Linafelt noted how problematic it is that God first admits, or "perhaps even brags" that God gave (נתן) Saul's women to David (2 Sam 12:8), and now God will take (לקח) David's women and give (נתן) them to his neighbor. Linafelt, "Taking Women in Samuel," 106–7.

63. McKenzie, *King David: A Biography,* 168. Similarly, David Daube wrote that Ahithophel's "atrocious handling" of the concubines had a motivation that "can be traced: he is the paternal grandfather of Bathsheba (2 Sam xi 3, xxiii 34), once treated by the king with the same ruthlessness." Daube, "Absalom," 320. Wesselius similarly suggested that "the reason why Ahithophel hated David" is because of what David had done to his granddaughter. Wesselius even titles the section where he talks about the connection between Ahithophel, Absalom and Bathsheba as "Bathsheba's revenge," not "Ahithophel's revenge." "Joab's Death," 350. Cf. Keith Bodner, *Rebellion of Absalom,* 78–79.

64. Kirkpatrick, *Second Book of Samuel,* 327.

65. When Bathsheba hears that Ahithophel is among Absalom's conspirators, Jill Eileen Smith wrote, "Bathsheba sucked in a soft breath, hoping no one heard or noticed her presence, though her heart beat fast and she suddenly felt faint. Sabba, Sabba . . . do you hate me so much? . . . Ahitophel had betrayed [David] because of her. Could David see the regret in her eyes? Could he sense the remorse, the sorrow, she carried for him? Oh, Adonai, let the blame rest on me! . . . By the looks of some of the Thirty, it was no more than she deserved for the ill will she had brought down on David's house. She'd grown used to the shunning. "I'm sorry for my grandfather's choices, my lord," she said loud enough to be heard for those standing closest to the king. "I'm sorry for all of the hurt I have caused you." She lowered her voice on the final words, meaning them for him alone." Smith, *Bathsheba: A Novel,* 288–289.

66. Amnon and Absalom were killed, and there is no mention of Abigail's son Chileab besides his name in 2 Sam 3:3 and 1 Chron 3:1. Rashi explained that some questioned whether Chileab's father was David or Abigail's first husband Nabal, and therefore God arranged that the son would resemble David. In Joseph Heller's novel *God Knows,* David explains that Chileab was born with a birth defect that made him unfit to take the throne. In L'Engle's novel *Certain Women,* Abigail's children die when they are young. Tomoo Ishida explained that the principle of primogeniture had been accepted in Israel, and therefore Adonijah was not wrong to assume that he would take the throne. Ishida, "Adonijah Son of Haggith," 171.

67. This is the same interrogative, הלוא, that introduced Bathsheba in 2 Sam 11:3.

68. Robert Alter observed that when Nathan gave Solomon a second name in 2 Sam 12:24, it might have reflected "a political calculation on the part of Nathan: he is already aligning himself with Solomon (and with Bathsheba), figuring that in the long run it will be best to have a successor to David under some obligation to him." Alter, *The David Story*, 263.

69. For example, Brueggemann believes David never made the promise. Brueggemann, *1 & 2 Kings*, 14. Seow is also skeptical, because of "the importance of such a tradition to the Davidic monarchy." "1 & 2 Kings," 19. David Marcus has argued that Nathan did invent this promise, but wrote that Bathsheba was willing to play a part in Nathan's invention to get back at David for what he did to her in 2 Sam 11. "The impetus for Bathsheba to act in consort with Nathan to deceive David, it may be supposed, was that David had at one time deceived her." Marcus, "David the Deceiver and the Dupe," 167.

70. A *midrash* on Ecc 4:12 identifies Bathsheba, David, and Nathan as the threefold cord in that verse.

71. Seow wrote, "This lack of knowledge on his part is telling, for the king was once assumed to have had great wisdom and the ability 'to know all things that are on earth' (2 Sam 14:20)." "1 & 2 Kings," 18.

72. Seow, "1 & 2 Kings," 33.

73. Aschkenasy, *Woman at the Window*, 115.

74. Brueggemann, *1 & 2 Kings*, 20. But Bathsheba does not simply repeat what Nathan told her to say; she adds phrases and nuances of her own. There are seven differences between what Nathan told Bathsheba to say, and what she actually says. First, Bathsheba makes into a statement what Nathan had as a question; second, Bathsheba tells David that he swore "by YHWH your God"; third, Bathsheba tells David that he did not know about Adonijah's actions; fourth, she gives David details about what Adonijah has done; fifth, when Bathsheba names Solomon as the person whom Adonijah did not invite to his feast, she refers to him as David's "servant"; sixth, Bathsheba tells David that "the eyes of all Israel" are on him to tell them who will succeed him on the throne; and seventh, she tells David that when he dies, she and her son Solomon will be counted as offenders (1 Kgs 1:21). That final phrase proves to be cryptic, something that interpreters receive differently.

75. The evidence that Bathsheba has, in fact, heard about Adonijah's actions is in the details she gives David about the feast; details that Nathan did not tell her, so she must have gotten the knowledge somewhere.

76. Seow, "1 & 2 Kings," 19.

77. Brueggemann, *1 & 2 Kings*, 16. Seow wrote, "With David's oath explicitly designating Solomon (vv. 28–30) and Bathsheba's benediction (v. 31), the story takes a decisive turn. Medieval Hebrew scholars noticed the shift and placed the strongest marker of a paragraph division after the words of Bathsheba (v. 31)—the only such marked in the chapter." Seow, "1 & 2 Kings," 20.

78. Smith wrote Bathsheba thinking, "*O Adonai, I don't want to lose him!* Despite the years, he was precious to her." *Bathsheba*, 327.

79. Montgomery, *Critical and Exegetical Commentary*, 92.

80. It is not entirely clear if Bathsheba was in a position of power before she became queen mother, or after. Some interpreters compare Bathsheba with a gebîrâ, or "mighty lady." The text never refers to her as such, as it does with Maacah in 1 Kgs 15:13. Cf. Gray, *I & II Kings*, 265; Andreasen, "Role of the Queen Mother," 188; Solvang, *A Woman's Place*. Bowen concludes that while Bathsheba should be seen as an extraordinary woman who plays a pivotal role in the outcome of the succession, she is not a gebîrâ. "The Quest for the Historical Gĕbîrǎ," 606. Beverly Cushman has argued that Bathsheba functions as a gᵉbîrâ in both chapters of 1 Kings, and that one of the particular roles of a gᵉbîrâ was to administrate the palace household, with special authority over the harem. Cushman, "Politics," 330. Nathan's choice of Bathsheba as a co-conspirator suggests that she did have some level of power before; though of course, power is not limited to official positions of hierarchy.

81. Bathsheba's previous words have also been brief: in 1 Kgs 2:13 when she asks Adonijah if he comes in peace, she uses only two words, השלם באך [do you come in peace?] Cogan has argued that the implication of that conversation "is that the rivalry between the two parties had not dissipated." Cogan, *1 Kings*, 175. Cogan wonders if the repetition of the name of Adonijah's mother, "Haggith" hints at rivalry between the mothers. Bodner also suggested a rivalry between the mothers, and suggested that Nathan had tried to exploit the maternal rivalry when he always used the language, "mother of" and "son of." Bodner, "Nathan," 50.

82. Bowen, "Quest," 605.

83. Whybray, *Succession Narrative*, 40.

84. Nicol, "Alleged Rape," 53 and Aschkenasy, *Woman at the Window*, 117.

85. In the book of Chronicles, she gets named "Bathshua," and in the Matthean genealogy of Jesus, she gets mentioned, but not by name: she is "wife of Uriah the Hittite" (Matt 1:6).

86. Kermode, "New Ways," 125.

2 — Bathsheba Revealed in Rabbinic Literature

1. Sternberg described this technique dismissively, referring to midrash as an example of "illegitimate gap-filling," which is for Sternberg, "launched and sustained by the reader's subjective concerns (or dictated by more general preconceptions) rather than by the text's own norms and directives." Sternberg, *Poetics*, 188. Jacob Neusner wrote that the rabbis impose upon Scripture and the Mishnah "their own judgment of its meaning." The uncharitable nature of such statements notwithstanding, they miss the point that there are particular and intentional reading strategies of midrash, which are better understood by better understanding the midrashic assumptions about the text, discussed below. Neusner, *Midrash in Context*, 136.

2. Boyarin, *Intertextuality*, 41.

3. Cf. Bassler, "A Man for All Seasons," 156–69; Shimoff, "David and Bathsheba," 246–56; and Valler, "King David," 129–42.

4. Another place where Bathsheba is not evoked is in R. Joshua b. Levi's warning to men about places where they may see immodest sights, in *b. Pesaḥ* 113a. Variant texts

read specifically "do not frequent roofs." But neither David nor Bathsheba is mentioned in this tractate.

5. Daniel Boyarin and Karin Zetterholm explain that the gaps can be theological or other; essentially, anything problematic or unclear that would require further explanation. Though the Talmud and Midrash share an overall hermeneutic of filling in the gaps, they are distinct literary collections. The Talmud consists of two parts: the Mishnah and the Gemara. The Mishnah is legal material attributed to rabbis in the first two centuries C.E., redacted in the beginning of the third century. The Gemara is the commentary on the Mishnah, including biblical citations. This commentary also is interested in filling in details perceived to be missing in the Mishnah. There are two Talmudim: the Palestinian or Yerushalmi Talmud was produced in Jerusalem until circa 400 C.E., and the Babylonian Talmud was composed by rabbis living in Babylonia from the third through the seventh or eighth century. Because the Babylonian Talmud was edited for so many more years, it is unsurprisingly more expansive, and more authoritative in Judaism. Zetterholm, *Jewish Interpretation*, 48. The Talmud is not a retelling of the biblical story, nor it is a verse-by-verse commentary; it references various biblical texts for the purposes of explicating both the Mishnah and other biblical texts. Therefore, certain elements in the biblical story are not mentioned in the Talmud. The word "Midrash" refers to a less formal document than the Talmud, though there are numerous compilations of midrash which range in dates from the 5th to 12th centuries.

6. For example, fundamentalists would not assume that there are problems in the text, especially when using terms such as "inerrant" which gets defined in the "Chicago Statement on Biblical Inerrancy" (CSBI) produced by the International Council on Biblical Inerrancy as "free from all falsehood, fraud, or deceit."

7. Kugel, *The Bible as It Was*, 18–22.

8. Ibid., 21. In *The Idea of Biblical Poetry*, Alter notes that parallelism is one way to unlock some of the additional meanings in a text. Alter, *Idea of Biblical Poetry*, 104–105.

9. Sommer has argued that it is not until the Middle Ages that there is a sense of longer textual units such as a whole poem or a complete story. Sommer, "Concepts of Scriptural Language," 67.

10. Kugel, "Two Introductions to Midrash," 145.

11. Sommer, "Concepts of Scriptural Language," 69.

12. Boyarin, *Carnal Israel*, 27.

13. Gerald Bruns explained that there is no conflict of authority in a conflict of interpretations, because it is the whole dialogue which is authoritative, not just the isolated interpretations that emerge from it. "Midrashic interpretation is multiform and extravagant but also holistic as a social practice; no one interpretation stands by itself, because no one rabbi speaks as a solitary reader—no one rabbi speaks purely and simply in his own name and on his own private authority. . . . This means that there is neither occasion nor cause to determine the authority or correctness of this or that isolated interpretation. Interpretations are not logical propositions concerning which we have to decide for and against, true or false. They are modes of participation in the dialogue with Torah." Bruns, "Midrash and Allegory," 632.

14. Breed, "Nomadology of the Bible," 318.

15. Bruns references a rabbinic saying from Peskita Rabbati, Piska 14:9, "Solomon has three thousand parables to illustrate each and every verse [of Scripture]; and a thousand and five interpretations for each and every parable," which adds up to 3,015,000 interpretations for every scriptural verse. Bruns, "Midrash and Allegory," 630.

16. Bruns, "Midrash and Allegory," 629.

17. Zetterholm, *Jewish Interpretation*, 2.

18. Polliack, "Concepts of Scripture," 86. Robert Harris explained that that omnisignificant, midrashic understanding of Scripture changed in the 11th to 13th centuries with the development of *peshat,* which he defines as "plain sense" or "contextual" exegesis. Robert Harris also described *peshat* as rooted in the Karaite and Rabbanite reactions to the rise of Islam. Karaite Judaism began in the medieval Islamic world, and exists today in Israel. Harris, "Concepts of Scripture," 107–18.

19. Brigitte Donnet-Guez did note variances in Bathsheba's characterization, but the "ambiguity" has to do with Bathsheba's varying roles as wife and queen mother, not with whether Bathsheba is the seductress. "L'ambiguïté du personage de Bethsabée," 65–84.

20. Redak is an acronym for Rabbi David Kimchi, the Spanish grammarian and scholar who was born in 1160 to a learned family: his father Rabbi Joseph Ben Isaac Kimchi was also a scholar who wrote about Hebrew grammar and culture. Under persecution of the Almohades dynasty in Spain, the family fled to Narbonne in France. Redak's commentary is similar in style to those of Rashi, as he includes reasoning and grammar in his explanations.

21. Rosenberg, ed., *Psalms, Volume 2,* 192.

22. Daniel Boyarin discusses the dialectic nature of the "evil inclination" in *Carnal Israel,* 61–76.

23. Rosenberg, ed., *Psalms, Volume 2,* 193.

24. Rashi reads this word as "beehive."

25. She wrote, "The moral of this whole passage is that David is not to blame for having an affair with a married woman. The moment Satan is introduced into the story, it changes into a story about God and Satan; hence, David can have no influence on the sequence of events." Valler, "King David," 138. Satan appears elsewhere in the Talmud; in *b. Kidd.* 81a he appears in the guise of a woman to tempt Rabbi Meir and Rabbi Akiba, but ultimately lets them go because it had been proclaimed in heaven that people should take heed of each rabbi and his teaching. In that tractate, the rabbis do not resist the temptation on their own strength; Satan relents.

26. Valler, "King David," 139.

27. Kabbalist Joseph Gikatila focuses on the "predestination" aspect of this teaching to explain that when God creates a male, at the same time God creates a female because the two are necessary to make a whole. Gikatila, *David et Bethsabée,* 52.

28. Valler, "King David," 139.

29. Ibid.

30. Rosenberg, ed., *Psalms, Volume II,* 191.

31. Rosenberg, ed., *Book of Samuel 2,* 317–18.

32. Ibid., 329. Abarbanel is a medieval scholar, born in Lisbon in 1437. He studied Talmud, philosophy, and secular studies.

33. Both Ahithophel and Absalom are included in *b. Sot 9b* in a list of people who "set their eyes upon that which was not proper for them; what they sought was not granted to them and what they possessed was taken from them." Others who did this are Korah, Cain, Balaam, Doeg, Gehazai, Adonijah, Uzziah, and Haman.

34. Freedman, trans., *Midrash Rabbah Genesis,* 249.

35. Rosenberg, *Book of Samuel 2,* 330.

36. The words are, "David was not the kind of man to do that act [with Bathsheba], as it is written, *My heart is slain within me;* nor were the Israelites the kind of people to commit that act [with the golden calf], for it is said, *O that they had such a heart as this always, etc.* Why, then, did they act thus? [5a] [God predestined it so] in order to teach thee that if an individual hath sinned [and hesitates about the effect of repentance] he could be referred to the individual [David], and if a community commits a sin they should be told: Go to the community."

37. This comment also highlights the sense of struggle, found in many interpretations through the years, over whether David's deeds were an aberration to his character.

38. B. *Šab.* 56a.

39. Shimoff, "David and Bathsheba," 253.

40. "Everyone who goes out into the war of the House of David writes for his wife a deed of divorce, for it is written, *And to thy brethren shalt thou bring greetings and take their pledge* [1 Sam 17:18]." *b. Ketub.* 9b.

41. B. *Šab.* 56a.

42. Rosenberg, *Book of Samuel 2,* 318.

43. Ibid., 320.

44. Ibid., 318.

45. Rosenberg, *Book of Samuel 2,* 323. Malbim connects this to the definition of (בעלה) in Hos 2:16; another example of using a verse in one section of the Hebrew Bible to explicate another one.

46. For example, the report from YHWH through Nathan 2 Sam 12:9–10 uses language that David had done evil in the sight of YHWH by putting Uriah to the sword because David took his wife. A plainer reading of the text would suggest that David's reason for the murder was not Uriah's insolence, but to cover up that David had cuckolded Uriah.

47. In Gen 6:5, YHWH sees that the inclination of the human heart is evil. B. *Kid. 30b* explains that God created the Torah as an antidote to this evil inclination.

48. From *b. Sukkah* 52b. Kimchi concurs with Rashi on this point. Cf. Coxon "A Note on 'Bathsheba' in 2 Samuel 12:1–6," 248.

49. Boyarin, *Carnal Israel,* 62.

50. Michael Saltow explained that the assumption is that a woman need not actively seduce a man to be tempting because women's mere existence is a temptation, so one way to avoid this would be to restrict men from being with women. A man's desire (יצר) could rise to "dangerous levels." Saltow, *Tasting the Dish,* 158. Both men and women were

thought to be sexually desirous. Only men, however, were thought capable of controlling "this overwhelming desire." According to Saltow, the rabbis who produced the Jerusalem Talmud were less optimistic than the Babylonian ones that men were able to exercise self-control. Ibid, 163–64.

51. Cf. Alice Bach, "Good to the Last Drop."

52. Regarding the gap about the nature of the sexual encounter between David and Bathsheba, the rabbis do not entertain the notion of rape. Either it is adultery, or not if Uriah is out of the picture. Saltow explained, "The tannaim conceptualized the 'rape' of a married woman entirely differently from that of a non-married woman. . . . Rape of married women, because outside of the biblical rape/seduction categories, is not considered here." In the Talmud, there is some discussion about the effects of rape on a married woman, but the discussions focus on whether or not she is permitted to return to her husband. Nor is sexuality discussed with the good of the woman in mind. Saltow, *Tasting the Dish.*

53. Rosenberg, *Book of Samuel 2*, 329. This is, obviously, not mentioned in the Hebrew Bible. The interpreters are filling in a gap as to the promise of succession, as well as a reason why David would promise that Solomon would be king.

54. It was thought that cohabitation during pregnancy was beneficial to the unborn child. *Midrash Rabbah Numbers*, 353, n. 1.

55. Regarding Bathsheba's message "I am pregnant" in v. 5, Rabbi Levi ben Gershom (Ralbag) and Rabbi Meir Leibush Malbim have noted, "Perhaps she immediately became aware of her pregnancy because she sensed that the area of her womb had lost its moisture, this being a sign of conception." Rosenberg, *Book of Samuel 2*, 319.

56. Solomon's age is calculated as seven when Ahithophel committed suicide by comparing 2 Sam 13:23, 2 Sam 13:38, and 2 Sam 14:28: Absalom killed Amnon two years after Solomon's birth; he was exiled for three years and he then lived two years in Jerusalem before his rebellion, in consequence of which Ahithophel hanged himself soon after; so two, three, and two equal seven. Ahithophel and Eliam are understood to be eight years old when they father their children based on Ahithophel's age of 26 when Solomon died. They factor that the three pregnancies added up to approximately two years, so that twenty-four years are left for the three generations (Ahithophel to Eliam to Bathsheba), which gives eight years for each.

57. Rosenberg, *Book of Samuel 2*, 329.

58. The interest in the "medical benefits" for keeping warm of a virgin gets repeated in the enlightenment, and in other eras.

59. Rosenberg and Reuven Hochberg, *Book of Kings 1*, 4. This interpretation is similar to that of Christian church father Isho'dad of Merv, discussed earlier.

60. Boyarin, *Carnal Israel*, 31–60. This is not the Platonic understanding that humans are best understood as spiritual beings and the body a shameful shell, bearing more resemblance to Aristotle's understanding of a soul as consisting of body. Cf. Christopher Shields, "Aristotle's Psychology" http://plato.stanford.edu/archives/spr2015/entries/aristotle-psychology/ [Accessed Dec. 3, 2015.]

61. Rosenberg and Hochberg, 10.

62. The editors of Mikraot Gedalot are careful to note that this has no basis in *halakah*! Rosenberg and Hochberg, 9.

63. Ibid., 9.

64. *Midrash Rabbah Ecclesiastes*, 121.

65. Rosenberg and Hochberg, 21.

66. Ibid., 21–22.

67. "Why was Solomon called Lemuel? R. Ishmael said: On the selfsame night that Solomon completed the work of the Holy Temple he married Bathiah, the daughter of Pharoah, and there was great jubilation on account of the Temple, and jubilation on account of Pharaoh's daughter, and the jubilation on account of Pharaoh's daughter exceeded that of the Temple; as the proverb says: 'Everybody flatters the king.' The reason why he was called Lemuel is because he cast off the yoke of the kingdom of heaven from his shoulders; as if to say *Lammah lo el*." *Midrash Rabbah Numbers*, 352. In the Hebrew אל לו למה, the lamed, mem, waw, aleph and lamed form the letters of Lemuel's name. A literal translation would be, "why to him God," which is here interpreted to mean, "why should there be to him what is divine?"

68. *Midrash Rabbah Numbers*, 353.

69. Ibid.

70. *Midrash Rabbah Leviticus*, 159–60.

71. *Midrash Rabbah Numbers*, 355.

72. *Midrash Rabbah Song of Songs*, 123. Apparently, R. Isaac was unaware of this reference, for he is recorded in Exodus Rabbah as confessing, "I have searched through the whole Bible but have not been able to find anywhere the statement that Bathsheba made a crown for Solomon." *Midrash Rabbah Exodus*, 579.

73. *Midrash Rabbah Exodus*, 579–80, cf. *Midrash Rabbah Song of Songs* 3:11, 173, *Midrash Rabbah Numbers* 12:8, 473.

74. *Midrash Rabbah Song of Songs*, 123–24.

3 — Bathsheba as a Type and Trope in the Patristics

1. Manlio Simonetti, *Biblical Interpretation in the Early Church*, 39. Those books functioned as a patristic canon within a canon, during a time when the canonization process itself was being debated. Cf. David Nienhuis, *Not By Paul Alone*, 1–6.

2. In fact, the church fathers gave a lot of attention to the typological connection between Eve and Mary (likely following the Apostle Paul's example), but they did not connect Bathsheba, the mother of Solomon, with Mary, the mother of Christ. That connection will not get made until the medieval era.

3. This happened with Jewish exegesis, as in the examples where Bathsheba and Solomon were compared to Israel and God, or where Bathsheba crowned Solomon with the tabernacle, and so on.

4. Simonetti, *Biblical Interpretation in the Early Church*, 26.

5. Ibid., 54–55.

6. Young, "Alexandrian School," 25.

7. The church fathers were neither the first nor the last to use allegory. It was

practiced in Judaism—by Philo, for example—and in readings of classical Greek texts like those of Homer.

8. For example, Bede read Dinah as a type of the church, her vengeful brothers who used trickery to defeat Shechem on the third day after Shechem's circumcision were representing Christ who used trickery to overcome the devil by rising on the third day. Joy A. Schroeder, *Dinah's Lament*, 14.

9. Augustine, *Confessions*, 115–16.

10. Ramsey, *Beginning to Read*, 29.

11. Wall, "The 'Rule of Faith' and Biblical Hermeneutics," 1–3.

12. Kugel and Greer, *Early Biblical Interpretation*, 197.

13. These critiques came from those outside Christianity; for example, from the Neoplatonic philosopher Porphyry who, in his *Against the Christians*, described Origen's allegories as absurd. Because Porphyry's writings were burned, we have only fragments of them preserved in the works of those Christians who refuted him. Porphyry wrote, "Some persons, desiring to find a solution to the baseness of the Jewish Scriptures rather than abandon them, have had recourse to explanations inconsistent and incongruous with the words written, which explanations, instead of supplying a defense of the foreigners, contain rather approval and praise of themselves. For they boast that the plain words of Moses are 'enigmas,' and regard them as oracles full of hidden mysteries; and having bewildered the mental judgment by folly, they make their explanations." Eusebius, *Church History*, 265. But there was also some concern from within Christianity, namely those in the so-called Antiochene school. Basil, for example, clearly rejected an allegorical interpretation of Genesis 1 in his *Homilies on the Hexameron*. Simonetti noted that Basil even described the allegorical interpretation of the firmament in Gen 1:7 as fantasy or old men's tales, a critique that is striking considering that such an interpretation came from Origen, whom Basil admired. Simonetti, *Biblical Interpretation in the Early Church*, 64–65.

14. For "Alexandrian" scholars like Hippolytus, Origen and others, the history of Israel was only of interest insofar as it might connect with Christ and the church. But in these later centuries, there was an interest in Israel's history in its own right. It was not that those in Antioch were uninterested in Christology; in fact, Antioch was the focus of the controversy over the teachings of Arius, and Theodore of Mopsuestia, a representative of the "Antiochene school" was the one who systematized Christ's dual nature in opposition to Arianism and Apollinarianism. The dual nature of Christ was given full expression by Nestorius, Theodore's disciple, whose Christology was repudiated by the councils of Ephesus in 431 and by those of Chalcedon in 451. Theodore's teacher, Didore, was condemned retrospectively by a synod in Constantinople in 499, and Theodore himself condemned posthumously by the second Council of Constantinople in 553.

15. Simonetti, *Biblical Interpretation in the Early Church*, 70.

16. Margaret Mitchell, "Allegory, Christianity," 797.

17. Another term which can be brought into the discussion is "figural readings," which is very close to typology; an Old Testament character can be seen as a figure of something spiritual, or as a figure of someone in the New Testament. Yet, a scholar like

Gerhard von Rad employed figural readings to help him both hold to historical critical readings of the Old Testament and to see a connection between the testaments. Christopher Seitz, "History, Figural History, and Providence," 4–5.

18. Theodore of Mopsuestia's views on prophecy also helped make the distinction clear: he believed that God's sending of the prophets was ultimately connected with God's plan for Christianity, but he was convicted that apart from David—whom he considered to be a prophet—none of the prophets spoke directly of Christ; their immediate vision was confined to the historical and theological framework of the Old Testament. Certain messages, however, could have had a dual historical application; for example, for Theodore, Zech 9:8–10 refers to Zerubbabel, but the language is so hyperbolic that the words are only fully true when they are applied to Christ. Thus, the Old Testament is still referring historically to itself and its own time, but a limited number of texts might refer to Christianity. Even "David's" prophecies in the psalms only referred to Christ in a few places, and others were prophetic for Israel's history, such as Psalm 51 which referred to the Babylonian exile. Norris, "Antiochene Interpretation," 31.

19. McLeod, *Theodore of Mopsuestia*, 18.

20. Rusty Reno and John O'Keefe suggested that the church fathers' intimate knowledge of the contents of both testaments is what enables them to move between them in such a facile manner. *Sanctified Vision*, 121–22. The rabbis, obviously, had a similar intimate knowledge of the contents of the Tanakh.

21. Bertrand de Margerie, *An Introduction to the History of Exegesis*, 5.

22. Bruns, "Midrash and Allegory," 635.

23. Jerome, "Against Jovinianus," *Letters and Select Works*, 363–64.

24. Isaac of Ninevah, *Ascetical Homilies 10*, 361.

25. Irenaus, *Against Heresies*, Book IV, chapter 27.

26. Both sins are mentioned twice. 2 Sam 12:9 reads, "Uriah the Hittite you have struck with a sword, his wife you took to be a wife for yourself, and him you have killed with the sword of the Ammonites." 2 Sam 12:10 repeats the "taking of Uriah's wife" when explaining the reason for the sword remaining in David's house forever, "because you despised me and you took the wife of Uriah the Hittite to be your wife."

27. Thomas O'Loughlin, "A Woman's Plight and the Western Fathers," 101. With that in mind, O'Loughlin noted that perhaps the pericope about the woman caught in the act of adultery was ignored because it challenged some deep-seated fears by men about women, sexuality, and religion. Ibid., 103.

28. Here is another contrast with the Jewish texts, where the rabbis were not in the least hesitant to discuss sex and sexuality. This difference has been noted by Peter Brown in *The Body and Society*, [add to Bib] 266–27; and by Daniel Boyarin, in *Carnal Israel*, nb. 2–10.

29. Ambrose, *Apologia*, 71.

30. Jerome, "Letter 22," *Letters and Select Works*, 26.

31. Pseudo-Clementine, "Two Epistles Concerning Virginity," 64.

32. de Margerie, *An Introduction to the History of Exegesis*, Volume 2, 85–86.

33. Ambrose did not disparage the literal sense of the text per se, but the literal sense

"shorn of its spiritual potential, as when a figure is not acknowledged as such and does not lead to the truth which is figured." Ibid., 80. In this way, Ambrose was similar to and even dependent upon Origen, acknowledging that there was a literal sense of the Old Testament, but that it was impoverished in comparison with the spiritual sense and the understanding to which the latter can lead.

34. Augustine, *Christian Instruction,* 3.21, 141.

35. There may be a connection between the arrow David purportedly shot, and Isaac of Ninevah's question in *Ascetical Homilies,* "was [David] not punished because of adultery with a woman, when he held her beauty with his eyes and was pierced in his soul by that arrow?" However, "Arrow" might be a common trope.

36. Chrysostom, "Homilies on Colossians," 299.

37. Chrysostom, *Homilies on the Gospel of St. Matthew,* 311.

38. Phyllis Trible, however, demonstrated that there are other ways to read Jezebel. "Exegesis for Storytellers and Other Strangers."

39. Augustine treated this in question 61 on the gospel story that the Lord fed the multitude on the mountain with five loaves of bread. "St. Augustine: Eighty-three different questions," 118–19.

40. Pacian, "Letter 1.5.3," 23. *The Fathers of the Church,* 267.

41. Jerome, "Letter 122," in *Letters and Select Works,* 227. Jerome also attributed to David more emotions than the text does, by describing David "bursting into tears" as David prayed the words of Psalm 51.

42. Referenced in Franke, *Joshua, Judges, Ruth, 1–2 Samuel, 3.*

43. Jerome, "Letter 85" in *Letters and Select Works,* 182.

44. Jerome, "Letter 22" in *Letters and Select Works,* 26.

45. Ibid., 22.

46. Ramsey explained, "Depending on the point he wished to make, in fact, the same Father could at different times allegorize the same passage in different ways." *Beginning to Read the Fathers,* 31.

47. An anonymous author of the *Incomplete Work on Matthew, Homily 1,* asserted that Solomon, who "is interpreted as 'peaceful' . . . was a figure of our peace-loving Christ, who, for all the people fleeing to him in faith and paying the spiritual taxes of good works, provided a peaceful kingdom, built with living stones—not only Jews but also Gentiles—so that he might build a living temple to the living God." *Patrologia Graeca* 56:621. This author, however, did not make the link between Bathsheba and Mary, just Solomon and Christ.

48. van Liere, "Literal Sense of the Books of Samuel and Kings," 62.

49. Theodore of Mopsuestia, who was a representative of the Antiochene school, interpreted Psalm 51 not to refer to David and Bathsheba, but as prophetic of Israel's experience in the exile, when they were being taunted by others. McLeod, *Theodore of Mopuestia,* 19.

50. Indeed, though the medieval period is when Bathsheba becomes a type of Mary, Bathsheba is also highlighted in that time period through commentaries and other treatments of the Psalms. As will be discussed in the next chapter, the Psalms becomes the primary OT book in the medieval era.

51. Cassiodorus, *Explanation of the Psalms,* 492–93.

52. When Simonetti discussed Hippolytus's treatment of Susanna, he rather disparagingly commented that the church father was "indifferent to the critical and linguistic dimensions of the Greek text of the Susanna episode." *Biblical Interpretation in the Early Church,* 48.

53. Isodore of Seville "Questiones in Vet. Testam, in Regum II," *Patrologia Latina* 83: 411, 2.

54. Possibly, this comes from the name of the Hittite fortress, "Hamath," which in Greek can be understood as "protected," or "cut off," though in a positive sense.

55. Isidore, "Questiones in Vet. Testam, in Regum II," 411, 8.

56. He wrote, "But what else did her husband Uriah signify, by the translation of his name, than the devil? This most evil marriage had bound all whom the grace of God sets free, so that the Church might be united to her savior without stain or wrinkle. For Uriah is translated as 'my light of God,' and Hittite as 'cut off,' either because he did not remain standing in virtue but was cut off by reason of his pride from his light from above, which he had from God, or because in falling he loses his true strength and yet transforms himself into an angel of light while still daring to say, 'My light is from God.'" *Answer to Faustus,* 364.

57. Ibid.

58. Ambrose, *Apologia,* 90.

59. Eucherius, "Commentarii in Libros Regum, Lib. II," *Patrologia Latina,* 50:1092. Recent scholarship has posited that the commentary attributed to Eucherius was actually written four centuries later, by Claudius of Turin, d. 827. Clearly, ideas about Bathsheba are not limited to a single historical period.

60. Gregory the Great, *Morals on the Book of Job,* 166.

61. The anonymous author of *Incomplete Work on Matthew, Homily 1* admitted as such when he explained that in the story of David and Bathsheba, "There is a prefiguring even here, though it may seem unlikely." *Patrologia Graeca* 56: 520.

62. Gregory the Great, *Morals,* 167.

63. Gregory the Great, *Corpus Christianorum Series Latina* 143, 148.

4 — Bathsheba in the Bath in the Medieval Period

1. Exum, *Plotted, Shot, and Painted,* 26. As discussed in chapter 1, the clause may also refer to purification after sexual intercourse, which would still make the washing something sexual.

2. By contrast, Adam and Eve in Gen 2:25 are naked, as is Saul in 1 Sam 19:24. Other bathing women in scripture include Bilhah, who in the pseudepigraphal *Testament of Reuben* is described as bathing "in a secret place." In the apocryphal addition to Daniel, the text makes clear that Susanna shut the doors of the garden so as not to be seen, but she is not described with the word naked. John Kessler wrote, "There is no reason to assume that Bathsheba was naked. . . . Public nudity was viewed as abhorrent and humiliating (cf. Hos 2:10). It seems unlikely that we are to envisage a naked woman in public view on the slopes of Jerusalem's eastern hill." Kessler, "Sexuality and Politics," 418.

3. Kunoth-Leifels, *Über die Darstellungen der «Bathsheba im Bade, "* 93ff. Another

image of Bathsheba bathing with clothes on is Pablo Picasso's 1949 lithograph, also discussed in Kunoth-Liefels's work.

4. Exum, *Plotted, Shot, and Painted,* 26–37.

5. Monica Walker Vadillo notes the increase of images of Bathsheba painted naked in the fifteenth century, and comments, "it is possible to conclude that Bathsheba clothed was less popular than Bathsheba nude." Walker Vadillo, *Bathsheba in Late Medieval French,* 38–40. Clare Costley King'oo confirmed that early Books of Hours had the seven Penitential Psalms glossed with an image of David repenting, but from the end of the fifteenth century, the illustration was commonly one of David peering at bathing Bathsheba. Kingoo, *Miserere Mei,* 31.

6. Henri de Lubac's magisterial two-volume work, *Medieval Exegesis,* is subtitled *The Four Senses of Scripture,* though in it he illustrated that some interpreters have emphasized three (historical, moral, allegorical) while others have employed between four and seven layers of meaning. There is often overlap in the types of interpretation, where tropological interpretation became moral, or anagogical interpretation was typological or figural, which may account for the difference in numbers.

7. Medieval scholars often date the shift from the more spiritual readings to the more literal and scholastic exegesis to the twelfth and thirteenth centuries. Frans van Liere has argued that in addition to the increased emphasis on literal exegesis, the understanding of what was "literal" also shifted between the work of the Victorines (Hugh, Andrew, and Richard), and that of Nicholas of Lyra. Van Liere, "The Literal Sense of the Books of Samuel and Kings," 60ff. A similar move took place between the so-called Alexandrian and Antiochene schools: the earlier interpretations were more spiritual, and the later interpretations shifted to something more literal and historical.

8. Peter von Moos, *Hildebert von Lavardin,* 374. Von Moos referred to this quote as a questionable addition to the biblical epigrams which suggests that it may not be authentic to Hildebert.

9. To use Deleuze's terms, a piece of art is an "actual" manifestation of what the text can do, though it might also have other "virtual" possibilities. Cf. Breed, "Nomadology of the Bible," 313–15.

10. Walker Vadillo, *Bathsheba in Late Medieval French Manuscript,* 90.

11. The same is true for other forms of art, including sculptures and film. How many people imagine David to look like Michaelangelo's statue, or imagine Charlton Heston as Moses? Cf. Pardes, "Moses Goes Down to Hollywood," 15–31.

12. John of Damascus in "Against Those Who Decry Holy Images," referenced in Weitzmann, *Miniatures of the Sacra Parellela,* 25.

13. Esmeijer, *Divina Quaternitas,* 24. Esmeijer dated the start of this type of exegesis to the fourth century, noting that the ideas about the nature and function of images diverged in the East and the West. It was in the 11th and 12th centuries, however, when typological representations assumed "a particularly important role."

14. Craven, "Iconography of the David," 226.

15. Walker Vadillo, *Bathsheba in Late Medieval French Manuscript,* 24.

16. Wormald, "Bible Illustration in Medieval Manuscripts," 309–37.

17. Jonathan Harthan, *Book of Hours*, 13–19.

18. Weick, *Painted Prayers*, 19.

19. van Liere, *Introduction to the Medieval Bible*, 248.

20. Wormald, "Bible Illustration in Medieval Manuscripts," 321.

21. There are many variations on the legend: some say that the seed for the tree came from the garden of Eden; others include the wood as the source of Moses's staff. Cf. Morris, *Legends of the Holy Rood*.

22. Costley, "David, Bathsheba and the Penitential Psalms," 1243.

23. Kuczynski, *Prophetic Song*, 37.

24. For example, Kunoth-Liefels, *Über die Darstellungen*. J. Cheryl Exum and others have discussed in detail Rembrandt's painting of Bathsheba (*Plotted, Shot, and Painted*), and Walker Vadillo and King'oo have also provided helpful examples and images. In addition to consulting their work, I spent time at the Getty Research Institute in Los Angeles working with their Photo Archive, which has hundreds of other images of Bathsheba.

25. This is held by the Bibliothèque nationale de France.

26. At least, that is the scholarly consensus of the date of the manuscript. Weitzmann has argued for a slightly earlier date, in the first half of the ninth century. Weitzmann, *Miniatures of the Sacra Parallela*, 23–25.

27. Ibid., 11–20.

28. Weitzmann, *Miniatures of the Sacra Parallela*, 8.

29. Meyer, "Theologizing or Indulging Desire." http://differentvisions.org/theologizing -indulging-desire-bathers-sacra-parallela-paris-bnf-gr-923/ [Accessed Apr. 11, 2016].

30. Walker Vadillo, *Bathsheba in Late Medieval French Manuscript Illumination*, 20.

31. One reason why one might surmise an error is because David is both bearded and has breasts. Meyer went on to argue that in the *Sacra Parallela*, the naked body might be identified as a "third gender" that transcends traditional gender boundaries. This, in turn, encourages the viewers to interpret the naked bathing bodies not in purely physical terms, but in exegetical and moral terms relating to the love of God. Meyer, "Theologizing or Indulging Desire."

32. Weitzmann explained, "Because the margin has been trimmed, the action of her right hand is not quite clear, but as her long hair falls over her right shoulder, she was presumably combing it in a manner similar to . . . the bathing Susanna." *Miniatures of the Sacra Parallela*, 83. Diane Wolfthal traces how the image of a comb was used in medieval Europe as a multivalent sign of sexuality, including courtly love, same-sex desire, fetishism, and saintly virginity. "The Sexuality of the Medieval Comb," 176–94.

33. Meyer, "Theologizing or Indulging Desire."

34. Walker Vadillo, *Bathsheba in Late Medieval French Manuscript Illumination*, 64–65. Renaissance painter Artemesia Gentileschi depicted both Susanna and Bathsheba in the 17th century, but Susanna's face is anguished, and she is holding out her arms as if to push away the elders who are leering at her from above. Bathsheba, in contrast, is painted by Gentileschi with a much more neutral expression, and her face is turned in the direction of David, who is watching her from his balcony. Gentileschi painted "Susannah and the Elders" when she was only seventeen years old. She herself was a

victim of rape by her father's colleague. When she took the case to trial, she was further victimized as she was subject to a public gynecological exam and tortured with metal rings tightened by strings around her fingers to verify her testimony. Garrard, *Artemisia Gentileschi,* 21.

35. Ziva Ben-Porat's theoretical definition of literary allusion may be helpful, though obviously she was discussing texts, and not allusion in visual works. Ben-Porat explained that the first stage in literary allusion is to notice the presence of a sign in a given text that alludes to another, independent text. The second stage is to identify the referent, and the third stage is to modify "the initial local interpretation of the signal" in light of the alluded text. Ben-Porat, "The Poetics of Literary Allusion," 110. There is a fourth stage, where having been alluded to, the entire text is activated, and even more patterns are formed which need not use the marker or marked as their components. Though most literary allusions have the potential for this fourth stage, Ben-Porat explained that completion of the first three stages is enough to determine the existence of an actual literary allusion. Ibid., 111.

36. Cf. Kitzinger, *Byzantine Art in the Making.*

37. Kalavrezou, Trahoulia, and Sabar. "Critique of the Emperor in the Vatican Psalter," 202.

38. Ibid., 207. For example, Psalm 64 begins with an illustration of David kneeling before Christ enthroned (fol. 197v); Psalm 2 depicts David in the same manner kneeling before Christ, who is accompanied by the archangel Michael, as the accompanying inscription states "And Christ is pardoning David" (fol. 20r). The inscription for Psalm 12 reads, "Christ is blessing David; and the Lord has forgiven your sin" (fol. 44r), while another inscription for the same psalm states, "Christ is forgiving David" (fol 45r).

39. "As a symbolic allusion to the emperor, the sinful David expresses the contemporary attitude of the church toward the conduct of both Constantine IX and Isaac Komnenos: committing adultery, communing openly with heretics, and causing the death of the patriarch were obviously grave sins in the eyes of the church and its officials. . . . As a stronghold of Keroularios and the traditional seat of opposition to heretical emperors, the monastery of Studios must have seethed with righteous indignation, which may very well have resulted in the production of Vat. gr. 752." Ibid., 204–12.

40. Ibid, 202.

41. Walker Vadillo, *Bathsheba in Late Medieval French Manuscript Illumination,* 89.

42. This tendency will occur in the Enlightenment period, based on the attention that commentators of that era give to the phrase in 2 Sam 11:4, "and she came to him." Kalavrezou, Trahoulia, and Sabar are not alone in highlighting Bathsheba's "sin"; in her work on the Queen Mary Psalter, Anne Rudloff Stanton described Bathsheba as follows, "Bathsheba is an important character; her seductiveness causes the death of her first husband, Uriah, and great calamities for her second, King David. While David is presented as a responsible leader throughout fifty-two scenes (nearly one-quarter of the drawings in the preface), the text makes clear that many of his choices are necessitated by his early, signal sin with Bathsheba. . . . David's murder of her husband Uriah leads directly into the incestuous rape of his own daughter, Tamar, by his son Amnon on fol. 58r, and the caption of this image emphasizes that the rape is the beginning of the punishment

of David for his sin with Bathsheba, a punishment that will finally involve almost all of David's immediate family. Thus Bathsheba, like Eve, lures a man into a sin that will echo through his lineage." Stanton, "Motherhood in the Queen Mary Psalter," 179.

43. Petersen, *"Sucispere Digneris,"* 61–63. Those additions include an obituary notice of the death of Eric duke of Jutland, son of king Abel of Denmark, and a prayer for a Duke Birger, also from Scandinavia.

44. Though this is not universally agreed upon; cf. Stones, "Questions of Style and Provenance in the Morgan Bible," 2005.

45. Mann, "Picturing the Bible in the Thirteenth Century," 39. About forty percent of the images refer to David's life.

46. These inscriptions were added later: the Latin ones probably date to the early fourteenth century. The Persian captions were likely added circa 1608, when the manuscript was presented as a diplomatic gift from France to the Persian ruler Shah Abbas. Weiss, "Portraying the Past, Illuminating the Present," 13. The Judeo-Persian inscriptions are last, and most likely date to 1722 or shortly after, as that year, Isfahan was sacked by the Afghans.

47. The accompanying Latin reads, "it happened one day that David was walking, after his midday sleep in a balcony in the palace, when he saw Bathsheba, a beautiful woman indeed, washing herself in a balcony over against him. Thereupon he fell in love with her and sent messengers to bring her to him." The Persian inscription, like the Latin, speaks of David's love, something the biblical text says nothing about. It reads, "He saw that a woman was washing her body in the bathhouse. Desire and love surfaced [in him] and he summoned her." This language reminds us that the Morgan Picture Bible is a product of its time, when chivalry and courtly love were of great interest, though ideas of love and romance in the medieval period are themselves broad, detailed and complicated. This is the era that popularized the story of the passion of Abelard and Heloise, the Romance of Tristan, and other subsequent Arthurian romances. Many scholars understood "courtly love" to be the idealization of sexual desire, but Sarah Kay helpfully lists varying definitions of that term, noting the tension between inner intensity and outward decorum. Kay, "Courts, Clerks, and Courtly Love," 84–85. Cf. May, *Love: A History.*

48. Wolfthal, *Images of Rape*, 41.

49. Richard Leson, http://www.themorgan.org/collections/swf/exhibOnline.asp?id =28 [Accessed July 21, 2010]. The accompanying marginal Persian inscription to their marriage scene explains, "After the king heard that the woman's husband was dead, he married her and his mind was free of discord."

50. Walker Vadillo, *Bathsheba in Late Medieval French Manuscript Illumination*, 13–14.

51. King'oo, *Miserere Mei*, 42.

52. Kren, "Looking at Louis XII's Bathsheba," 44.

53. Walker Vadillo, *Bathsheba in Late Medieval French Manuscript Illumination*, 91.

54. Kren, "Looking at Louis XII's Bathsheba," 44.

55. Sam 11:4 does not specify that David sends a letter to Bathsheba, just that he sends messengers, so there may be a conflation with the letter sent to Joab by the hand of Uriah in 2 Sam 11:14–15.

56. Bryne, "Admiral Prigent de Coëtivy," 249. Similar images of penitent David above

a smaller bathing Bathsheba also appear in the *Hours of Charlotte of Savoy*, dated between 1420 and 1425, and *The Book of Hours*, Use of Lisieux, from Rouen, circa 1460–1470.

57. King'oo noted how the story of David and Goliath is not previously associated with the Penitential Psalms, but "in some of the most extravagant of the later primers, the Penitential Psalms are illustrated with seven images that together combine the story of David and Bathsheba with additional incidents from the long sweep of Davidic biography." *Miserere Mei*, 46.

58. This image is similar to Ms. M. 1004, fol. 78r, where David killing Goliath is also part of the image. However, in this one, there is no penitential David, as there was in that one.

59. King'oo, *Miserere Mei*, 50.

60. Exum, *Plotted, Shot, and Painted*, 25; and Gunn, "Bathsheba Goes Bathing in Hollywood," 75–79.

61. Gunn has argued that as the medieval era progresses, Bathsheba becomes more clothed to reflect sanitary practices influenced by outbreaks of the plague and syphilis. When doctors connected public bathhouses with the spread of such diseases, bathing changed to the extent that washing was limited to hands, face, and feet. Gunn, "Bathsheba Goes Bathing in Hollywood," 84. This argument accounts for changes in Bathsheba's iconography in texts produced in the early Reformation, but does not quite match the iconographic evidence, nor does it take into account why Bathsheba nude persists through the subsequent centuries.

62. Erasmus, *The Collected Works*, 430. King'oo, however, has argued that Erasmus is biased against artists, and is atypical in his time for finding problems in representations of the scene of temptation. *Miserere Mei*, 53.

63. Harthan, *The Book of Hours*, 34.

64. Wieck, *Painted Prayers*, 95.

65. King'oo, *Miserere Mei*, 50; cf. Costley, "David, Bathsheba, and the Penitential Psalms," 1252.

66. Tentler, *Sin and Confession*, 165.

67. She wrote, "From a modern psychological perspective, the sexual subject matter of the David and Bathsheba illustrations seems utterly inappropriate in either a religious or an educational context: post Freud, it is difficult not to read these persistent images as *pretending* to give a pious warning while *in reality* appealing to the viewer's prurience. But such a reading simply naturalizes and universalizes modern intuitions. Moreover, it absurdly proposes that adult Christians not only derived a furtive pleasure out of images of David and Bathsheba but also made that furtive pleasure the compulsory entrance into literacy for their children. And evidence from the late medieval and early modern texts fails to support this theory. It was not until the nineteenth century, and the dominance of new conceptions of childhood innocence, that such images . . . were no longer considered appropriate gateways to literacy. Until then depictions of Bathsheba bathing and David sneaking a peek formed a habitual, and even valuable, part of both day-to-day piety and institutionalized pedagogical practice." King'oo, *Miserere Mei*, 61.

68. Labriola and Smeltz, *Bible of the Poor*, 135.

69. The marriage scene is evident in their pose of holding right hands, a gesture referred to as the *dextrarum junction*, one which became a convention in artistic depictions of marriage from the fourth century on. Craven, "The Iconography of the David and Bathsheba Cycle," 234.

70. Craven, "Iconography of the David and Bathsheba Cycle," 235.

71. Obviously, a number of the Jewish interpretations discussed in chapter 2 were produced during the medieval period, but their social situation and their content are so different from most of the other interpretations of Bathsheba from this period that they are treated in a separate chapter.

72. *Catena Aurea*, 25. The *Catena* includes the work of the Church Fathers, but was compiled and summarized during the medieval period, and both Remigius and Rabanus date to the medieval period. The Ordinary Gloss in the *Catena* for Matthew 1:6 affirms, "Besides, he does not name Bathsheba, that, by naming Urias, he may recall to memory that great wickedness which *she* was guilty of towards him." Ibid.

73. Maurus, *Exposito in Matthaeum*, 16.

74. Carthusianorum, *Institutoris Opera Omnia*, 104.

75. Referenced in Craven, "The Iconography of the David and Bathsheba Cycle," 237.

76. Maurus, *Exposito in Matthaeum*, 16.

77. Savage and Watson, *Anchoritic Spirituality*, 16. The penitential element fits well with the connection between David and Bathsheba and the penitential psalms in the medieval era.

78. Ibid., 349. In fact, the question of how to evaluate the status of women in the medieval era is a complex one, with some scholars arguing for it as helpful for women because the church allowed them status as nuns. Others see patriarchy so engrained in this time that it's particularly harmful for women. Cf. Judith Bennett, "Medievalism and Feminism," 309–31.

79. According to Joy Schroeder, this is not an uncommon critique of Dinah, even if it is an unfair one. Schroeder, *Dinah's Lament*.

80. Savage and Watson, *Anchoritic Spirituality*, 68.

81. Ibid., 69.

5 — Bathsheba Reformed in the Reformation

1. Thompson, "General Introduction," xxvii.

2. Calvin wrote, "It was when David came in to Bathsheba that Nathan came to him. By that sinful step he had placed himself at a distance from God; and the Divine goodness was signally displayed in contemplating his restoration." *Sermons on 2 Samuel*, 523.

3. Typology did not disappear in the Reformation; Calvin did refer to David as a type of Christ. In the Geneva Bible, "the argument" for 2 Samuel notes: "In the person of David the Scripture setteth forth Christ Jesus the chiefe King, who came of David according to the flesh, and was persecuted on every side with outward and inward enemies, as well as in his own person, as in his members, but at length hee overcommeth all his enemies and giveth his church victorie against all power both spirituall and temporall: and so reigneth with them, King forevermore," 121.

4. Calvin, *Sermons on 2 Samuel,* 476.

5. Zwingli, *Writings, In Search of True Religion,* 98.

6. Wesley, "The Great Privilege of those that are Born of God." http://wesley.nnu .edu/john-wesley/the-sermons-of-john-wesley-1872-edition/sermon-19-the-great-privilege -of-those-that-are-born-of-god/ [Accessed Oct. 25, 2012].

7. Thompson, "Biblical Interpretation in the Works of Martin Luther," 299.

8. Luther, *Church and Ministry I,* 164.

9. Luther, *Lectures on Galatians 5–6,* 386.

10. Luther, *Lectures on Genesis 31–37,* 170.

11. Luther, *A Commentary on Galatians,* 253.

12. Schroeder, *Dinah's Lament,* 41.

13. Luther, *Selected Psalms II,* 205.

14. Ibid.

15. According to 2 Sam 11:27, the thing that David did was evil in YHWH's eyes; he was not simply a fool. However, Nabal, Abigail's husband, is certainly the antagonist, so it's not as if "fool" is a compliment.

16. Luther, *Lectures on Genesis 15–20,* 45.

17. Calvin, *Sermons on 2 Samuel,* 486. Calvin went on to tell his congregation that when the Bible uses the word "sleep," we know that it means something else; but then Calvin referenced Ephesians 5:3, which says 'let adultery and all other uncleanness not even be named among you.'

18. Luther, *Schriften, 4. Band, Psalmenvorlesung 1513/15 (Ps. 85–150).*

19. Luther, *Selected Psalms III,* 173.

20. Luther continued to "prove" that the reason the reference does not apply to Solomon is because in 1 Kgs 1, Solomon becomes king during David's lifetime and receives orders from David; and in 1 Chron 28–29, David gives Solomon a plan for building the temple and ordering the kingdom and the priesthood. Luther does an interesting mix of reading the text literally and canonically (including Chronicles as part of the Davidic history), and also reading it more Christologically: namely, that the temple built after David's death does not refer to the first temple, but to the eschatological and spiritual temple of Jesus (cf. John 2:19). Luther, *Christian in Society IV,* 197–98.

21. Luther, *Lectures on Genesis Chapters 38–44,* 35.

22. Luther, *Career of the Reformer III,* 26.

23. Thompson, "Biblical Interpretation," 305.

24. Luther, *Lectures on Genesis 31–37,* 326.

25. Jaroslav Pelikan commented, "Thus it would seem to have been from Lyra's account 'of the many ways in which the Jews attempt to subvert the interpretation' of Gen 49:10 as a prophecy of the coming of Christ (as well as from other sources) that Luther learned about the rabbinic exegesis that he refuted in his account of this verse." Pelikan, *Reformation of the Bible,* 26.

26. Timothy George observed that Luther had a positive approach to Jews in his early career, in contrast with "his brutal attacks on them later on," and that Luther had gathered a group of Hebrew scholars around him in Wittenberg, referring to them as his

"Sanhedrin." George, *Reading Scripture with the Reformers*, 87. George noted a contrast between Luther's appreciation for the Old Testament and Erasmus' disparaging words about Hebrew and the Old Testament. Still, the relatively positive approaches do not cancel out the disturbing anti-Judaic elements and their consequences.

27. Calvin, *Sermons on 2 Samuel*, 477.

28. "Who was it that moved David to marry this woman? It was not she who solicited it, for we must carefully note that he ordered her to be fetched back into his palace, and celebrated the wedding while she was pregnant. Now that is absolutely clear. No-one needs to discuss this any longer or offer any further conjecture." Ibid., 514.

29. Barbara Pitkin has noted, "as an exegete, Calvin was always pressed for time. When writing a commentary, preparing a lecture, or thinking about one of the eight sermons he might preach in a given week, he had little time to consult his sources but instead relied chiefly on his memory, theological instincts and rhetorical skill in crafting his comments. Sometimes Calvin's alleged 'independence' may have stemmed simply from the fact that he worked in haste." "John Calvin and the Interpretation of the Bible," 348–49.

30. These days included Wednesday, August 12; Thursday, August 13; Friday, August 14; Saturday, August 15; and then Monday, August 24; Tuesday, August 25; Wednesday, August 26; Thursday, August 27; and Friday, August 28.

31. Perhaps Calvin used this language because Bathsheba is married, not single. He did refer to the rape of Tamar, but Bathsheba was always the adulteress. When preaching on David taking Bathsheba in marriage, Calvin talked about how bad it is for someone to get married to one with whom he has committed adultery, "for that would be opening the door to any wicked person or anyone who wanted to poison their spouse. If a man who had committed adultery with a married woman were permitted to take her, after the woman had attempted to kill her husband, it is certain that any parity would be immediately perverted, and the strongest would take over. In brief, such a thing should be considered contrary to nature." Calvin, *Sermons on 2 Samuel*, 515. Calvin clarified, "Now we are referring to a man who has committed adultery, that is, with an adulteress. It is different if a man who has raped a girl is touched with repentance. If, in that case, he takes her in marriage, it is a fruit of his repentance that he will not allow this girl to be condemned. Rather, he is displeased with what he has done, and says: 'We are two poor creatures and miserable sinners. Very well, we have been ill advised. But now let us endeavor to serve God, and to repair the ill already committed.' Therefore, when a man has committed fornication with a girl or with a woman who is not married, he may very well take her as wife." Ibid. It would seem that because Bathsheba is a married woman, there is no conversation about whether the sexual act was forced.

32. Calvin, *Sermons on 2 Samuel*, 481.

33. Calvin, *Sermons on 2 Samuel*, 487. In a later sermon, Calvin referred to Lev 14:7 and Num 8:7, explaining "Yet she used the sprinkling which God had commanded in his Law in order to wash herself," 516.

34. Ibid., 487–88.

35. Calvin, *Sermons on 2 Samuel*, 516.

36. Ibid.

37. Ibid.

38. Ibid.

39. Ibid., 485.

40. Calvin, *Sermons on 2 Samuel*, 599.

41. Calvin quantified this misery by explaining, "Here is David, who was like someone with no principles for a time, and Bathsheba, a miserable fornicator who abandoned her principles, breaking faith with her husband, and then seeing her husband killed because of her." Ibid., 600–601.

42. Ibid., 601.

43. Calvin, *Opera Quae Supersunt Omnia*, 292.

44. It is also known as the "Breeches" bible, based on its translation of Gen 3:7 that Adam and Eve clothe themselves in "breeches" made from fig leaves.

45. *Geneva Bible*, 133.

46. Ibid., re. 2:19.

47. The rabbis also did this in *Numbers Rabbah* and *Leviticus Rabbah*, identifying the mysterious "Lemuel" as Solomon.

48. *Geneva Bible*, 253.

49. Tyndale, *Matthew-Tyndale Bible*, 461.

50. Panizza, "Introduction," 33.

51. It was not published until 1654, after Tarabotti had died. The controversial nature of the content caused it to be banned, but the writing was saved. Panizza, "Introduction," 33.

52. Passi's work was published in 1599, and also occasioned Lucrezia Marinella's written response, *The Nobility and Excellence of Women and the Defects and Vices of Men,* in 1600. Marinella reversed Passi's arguments, attacking men for those very same defects Passi accused women of having. Lucrezia Marinella, *The Nobility and Excellence of Women.*

53. Tarabotti, *Paternal Tyranny,* 112.

54. Ibid.

55. Tarabotti, *Paternal Tyranny,* 115.

56. Ibid., 118.

57. Ibid.

58. Schroeder, *Dinah's Lament,* 135. This is similar to how adultery was viewed and punished in the Patristic period, according to Thomas O'Loughlin, "A Woman's Plight."

59. She was understood to have committed adultery based on translating Judg 19:2 as "and she prostituted herself upon/against him," with some variation on how to translate the Hebrew preposition עַל. Brenz allowed that "the citizens manifested a savage crime against this woman," but explained, "nevertheless by this heinous and abominable form of death our Lord God punished this woman's adultery which she had committed earlier," 138. Martin Bucer and Martin Borrhaus also wrote that the concubine's death was God's punishment for her adultery. Schroeder, *Dinah's Lament,* 138–42.

60. Schroeder, *Dinah's Lament,* 199–202.

6 — Bathsheba Enlightened in the Enlightenment

1. Legaspi, *Death of Scripture.* Legaspi focused on Johann David Michaelis, using that single scholar as a lens through which to view the broader intellectual ethos of the era. Even people of personal faith would be careful to include language like "hypothesis," "evidence," and "reason." John Lange's *Commentary on the Holy Scriptures: Critical, Doctrinal and Homiletical: Samuel* is divided into separate sections: "Textual and Grammatical Notes," "Exegetical and Critical," "Historical and Theological," and "Homiletical and Practical." Lange's evaluation of other "English Commentaries" is illustrative. He explained, "Wall's Critical Notes are nearly useless; GILL has references to Jewish authorities; HENRY is devout; CLARKE is learned, but sometimes erratic and untrustworthy; the Comprehensive Commentary is a compilation not without value. Of the later, Bishop WORDSWORTH's Holy Bible with Notes is devout and conservative, and has some useful quotations from patristic writers, but is marred by excessive literalness and allegorizing." Lange, *Commentary on the Holy Scriptures,* 41–42.

2. Kermode, "New Ways with Biblical Stories," 122. Kermode is following Hans Frei's overarching argument in *The Eclipse of Biblical Narrative.* The emphasis on historical factuality has continued in biblical studies today, with scholars like Dale B. Martin and Roland Boer urging that other approaches to the text be considered, including the patristic way of reading texts. Cf. Martin, *Pedagogy of the Bible;* and Boer, *The Sacred Economy of Ancient Israel.*

3. Sheehan, *The Enlightenment Bible,* 217.

4. Moore and Sherwood, *Invention of the Biblical Scholar,* 46–81. They describe Kant's concern with the ways in which the Bible might appear in part to be morally dangerous, explaining that "Far from being unique, Kant's formulation was the culmination of certain tense and explicit renegotiations between the Bible and morality that had been taking pace, publicly in print, since at least the late seventeenth century. This debate on biblical error orbited obsessively around such iconic biblical crimes as the divinely mandated genocide of the Canaanites, Abraham's willingness to offer Isaac as a bloody sacrifice, and the manifest moral sins of David." Ibid., 50.

5. Lange, *Commentary on the Holy Scriptures: Samuel,* 465.

6. Calvin did this to some extent, but it happens much more in these sources.

7. This is in contrast with the radical Enlightenment, which he described as "That cabal of philosophers and libertines who haunted many of Europe's devout." Sheehan, *The Enlightenment Bible,* xi–xii.

8. Sheehan, *The Enlightenment Bible,* 4.

9. Sheehan, *The Enlightenment Bible,* 183. Anti-Judaism has not gone away in this historical time period. Another who wanted to remove the Hebrew idioms was Johann Lorenz Schmidt, who produced the Wertheimer Bible: a translation of the Pentateuch that attempted to "cleanse" it of "imperfections" created by "Moses' 'base manner of speaking.'" In fact, Schmidt used the metaphor of fertilizer, explaining, "When shit lies in

the street in front of the houses, it is, in that place, an evil thing. But as soon as someone carries it off to the fields, the same stuff is no longer disreputable and contributes to the fertility of the land." Sheehan, *The Enlightenment Bible*, 128–29. Sheehan comments, "Clearing away the shit might be an appropriate metaphor for Schmidt's task. And the shit, in this case, was the Hebrew idiom, which may have been proper to the ancient Jews but which stood as a barrier between modern man and the truths of the Bible. To sanitize the Bible . . . one needed a "free" translation, one aimed not at verbal but at conceptual fidelity." Ibid., 129.

10. Lowth specifically references Nathan's parable as an example of a type of allegory. He wrote, "It is also essential to the elegance of a parable, that the imagery should not only be apt and beautiful, but that all its parts and appendages should be perspicuous and pertinent. It is, however, by no means necessary, that in every parable the allusion should be complete in every part; such a degree of resemblance would frequently appear too minute and exact: but when the nature of the subject will bear, much more when it will even require a fuller explanation; and when the similitude runs directly, naturally, and regularly, through every circumstance, then it cannot be doubted that it is productive of the greatest beauty. Of all these excellencies, there cannot be more perfect examples than the parables which have been just specified. I will also venture to recommend the well-known parable of Nathan, though written in prose." Lowth, *Lectures on the Sacred Poetry of the Hebrews*, 228–29.

11. Edward Said's observations on "Orientalism" are applicable here, especially the Eurocentricism of the terminology. In the preface to his 2003 edition, he described the concept of the "Orient" as "semi-mythical construct which since Napoleon's invasion of Egypt in the late eighteenth century has been made and re-made countless times by power acting through an expedient form of knowledge to assert that this is the Orient's nature, and we must deal with it accordingly." Said, *Orientalism*, xiii. His larger point has to do with how this concept gets played out in contemporary history and politics, but it also applies to the powerful Enlightenment scholars who used their knowledge to make rather paternalistic assumptions that the cultures discussed had not changed at all, as if it were no problem to apply their current social practices in a certain part of the world to texts that described a society that existed thousands of years earlier.

12. Smith, Henry P. *Critical and Exegetical Commentary on the Books of Samuel*, 318. Smith is referencing William Robertson Smith's 1885 *Kinship and Marriage in Early Arabia*.

13. Clarke, *The Old Testament: Volume II*, 383, 387.

14. Kirkpatrick, *Second Book of Samuel*, 327.

15. Lange, *Commentary on the Holy Scriptures: Samuel*, 465.

16. Benson, *Critical and Explanatory Notes*, 892.

17. Patrick, *Commentary Upon the Two Books of Samuel*, 428. His mythological details are slightly inaccurate; Proserpina was associated not with Jupiter, but with Pluto, God of the underworld.

18. Clarke, *The Old Testament: Volume II*, 334.

19. Ibid., 337. Clarke does not want to paint anyone except Uriah in this narrative with a positive brush. After a fairly lengthy review of the characters in which he attempts

to "sum up and apportion the quantity of vice chargeable on each," he concludes, "Let *David*, once a pious, noble, generous, and benevolent hero, who, when almost perishing with thirst, would not taste the water which his brave men had acquired at the hazard of their lives; let this David, I say, be considered an awful example of *apostasy* from religion, justice, and virtue; *Bath-sheba*, of lightness and conjugal infidelity; *Joab*, of base, unmanly, and cold-blooded cruelty; *Uriah*, of untarnished heroism, inflexible fidelity, and unspotted virtue; and then justice will be done to each character. For my own part, I must say I *pity* David; I *venerate* Uriah; I *detest* Joab; and *think meanly* of Bath-sheba."

20. Kirkpatrick, *Second Book of Samuel*, 326.

21. Lange, *Commentary on the Holy Scriptures*, 465.

22. Smith, *Samuel*, 327.

23. Keil and Delitzsch, *Biblical Commentary on the Books of Samuel*, 383.

24. Lange, *Commentary on the Holy Scriptures*, 466.

25. Hall, "David with Bathsheba and URIAH," 240.

26. Benson, *Critical and Explanatory Notes Vol 1*, 892. Benson also referred to Bathsheba's fear of infamy, and perhaps of being stoned by Uriah. Ibid., 893.

27. Ibid., 899.

28. Henry, *Exposition of the Old and New Testaments*, 1035.

29. Henry, *Exposition of the Old and New Testaments*, 1037.

30. Trapp, *Royal Sin*, 7. Trapp also described Bathsheba as "the adulteress." When Trapp discussed their marriage, Trapp explained that David is "highly satisfied, no doubt, with the undisturb'd possession of the woman whom so many difficulties had endeared to him."

31. Kirkpatrick, *Second Book of Samuel*, 330.

32. Henry, *Exposition of the Old and New Testaments*, 1037.

33. Clarke, 336. *The Old Testament, Volume II*.

34. Stanton, *The Woman's Bible*, 57.

35. Henry, Gill and Pink, *An Exposition of I & II Samuel*, 402.

36. Smith, *Samuel*, 321.

37. Ibid., 11.

38. Clarke, 340.

39. Henry, *Exposition of the Old and New Testaments*, 1036. Henry is not the only one to suggest that David might divorce Bathsheba; Kirkpatrick noted the absence of any mention of divorce in 2 Sam 12:14, writing, "To divorce Bath-sheba now would be a further wrong." Kirkpatrick, *Second Book of Samuel*, 335.

40. Kirkpatrick, *Second Book of Samuel*, 334.

41. Ibid., 327.

42. Obviously, an appeal to proof cannot be sustained as something entirely unique in this time; Rashi and other Jewish interpreters in Medieval Spain sought to use methods which we might describe as scientific and thoroughly academic. A difference between that period and the Enlightenment, however, is the positivism that is attached to an interpretation during the Enlightenment, when the study concludes in a single right answer.

43. Kirkpatrick, *Second Book of Samuel*, 334.

44. Montgomery, *Book of Kings*, 92.

45. Lumby, *First Book of the Kings,* 21; Keil, *Commentary on the Books of Kings,* 32.

46. Clarke, 384.

47. Ibid.

48. Matthew Henry described Bathsheba using similar terms. He wrote, "Bath-sheba lived retired, and knew nothing of it [Adonijah's attempt at the throne], till Nathan informed her. Many get very comfortably through this world, that know little how the world goes." Henry, *Exposition of the Old and New Testaments,* 1015. Henry also thinks that Solomon did know of Adonijah's attempt at the throne, but "quietly composed himself and left it to God and his friends to order the matter." Ibid.

49. Benson, *Critical and Explanatory Notes Vol II,* 5. Benson also explained Nathan's twofold motivations for speaking as "his piety, that he might fulfill the will of God declared to him concerning Solomon's succession, 2 Sam. vii. 13; and by his prudence, knowing that Adonijah hated him for being the principal instrument of Solomon's advancement." *Ibid.*

50. Benson, *Critical and Explanatory Notes Vol II,* 6.

51. Lumby, *The First Book of the Kings,* 6.

52. Henry, *Exposition of the Old and New Testaments,* 1015.

53. Stanton, *The Woman's Bible,* 59.

54. Henry, *Exposition of the Old and New Testaments,* 1015.

55. Gage, *The Woman's Bible,* 61.

56. Ibid.

57. Gage gives examples of a legal case in England where the father was granted control over the religious education of his children, though he and his wife had previously had a prenuptial agreement. *The Woman's Bible,* 61.

58. Montgomery, *The Book of Kings,* 67.

59. Lumby, *First Book of the Kings,* 20.

60. Benson, *Critical and Explanatory Notes Vol II,* 11.

61. Keil, *Commentary on the Books of Kings,* 32.

62. Lumby, *The First Book of the Kings,* 21.

63. Keil, *Commentary on the Books of Kings,* 32.

64. Lumby, *First Book of the Kings,* 21.

65. Whybray, *Succession Narrative,* 40.

66. Montgomery, *The Book of Kings,* 92.

67. Driver, *Notes on the Hebrew Text of the Books of Samuel,* 222.

7 — Bathsheba Told, Sung, Acted, and Politicized in the Contemporary World

1. Sherwood, *A Biblical Text and Its Afterlives,* 150.

2. Ibid., 151, fn. 166.

3. *The Bible* miniseries is another interpretation of Bathsheba that would seem to be concerned with the authority of the Bible, as evidenced in the quote that appears at the start of the credits: "This program is an adaptation of biblical stories that changed our world. It endeavors to stay true to the spirit of The Book." And yet, as will be discussed below, this interpretation of David is one of the less reverent ones, so it too, might better be classified as "mixed."

4. Though the technology of screens is new, this tendency to skip around in the Bible is not. When texts were printed on scrolls, people would have to roll through to get to a later section, but when they were printed and bound in a codex it became easier to flip through.

5. Beal, *The Rise and Fall of the Bible*, 79–81.

6. Cf. Leneman, "Portrayals of Power in Delilah and Bathsheba," 227–43.

7. The term also may be abbreviated to fan fic, fanfic, or fic.

8. As of June 2016, there were over 80,000 stories on the HarryPotterFanfiction.com website, and author E. L. James's fanfiction of *Twilight* was eventually published in book form as the series *Fifty Shades*.

9. Both books are part of a series on biblical women. Rivers's five-book series is titled "A Lineage of Grace," with a book on each of the five women mentioned in Jesus' genealogy in Matthew: Tamar, Rahab, Ruth, Bathsheba, and Mary. Smith's book about Bathsheba is part of her three-book series on "The Wives of King David" (which include Michal and Abigail), but she has also written series on "The Wives of the Patriarchs," "The Loves of King Solomon," and "Daughters of the Promised Land."

10. Rivers's website explains that she wrote her first novel about Hosea and Gomer as a statement of faith "shortly after becoming a born-again Christian in 1986." http://francinerivers.com/about [Accessed Apr. 21, 2014].

11. Rivers, *Unspoken: Bathsheba*, 47.

12. Ibid.

13. Smith, *Bathsheba: A Novel*, 130.

14. Ibid., 45–46.

15. Ibid., 129.

16. Rivers, *Unspoken: Bathsheba*, 88.

17. Ibid., 48.

18. Ibid., 52–53. For example, Rivers wrote, "She put her hands against his chest. She knew she should say something to stop him. She should be like Abigail and make him aware of the sin he was about to commit. But her resolve weakened when she felt his heart pounding faster and harder than her own. . . . When his mouth took hers, Bathsheba felt herself being pulled down with him into a vortex of desire. His fingers raked through her hair. He moaned her name, and the words of warning died in her throat. As her body caught fire, she clung to him and didn't say a word." Ibid., 53.

19. Smith described Bathsheba's early encounter with David as follows: "Thoughts of Uriah filled her with shame. He would not understand her desire to talk with this man, even if he was the king. She did not understand it herself, but she sensed that she should not be here, should not continue a conversation that could only grow more intimate. Was the king attracted to her? The thought made her pause, as she self-consciously pulled the veil across her mouth again. It couldn't be. The king had many wives to choose from, some far more beautiful than she. And he could have any woman in the kingdom. A strange regret filled her at that thought. Was it she who was attracted to him? Confusion crept in, filling her with uncertainty." *Bathsheba: A Novel*, 56.

20. Smith, *Bathsheba: A Novel*, 141.

21. Ibid., 143.

22. Rivers, *Unspoken: Bathsheba*, 147.

23. In Matthew Quick's novel *Love May Fail*, he has a character who was a pornographer find religion, and the woman with whom he had an affair explains, "Father Martin calls Ken King David. Says God's called him to a new life. He says I am Ken's Bathsheba—that our pairing came of sin, but that we will redeem ourselves." *Love May Fail*, 361. Quick also wrote the book-turned-movie, *Silver Linings Playbook*. In Julius Lester's *The Autobiography of God*, God is describing God's attempt to get humans to read God's autobiography, and says, "I have to admit it was daunting to think King David would be reading something I wrote. Now there was a man who could write! I was so eager for his opinion. But I made the mistake of putting the manuscript on his night table while he was carrying on with that Bathsheba woman. I don't think he ever realized it was there." Lester, *The Autobiography of God*, 154. Also, Thomas Hardy named his main character in *Far from the Madding Crowd* after biblical Bathsheba.

24. L'Engle, *Certain Women*, 350.

25. Ibid., 42.

26. Ibid., 212.

27. Ibid., 47.

28. Ibid., 289.

29. Ibid., 252.

30. Ibid., 259.

31. Ibid., 289.

32. Ibid., 343.

33. Englehard, *The Bathsheba Deadline*, 2.

34. Ibid., 4–5.

35. Ibid., 6.

36. Perhaps trying to mitigate the incredulous nature of this as a plot device, the character asks, "Another coincidence, or truly, am I being followed by the prophets?" Ibid., 228.

37. L'Engle, *Certain Women*, 84.

38. Ibid., 326.

39. Ibid.

40. Cliff Graham is currently writing a series called *Lion of War*, which his website describes as follows: "Conceived as gritty, intense, and exciting novels that would help a new generation connect with the Bible . . . the story of the Mighty Men—a disgruntled army of mercenaries and outcasts forged into an elite fighting force by a young warlord named David." The first book was released in 2011, and does not include Uriah. Likely, later books will talk about Uriah and Bathsheba, but the focus is on David as warrior, not lover. Another book titled *Midbar III*, self-published by author Lynny Harris in 2013, similarly sets the story of Bathsheba in the ancient past. I was not able to get Geraldine Brooks's 2015 novel, *The Secret Chord* before this went to print; clearly there is more that is and will be written on Bathsheba.

41. Heller, *God Knows*, 26. Heller also has a conversation between Joab and David in which Joab talks about wanting to conquer "Russia, including the towns of Leningrad, Moscow, Stalingrad, Rostov, Kiev and Odessa." Ibid., 260.

42. Schmitt, *David the King,* 438.

43. Ibid., 441.

44. Ibid., 420.

45. Ibid., 589.

46. Massie, *King David,* 4.

47. Heym, *King David Report,* 155–56.

48. Ibid., 184.

49. Tumanov, *Divine Silence in Stefan;* and Heym, *The King David Report.*

50. Heller, *God Knows,* 283–84.

51. For example, ibid., 276. Heller also has Bathsheba writing Psalm 23. When she writes "the Lord is my shepherd," David responds as follows "Are you crazy? How fantastic can you get? That's crap, Bathsheba, pure crap. Where's your sense of metaphor? You're turning God into a laborer and your audience into animals. That's practically blasphemy. Shall not want what? You're raising questions instead of answering them." Ibid., 272.

52. Ibid., 289.

53. Ibid., 19.

54. Schmitt, *David the King,* 589.

55. Sting, *Lyrics,* 1.

56. Ibid.

57. Leneman, *The Performed Bible* and *Love, Lust, and Lunacy.* For example, Leneman observed how Darius Milhaud's opera *David* has a scene in which David and Bathsheba converse about their dying baby. In that scene, "When David asks if the child is out of danger, his voice rises much higher than in his opening phrase, betraying emotion, while Bathsheba's response in marked contrast lies very low in the soprano register and includes a diminished octave leap from *b' to c'* . . . David's voice rises and grows stronger after he speaks of God's power, and he is accompanied by muted trumpets. . . . This suggests both a martial sound and a foretelling of death." *Love, Lust, and Lunacy,* 293.

58. During a Coldplay concert I attended in 2012, lead singer Chris Martin introduced the song "Us Against the World" by explaining that it could be about a breakup or it could be about the Seattle Mariners, encouraging the audience to participate in making it mean what we wanted it to mean.

59. See, for example, the website songmeanings.com, where people are able to contribute their interpretation of the meaning of different songs.

60. Sting, *Lyrics,* 149; and interview with Timothy White, quoted on http://sting.com/discography/index/album/albumId/17/tagName/Albums [Accessed Mar. 18, 2014].

61. On Sting.com. http://sting.com/discography/index/album/albumId/17/tagName/Albums [Accessed Mar. 18, 2014].

62. In his *Lyrics,* Sting introduces "Mad About You" by writing: "The second book of Samuel, chapter 11. King David falls in lust with Bathsheba, the beautiful wife of Uriah the Hittite. King David arranges for Uriah the Hittite to be killed in battle. The king makes love to Bathsheba. God is not pleased. Punishment comes in Chapter 12." Sting, *Lyrics,* 149. To White, Sting said, "The inspiration for the song was the story of King David who at the height of his political power fell in love with someone else's wife. This

man was a soldier, so he manufactured some war and sent the soldier off to fight in the front line. He of course died, and he then made love to the wife and regretted it for the rest of his life." http://sting.com/discography/index/album/albumId/17/tagName/Albums [Accessed Mar. 18, 2014].

63. http://sting.com/discography/index/album/albumId/17/tagName/Albums [Accessed Mar. 18, 2014].

64. This album made *Rolling Stone's* list of top 500 albums of all time, and Kurt Cobain acknowledged the Pixies' influence on the sound in "Smells Like Teen Spirit." http://www.rollingstone.com/music/lists/500-greatest-albums-of-all-time-20120531/pixies -doolittle-20120524#ixzz2yKRH7MHY [Accessed Mar. 20, 2014]. Another song on Dolittle, "Gouge Away," alludes to Samson and Delilah, but does not use their names, just lyrics like "you stroke my locks," and, "chained to the pillars / a 3-day party / i break the walls / and kill us all / with holy fingers." Several musical interpretations relate David and Bathsheba with Samson and Delilah, such as Leonard Cohen's "Hallelujah." While the Pixies do not combine the two in a single song, it is still noteworthy that these are the two biblical stories drawn on for this album.

65. According to producer John Lissauer, the song "Hallelujah" was thought to be the standout single of the album, but when Walter Yetnikoff, then president of CBS Records, heard it, he said, "What is this? This isn't pop music. We're not releasing it. This is a disaster." In that same year, the Billboard top song of 1984 was Prince's "When Doves Cry," the lead single from his album *Purple Rain,* and also featured in the film; Madonna had released her self-titled debut studio album in the previous year; and Michael Jackson's *Thriller* was two years old. Cohen's dramatic, synthesizer heavy sound did not even register on the charts. Fetters, "How Leonard Cohen's 'Hallelujah' Became Everybody's 'Hallelujah'."

66. It was Buckley's version that became so well known, to the extent that many people—including Jon Bon Jovi—thought that Buckley wrote the song. When Buckley suddenly, and tragically, died in a drowning accident in 1997, his association with the song made it even more poignant/famous. Other artists who recorded the song include Bono in 1985, Rufus Wainwright for the movie *Shrek* in 2001, Imogen Heap's version for the TV show "The O.C."; K.D. Lang; and Justin Timberlake in 2010, in a relief concert for the Haiti earthquake. Alan Light, *The Holy or the Broken,* xvii, 148.

67. Light, *The Holy or the Broken,* x.

68. Ibid., 20.

69. Ibid., xvii.

70. Barthel wrote that the repeated use of the song to indicate sadness has "erased the line-by-line, verse-by-verse meaning and replaced it with an overall feeling of sadness. You hear those opening chords now and the words hardly matter. The visual emotions it was used to counterpoint have taken over the lyrical content." Ibid., 118–19.

71. Ibid., xvii.

72. For example, John Cale of the band The Velvet Underground rerecorded the song but shifted the order so that it says, "she broke your throne, she cut your hair / love is not a victory march." A contrast can be made with the time artist CeeLo Green did a

performance of John Lennon's "Imagine." When Green changed the lyrics from "Imagine there's no heaven, and no religion, too," to "imagine there's no heaven, and all religion's true," there was an outcry. http://www.rollingstone.com/music/news/cee-lo-green -outrages-john-lennon-fans-by-changing-lyrics-to-imagine-20120102 [Accessed Apr. 7, 2014].

73. Light, *The Holy or the Broken,* 226.

74. Cf. *Plotted, Shot, and Painted.* Julie Kelso also discussed the 1951 film in her "Gazing at Impotence in Henry King's *David and Bathsheba.*"

75. That sentence is part of the logo: http://logos.wikia.com/wiki/File:VeggieTales _Logo_2_c_Sunday_Morning_Values_Saturday_Morning_Fun_Since_1993.png [Accessed Aug. 4, 2015].

76. There are larger debates about whether, or in what ways, the Bible should be edited for children. Cf. Bottigheimer, *The Bible for Children;* Vander Stichele and Pyper, *Text, Image, and Otherness in Children's Bibles;* Landy, "Noah's Ark and Mrs. Monkey"; and du Toit, "Seeing Is Believing."

77. Cf. http://www.outreach.com/campaigns/the-bible-resources.aspx [Accessed Aug. 25, 2015].

78. Again, this was how David and Bathsheba met in Schmitt's novel *David the King.*

79. The miniseries does not show any scenes of Solomon except the one when he is a toddler; we have to take the narrator's word that he finds it impossible to follow the commandments. This theme is repeated in the episode titled, "Mission," which covers Jesus' ministry; a narrator explains that the people were "guided by Pharisees, guardians of the commandments. . . . Pharisees believe that the well-being of the nation depends on strictly observing the laws God gave to Moses." In the scene that dramatizes the woman caught in adultery (John 7:53–8:11), Jesus says, "I'll give my stone to the first man who tells me that he has never sinned."

80. https://www.youtube.com/watch?v=W5fEIkgijE8 [Accessed Aug. 25, 2015].

81. Ibid.

82. Ibid.

83. While the boards are covering Larry's face, the man cuckolding him tells him—with some amount of double entendre—"Nailing it down. So important."

84. Jacobson, *Does David Still Play Before You?,* 18. In 1970, Peres had written a book about the history of Israel's military development titled *David's Sling.*

85. Ibid.

86. Ludwig and Longenecker, "The Bathsheba Syndrome," 265.

87. Thom Shanker, "Concern Grows Over Top Military Officer's Ethics."

88. Owen, "Petraeus's Bathsheba Syndrome: Why Did a Man We So Respected Succumb to Temptation?"

89. Cf. Marcia Mount Shoop, "The David Syndrome." http://feminismandreligion .com/2012/11/17/the-david-syndrome-by-marcia-mount-shoop/ [Accessed June 20, 2014].; Carl W. Kenney II, "Jesse Jackson Jr.: Living with the David Syndrome." http://rev-elution .blogspot.com/2012/07/jesse-jackson-jr-living-with-david.html [Accessed June 20, 2014]; and Carol Burbank, "Enough about the Bathsheba Syndrome: Let's Talk about King

David Syndrome." http://leadershipspirit.wordpress.com/2013/05/13/enough-about-the
-bathsheba-syndrome-lets-talk-about-king-david-syndrome/ [Accessed June 20, 2014].
Burbank also identifies other possibilities, including, "The Petraeus Syndrome." Burbank, "The Petraeus Syndrome and Leadership Stories: A Rotten Rose by Any Other
Name?" https://leadershipspirit.wordpress.com/2014/01/10/the-petraeus-syndrome-and
-leadership-stories-a-rotten-rose-by-any-other-name/ [Accessed June 20, 2014].

90. Bathsheba did get referenced in a sidebar to the July 12, 2004 *Newsweek* article,
"The Secret Lives of Wives" by Lorraine Ali and Lisa Miller. The sidebar was titled,
"Wayward Wives 101," and introduced with these words: "Throughout history, women,
both real and imagined, have shown that when it comes to infidelity, it's not solely a
man's world. Here's a crash course." Bathsheba was the first of several examples which
included Guinevere, Catherine the Great, Hester Prynne, Emma Bovary, Anna Karenina,
Ingrid Bergman, Elizabeth Taylor, Mrs. Robinson, and Camilla Parker Bowles. Bathsheba
was described as follows: "Spotted bathing by a voyeuristic King David, the married
Bathsheba obliges his demands for a royal romp. Pregnant with David's child, Bathsheba
stands by as he murders her husband; the child conceived with the king dies." Ali and
Miller, "Wayward Wives 101," 49–52.

91. John, "Still On Immodest Dress Code." http://www.thetidenewsonline.com/2015/
08/03/still-on-immodest-dress-code/ [Accessed Aug. 4, 2015].

92. All Woman, "How I Stole Him Away." http://www.jamaicaobserver.com/magazines/
allwoman/How-I-stole-him-away_18429049 [Accessed Feb. 24, 2015].

93. Muivah, "Are Women as Powerless as They Appear? Part 2." http://e-pao.net/
epSubPageExtractor.asp?src=leisure.Essays.Essay_on_Faith_Spirituality.Are_Women_As
_Powerless_As_They_Appear_Part_2_By_Bienhome_Muivah. [Accessed Jan. 31, 2014].

Conclusion

1. Though Bathsheba is hardly the "hero" of the story in any conventional sense, for
Bakhtin, the hero is any subject. Not just those in the narrative spotlight are heroes; all
characters matter. In fact, Mieke Bal has identified what she called, "the problem of the
hero," explaining that "Lots of problematic features have accrued to the term, so much so
that it is better left alone. . . . The problem of the hero has ideological relevance, if only
because of the connotations of the concept itself. It is obvious that heroines display different features from male heroes, black from white heroes, in the large majority of the
narratives. The suspicion that the choice of a hero and of the features attributed to him
or her betrays an ideological position is a reason not to ignore the problem but rather to
study it." Bal, *Narratology*, 131–32.

2. Bakhtin, *Problems of Dostoevsky's Poetics*, 61.

3. Morson and Emerson, *Mikhail Bakhtin*, 36–37.

4. Jean-Gilles, Jovaneca. http://www.theupcoming.co.uk/2013/06/09/british-lifestyle
-brand-bathsheba-launches-beach-and-home-wear/ [Accessed June 9, 2013].

5. *Mikraot Gedalot to 2 Sam*, 329; and *Num. Rab.*, 353.

6. *Numbers Rabbah*, 352–53.

7. As discussed earlier, both *Numbers Rabbah* and *Leviticus Rabbah* have her waking Solomon from his slumber so that he can go and participate in the dedication of the temple.

8. Cf. Jerome's letter 85 to Paulinus.

9. Pay special attention to Joseph Heller's *God Knows* for the most salient example of that reception.

10. Baumgardner and Richards, *ManifestA*, 246.

BIBLIOGRAPHY

Adam, A. K. M. *Faithful Interpretation: Reading the Bible in a Postmodern World.* Minneapolis: Fortress, 2006.

Adelman, Rachel. *The Female Ruse: Women's Deception and Divine Sanction in the Hebrew Bible.* Sheffield: Sheffield Phoenix, 2015.

Ali, Lorraine, and Lisa Miller. "Wayward Wives 101," "The Secret Lives of Wives," *Newsweek*, July 12, 2004: 47–54.

Alter, Robert. *The Art of Biblical Poetry.* New York: Basic Books, 1985.

———. *The David Story: A Translation with Commentary of 1 and 2 Samuel.* New York: Norton, 1999.

Ambrose, *De Apologia David ad Theodosium Augustum.* Turnhout: Brepols, 2010.

Andreasen, Niels-Erik A. "The Role of the Queen Mother in Israelite Society," *Catholic Biblical Quarterly* 45 (Apr. 1983): 179–94.

Aschkenasy, Nehama. *Woman at the Window: Biblical Tales of Oppression and Escape.* Detroit: Wayne State University Press, 1998.

Auerbach, Erich. *Mimesis: The Representation of Reality in Western Literature.* Garden City, N.Y.: Doubleday Anchor, 1957.

Augustin, Matthias. "Die Inbesitznahme der schönen Frau aus der unterschiedlichen Sicht der Schwachen und der Mächtigen: Ein kritischer Vergleich von Gen 12, 10–20 und 2 Sam 11, 2–27a." *Biblische Zeitschrift* 27 (1983): 145–54.

Augustine. *Answer to Faustus, a Manichean.* Translated with notes by Roland Teske. Hyde Park: New City Press, 2007.

Augustine. *Christian Instruction.* Translated by John J. Gavigan. Vol. 2 of *The Fathers of the Church.* New York: Cima, 1948.

Augustine, *The Confessions.* London: Penguin, 1961.

Augustine. "St. Augustine: Eighty-Three Different Questions." Translated by David L. Mosher. Vol. 70 of *The Fathers of the Church.* Washington, D.C.: Catholic University of America Press, 1977.

Bach, Alice. "Good to the Last Drop: Viewing the Sotah (Numbers 5.11–31) as the Glass Half Empty and Wondering How to View It Half Full." Pages 26–54 in *The New Literary Criticism and the Hebrew Bible.* Edited by J. Cheryl Exum and David Clines. Journal for the Study of the Old Testament: Supplement Series 143. Sheffield: Almond Press, 1993.

Bailey, Randall C. *David in Love and War: The Pursuit of Power in 2 Samuel 10–12*. Journal for the Study of the Old Testament: Supplement Series 75. Sheffield: Sheffield Academic Press, 1990.

Bakhtin, Mikhail. *Problems of Dostoevsky's Poetics*. Edited and translated by Caryl Emerson. Minneapolis: University of Minnesota Press, 1984.

Bal, Mieke. *Lethal Love: Feminist Literary Readings of Biblical Love Stories*. Bloomington: Indiana University Press, 1987.

———. *Narratology: Introduction to the Theory of Narrative*. Toronto: University of Toronto Press, 1997.

Bassler, Judith. "A Man for All Seasons: David in Rabbinic and New Testament Literature." *Interpretation* 40 (1986): 156–69.

Baumgardner, Jennifer, and Amy Richards. *ManifestA: Young Women, Feminism, and the Future*. New York: Farrar, Straus and Giroux, 2000.

Beah, Ismael. *Radiance of Tomorrow*. New York: Sarah Crichton, 2014.

Beal, Timothy. "Reception History and Beyond: Toward the Cultural History of Scriptures." *Biblical Interpretation* 19 (2011): 357–72.

Beal, Timothy. *The Rise and Fall of the Bible*. Boston: Houghton Mifflin, 2011.

Ben-Porat, Ziva. "The Poetics of Literary Allusion." *PTL* 1 (1976): 105–28.

Bennett, Judith. "Medievalism and Feminism." *Speculum: A Journal of Medieval Studies* 68 (1993): 309–31.

Benson, Joseph. *Critical and Explanatory Notes Vol 1: Genesis to the Second Book of Samuel*. New York: T. Mason and G. Lane, 1841.

Benson, Joseph. *Critical and Explanatory Notes Vol II: The First Book of Kings to Proverbs*. New York: T. Mason and G. Lane, 1839.

Berlin, Adele. "Characterization in Biblical Narrative: David's Wives." Pages 219–33 in *Beyond Form Criticism*. Edited by Paul R. House. Winona Lake, Ind.: Eisenbrauns, 1992.

Besançon, Maria. *"L'affaire" de David et Bethsabee et la genealogie du Christ*. Saint-Maur: Parole et Silence, 1997.

Biederman, Patricia Ward. "Gracie Acts More Like Hairy Houdini." http://articles.latimes .com/2004/jan/22/local/me-zoo22. Accessed Jan. 16, 2015.

Bodi, Daniel. *The Demise of the Warlord: A New Look at the David Story*. Hebrew Bible Monographs, 26. Sheffield: Sheffield Phoenix, 2010.

Bodner, Keith. *David Observed: A King in the Eyes of His Court*. Sheffield: Sheffield Phoenix, 2005.

Bodner, Keith. "Nathan: Prophet, Politician and Novelist?" *Journal for the Study of the Old Testament* 95 (2001): 43–54.

Bodner, Keith. *The Rebellion of Absalom*. Hoboken: Taylor and Francis, 2013.

Boer, Roland. "Against Reception History," http://www.bibleinterp.com/opeds/boe358008 .shtml. Accessed Dec. 12, 2014.

Boer, Roland. *The Sacred Economy of Ancient Israel*. Philadelphia: Westminster/John Knox, 2015.

Bottigheimer, Ruth. *The Bible for Children: From the Age of Gutenberg to the Present*. New Haven, Conn.: Yale University Press, 1996.

Bowen, Nancy. "The Quest for the Historical Gĕbîrâ." *CBQ* 63 (2001): 597–618.

Boyarin, Daniel. *Carnal Israel: Reading Sex in Talmudic Culture.* Oakland: University of California Press, 1995.

Boyarin, Daniel. *Intertextuality and the Reading of Midrash.* Bloomington: Indiana University Press, 1994.

Breed, Brennan. *Nomadic Text: A Theory of Biblical Reception History.* Bloomington: Indiana University Press, 2014.

Breed, Brennan. "Nomadology of the Bible: A Processual Approach to Biblical Reception History." *Biblical Interpretation* 1 (2012): 299–320.

Brueggemann, Walter. *David's Truth in Israel's Imagination and Memory.* Philadelphia: Fortress, 1985.

Brueggemann, Walter. *1 & 2 Kings.* Macon: Smyth & Helwys, 2000.

Bruns, Gerald L. "Midrash and Allegory: The Beginnings of Scriptural Interpretation." Pages 625–46 in *The Literary Guide to the Bible.* Edited by Robert Alter and Frank Kermode. Cambridge: Belknap Press, 1987.

Bryne, Donal. "The Hours of the Admiral Prigent de Coëtivy." *Scriptorium* 28 (1974): 248–61.

Burbank, Carol. "Enough about the Bathsheba Syndrome: Let's Talk about King David Syndrome." *Lead Me On* (blog), May 13, 2013. http://leadershipspirit.wordpress .com/2013/05/13/enough-about-the-bathsheba-syndrome-lets-talk-about-king-david -syndrome/. Accessed June 20, 2014.

Burbank, Carol. "The Petraeus Syndrome and Leadership Stories: A Rotten Rose by Any Other Name?" *Lead Me On* (blog), Jan. 10, 2014. https://leadershipspirit.wordpress .com/2014/01/10/the-petraeus-syndrome-and-leadership-stories-a-rotten-rose-by-any -other-name/. Accessed June 20, 2014.

Burnes, Brian. "Seven Chimpanzees Use Ingenuity to Escape Their Enclosure at the Kansas City Zoo." *Kansas City Star.* http://www.kansascity.com/news/local/article344810/ Seven-chimpanzees-use-ingenuity-to-escape-their-enclosure-at-the-Kansas-City-Zoo .html#storylink=cpy. Accessed Jan. 16, 2015.

Cady Stanton, Elizabeth. *The Woman's Bible.* Seattle: Coalition Task Force on Women and Religion, 1974.

Călinescu, Matei. *Rereading,* New Haven, Conn.: Yale University Press, 1993.

Calvin, John. *Opera Quae Supersunt Omnia.* Vol. XLVIII of *Corpus Reformatorum Volume LXXVI.* Edited by Guilielmus Baum, Eduardus Cunitz, and Eduardus Reu. Brunsvigae: Appelhans and Pfennigstorff, 1892.

Calvin, John. *Sermons on 2 Samuel: Chapters 1–13.* Translated by Doug Kelly. Edinburgh: Banner of Truth Trust, 1992.

Carthusianorum, S. Brunonis. *Institutoris Opera Omnia.* Paris: Migne, 1853.

Cassiodorus. *Explanation of the Psalms, Vol. 1 Psalms 1–50.* Translated by P. G. Walsh. Ancient Christian Writers, no. 51. New York: Paulist, 1990.

Chrysostom, John. "Homilies on Colossians." *Chrysostom: Homilies on Galatians, Ephesians, Philippians, Colossians, Thessalonians, Timothy, Titus, and Philemon.* Nicene and Post-Nicene Fathers First Series, 13. Peabody, Mass.: Hendrickson, 2004. First published 1889 by Christian Literature Publishing.

Chrysostom, John. *Homilies on the Gospel of St. Matthew.* Translated by George Prevost and revised by M. Riddle. Nicene and Post-Nicene Fathers, 10. Grand Rapids, Mich.: Eerdmans, 1956.

Clarke, Adam. *The Old Testament: Volume II—Joshua to Esther.* New York: Methodist Book Concern, 1828.

Cogan, Mordechai. *I Kings: A New Translation with Introduction and Commentary.* Anchor Bible Commentary, Vol. 10. New Haven, Conn.: Yale University Press, 2008.

Cohen, H. Hirsch. "David and Bathsheba," *JBR* 33 (1965): 144.

The Commentators' Bible: The Rubin JPS Miḳra'ot Gedolot. Edited by Michael Carasik. Philadelphia, Penn.: Jewish Publication Society, 2005.

Conti, Marco, ed. *1–2 Kings, 1–2 Chronicles, Ezra, Nehemiah, Esther.* Edited by Thomas C. Oden. Vol. 5 of *Ancient Christian Commentary on Scripture: Old Testament.* Downers Grove, Ill.: InterVarsity, 2008.

Cosgrove, Charles "Toward a Postmodern Hermeneutica Sacra: Guiding Considerations in Choosing Between Competing Plausible Interpretations of Scripture." Pages 39–61 in *The Meanings We Choose: Hermeneutical Ethics, Indeterminacy and the Conflict of Interpretations.* Edited by Charles H. Cosgrove. London: T. & T. Clark, 2004.

Costley, Clare. "David, Bathsheba, and the Penitential Psalms." *Renaissance Quarterly* 57 (2004): 1235–77.

Coxon, Peter. "A Note on 'Bathsheba' in 2 Samuel 12:1–6." *Biblica* 62 (1981): 247–50.

Craven, Wayne. "The Iconography of the David and Bathsheba Cycle at the Cathedral of Auxerre." *Journal of the Society of Architectural Historians* 34 (1975): 226–37.

Cushman, Beverly. "The Politics of the Royal Harem and the Case of Bat-Sheba." *Journal for the Study of the Old Testament* 30 (2006): 327–43.

Daube, David. "Absalom and the Ideal King." *Vetus Testamentum* 48 (1998): 315–25.

de Margerie, Bertrand. *An Introduction to the History of Exegesis.* Volume 2, the Latin Fathers. Petersham, Mass.: Saint Bede's Publications, 1991.

de Lubac, Henri. *Medieval Exegesis: The Four Senses of Scripture.* Edinburgh: T. & T. Clark, 1959.

de Vaux, Roland. *Ancient Israel: Its Life and Institutions.* Translated by John McHugh. New York: McGraw Hill, 1961.

Deleuze, Giles. *Difference and Repetition.* Translated by Paul Patton. New York: Columbia University Press, 1994.

Deleuze, Giles. *The Fold: Leibniz and the Baroque.* Translated by Tom Conley. London: Athlone Press, 1993.

Donnet-Guez, Brigitte. "L'ambiguïté du personage de Bethsabée à travers la littérature rabbinique." Pages 65–84 in *L'Historie de David et Bethsabée—Etude interdisciplinaire.* Yod 8. Edited by Daniel Bodi and Masha Itshaki, 2004.

Driver, S. R. *Notes on the Hebrew Text of the Books of Samuel.* Oxford: Clarendon Press, 1890.

du Toit, Jaqueline. "Seeing Is Believing: Children's Bibles as Negotiated Translation." Pages 101–112 in *Ideology, Culture and Translation.* Edited by Scott S. Elliott and Roland Boer. Society of Biblical Literature: Semeia Studies 69, 2012.

Emery, Brent. "Comparing Texts in Hebrew Scripture Helps Clarify Claims of Rape." Nov. 13, 2015. *The News Tribune.* http://www.thenewstribune.com/news/local/community/gateway/g-living/article44756976.html. Accessed Nov. 14, 2015.

Englehard, Jack. *The Bathsheba Deadline: An Original Novel.* Bloomington, Ind.: iUniverse, 2007.

Erasmus, Desiderius. *The Collected Works.* Edited by John W. O'Malley and Louis A. Perraud. Toronto: University of Toronto Press, 1999.

Esmeijer, Anna. *Divina Quaternitas.* Amsterdam: Van Gorcum Assen, 1978.

Eucherius. "Commentarii in Libros Regum, Lib. II." In *Patrologia Latina* 50, edited by J. P. Migne. Paris: Garnier Frères, 1859.

Eusebius. *Church History.* Nicene and Post-Nicene Fathers, 2nd Series. Edited by P. Schaff and H. Wace. Reprint, Grand Rapids, Mich.: Eerdmans, 1955.

Exum, J. Cheryl. "Bathsheba Plotted, Shot, and Painted." *Semeia* 74 (1996): 47–73.

Exum, J. Cheryl. *Plotted, Shot, and Painted: Cultural Representations of Biblical Women.* Sheffield: Sheffield Academic, 1996.

Exum, J. Cheryl. *Tragedy and Biblical Narrative: Arrows of the Almighty.* Cambridge: Cambridge University Press, 1992.

Fetters, Ashley. "How Leonard Cohen's 'Hallelujah' Became Everybody's 'Hallelujah.'" *Atlantic,* Dec. 4, 2012. http://www.theatlantic.com/entertainment/archive/2012/12/how-leonard-cohens-hallelujah-became-everybodys-hallelujah/265900/. Accessed Apr. 14, 2014.

Fokkelman, J. P. *Narrative Art and Poetry in the Books of Samuel: A Full Interpretation Based on Stylistic and Structural Analyses.* Studia Semitica Neerlandica. Assen Netherlands: Van Gorcum, 1981.

Franke, John R., ed. *Joshua, Judges, Ruth, 1–2 Samuel.* Vol. 4 of *Ancient Christian Commentary on Scripture: Old Testament.* Edited by Thomas C. Oden. Downers Grove, Ill.: InterVarsity Press, 2005.

Freedman, David Noel. "Dinah and Shechem: Tamar and Amnon." *Austin Seminary Bulletin Faculty Edition* 105 (1990): 51–63.

Freedman, Rabbi Dr. H., trans. *Midrash Rabbah Genesis.* Edited by H. Freedman and Maurice Simon. London: Soncino, 1983.

Frei, Hans. *The Eclipse of Biblical Narrative: A Study in Eighteenth and Nineteenth Century Hermeneutics.* New Haven: Yale University Press, 1974.

Frymer-Kensky, Tikva Simone. *Reading the Women of the Bible.* 1st ed. New York: Schocken, 2002.

Gadamer, Hans-Georg. *Truth and Method.* Translation revised by Joel Weinsheimer and Donald G. Marshall. New York: Continuum, 1999.

Garrard, Mary. *Artemisia Gentileschi: The Image of the Female Hero in Italian Baroque Art.* Princeton, N.J.: Princeton University Press, 1991.

Garsiel, Moshe. "The Story of David and Bathsheba: A Different Approach." *Catholic Biblical Quarterly* 55 (1993): 244–62.

George, Timothy. *Reading Scripture with the Reformers.* Downers Grove: IVP Academic, 2011.

Gikatila, R. Joseph. *David et Bethsabée: Le Secret du Mariage.* Edited and translated by Charles Mopsik. Paris-Tel Aviv: Éditions de L'Éclat, 2003.

Gray, Mark. "Amnon: A Chip off the Old Block? Rhetorical Strategy in 2 Samuel 13.7–15: The Rape of Tamar and the Humiliation of the Poor," *Journal for the Study of the Old Testament* 77 (1993): 39–54.

Gray, John. *I & II Kings: A Commentary.* Old Testament Library. Philadelphia: Westminster, 1963.

Gravett, Sandie. "Reading 'Rape' in the Hebrew Bible: A Consideration of Language." *Journal for the Study of the Old Testament* 28 (2004): 279–99.

Gregory the Great, *Morals on the Book of Job.* Vol. 1, parts 1–2. Translated by John Henry Parker. London: Oxford, 1844.

Gunn, David. "Bathsheba Goes Bathing in Hollywood: Words, Images and Social Locations." *Semeia* 74 (1996): 75–102.

Gunn, David. "David and the Gift of the Kingdom (2 Sam. 2–4, 9–20, 1 Kings 1–2)." *Semeia* 3 (1975): 14–45.

Hall, Joseph. "David with Bathsheba and URIAH," *Contemplations Upon the Old Testament, Vol. 5.* London: E[dward] G[riffin] for Nathaniel Butter, 1620, book 15, 232–57.

Hankins, Davis. "The Book of Job's Past, Present, and Future Consequences." http://marginalia.lareviewofbooks.org/the-book-of-jobs-past-present-and-future-consequences-by-davis-hankins/. Accessed Jan. 25, 2015.

Harris, Robert A. "Concepts of Scripture in the School of Rashi." Pages 102–122 in *Jewish Concepts of Scripture: A Comparative Introduction.* Edited by Benjamin Sommer. New York: New York University Press, 2012.

Harthan, Jonathan. *The Book of Hours.* New York: Thomas Y. Cromwell, 1977.

Häusl, Maria. *Abischag und Batscheba: Frauen am Königshof und die Thronfolge Davids im Zeugnis der Texte 1 Kön 1 und 2.* St. Ottilien: EOS-Verlag, 1993.

Hebrew-English Edition of the Babylonian Talmud "'Abodah Zarah." Edited by Isidore Epstein. London: Soncino, 1988.

Hebrew-English Edition of the Babylonian Talmud "'Erubin." Edited by Isidore Epstein. Translated by Israel Slotki. London: Soncino, 1983.

Hebrew-English Edition of the Babylonian Talmud "Kethuboth." Edited by Isidore Epstein. Translated by Samuel Daiches and Israel Slotki. London: Soncino, 1989.

Hebrew-English Edition of the Babylonian Talmud "Kiddushin." Edited by Isidore Epstein. Translated by Harry Freedman. London: Soncino, 1990.

Hebrew-English Edition of the Babylonian Talmud "Megillah." Edited by Isidore Epstein. Translated by Maurice Simon. London: Soncino, 1990.

Hebrew-English Edition of the Babylonian Talmud "Mo'ed Katan." Edited by Isidore Epstein. Translated by Israel Slotki. London: Soncino, 1990.

Hebrew-English Edition of the Babylonian Talmud "Pesahim." Edited by Isidore Epstein. Translated by Harry Freedman. London: Soncino, 1990.

Hebrew-English Edition of the Babylonian Talmud "Šabbath." Edited by Isidore Epstein. Translated by Harry Freedman. London: Soncino, 1972.

Hebrew-English Edition of the Babylonian Talmud "Sanhedrin." Edited by Isidore Epstein. Translated by Jacob Shatcher and Harry Freedman. London: Soncino, 1994.

Hebrew-English Edition of the Babylonian Talmud. "Sukkah." Edited by Isidore Epstein. Translated by Israel Slotki. London: Soncino, 1990.

Hebrew-English Edition of the Babylonian Talmud "Yoma." Edited by Isidore Epstein. Translated by Leo Jung. London: Soncino, 1989.

Heller, Joseph. *God Knows.* New York: Knopf, 1984.

Henry, Matthew. *An Exposition of the Old and New Testaments.* Philadelphia: Alexander Towar and Hogan & Thompson, 1833.

Henry, Matthew, John Gill, and Arthur Walkington Pink. *An Exposition of I & II Samuel.* Mac Dill AFB, Fla.: MacDonald, 1900.

Heym, Stefan. *The King David Report: A Novel.* London: Hodder and Stoughton, 1973.

Holub, Robert C. *Reception Theory: A Critical Introduction.* New York: Methuen, 1984.

Irenaeus. *Against the Heresies.* New York: Paulist Press, 2012.

Iser, Wolfgang. "The Reading Process: A Phenomenological Approach." *New Literary History* 3 (1972): 279–99.

Iser, Wolfgang. "Indeterminacy and the Reader's Response in Prose Fiction." Pages 1–45 in *Aspects of Narrative; Selected Papers from the English Institute.* Edited by J. Hillis Miller. New York: Columbia University Press, 1971.

Ishida, Tomoo. "Adonijah Son of Haggith and His Supporters: An Inquiry into Problems about History and Historiography." Pages 165–87 in *The Future of Biblical Studies: The Hebrew Scriptures.* Edited by Richard Elliott Friedman and H. G. M. Williamson. Atlanta: Scholars, 1987.

Isodore of Seville. "Questiones in Vet. Testam, in Regum II." *Patrologia Latina* 83. Edited by J. P. Migne. Paris: Garnier Frères, 1850.

Jacobson, David. *Does David Still Play Before You? Israeli Poetry and the Bible.* Detroit: Wayne State University Press, 1997.

Jean-Gilles, Jovaneca. "British Lifestyle Brand Bathsheba Launches Beach and Home Wear" June 9, 2013. http://www.theupcoming.co.uk/2013/06/09/british-lifestyle-brand -bathsheba-launches-beach-and-home-wear/. Accessed June 9, 2013.

Jerome, *Letters and Select Works.* NPNF, ser. 2, vol. 6. Edited by Philip Schaff and Henry Wace. Edinburgh: T. & T. Clark. Reprint, Grand Rapids, Mich.: Eerdmans, 1954.

Jobling, David. *1 Samuel.* Berit Olam. Collegeville, Minn.: Liturgical Press, 1998.

John, Tagwana. "Still on Immodest Dress Code." *The Tide,* Aug. 3, 2015. http://www.the tidenewsonline.com/2015/08/03/still-on-immodest-dress-code/. Accessed Aug. 4, 2015.

Junior, Nyasha. "Re/Use of Texts." http://www.atthispoint.net/editor-notes/reuse-of-texts/ 265/. Accessed July 29, 2015.

Kalavrezou, Ioli, Nicolette Trahoulia, and Shalom Sabar. "Critique of the Emperor in the Vatican Psalter gr. 752." *Dumbarton Oaks Papers* 47 (1993): 195–219.

Kay, Sarah. "Courts, Clerks, and Courtly Love." Pages 81–96 in *The Cambridge Companion to Medieval Romance.* Edited by Roberta L. Krueger. Cambridge: Cambridge University Press, 2000.

Keil, Carl Friedrich, *Commentary on the Books of Kings.* Translated by James Martin. Edinburgh: T. & T. Clark, 1857.

Keil, Carl Friedrich and F. Delitzsch, *Biblical Commentary on the Books of Samuel.* Translated by James Martin. Edinburgh: T. & T. Clark, 1868.

Kelso, Julie. "Gazing at Impotence in Henry King's *David and Bathsheba.*" Pages 155–87 in *Screening Scripture: Intertextual Connections Between Scripture and Film.* Edited by George Aichele and Richard Walsh. Harrisburg: Trinity Press International, 2002.

Kenney II, Carl W. "Jesse Jackson Jr.: Living with the David Syndrome." *Rev-elution.* July 16, 2012. http://rev-elution.blogspot.com/2012/07/jesse-jackson-jr-living-with-david .html. Accessed June 20, 2014.

Kermode, Frank. "New Ways with Biblical Stories." Pages 121–35 in *Parable and Story in Judaism and Christianity.* Edited by Clemens Thoma and Michael Wyschogrod. Mahwah, N.J.: Paulist, 1989.

Kessler, John. "Sexuality and Politics: The Motif of the Displaced Husband in the Books of Samuel." *Catholic Biblical Quarterly* 62 (2000): 409–23.

Keys, Gillian. *The Wages of Sin: A Reappraisal of the 'Succession Narrative.'* Journal for the Study of the Old Testament: Supplement Series 221. Sheffield: Sheffield Academic Press, 1996.

King'oo, Clare Costley. *Miserere Mei: The Penitential Psalms in Late Medieval and Early Modern England.* Notre Dame: University of Notre Dame Press, 2010.

Kirk-Duggan, Cheryl. "Slingshots, Ships, and Personal Psychosis: Murder, Sexual Intrigue, and Power in the Lives of David and Othello." Pages 37–70 in *Pregnant Passion: Gender, Sex and Violence in the Bible.* Edited by Cheryl Kirk-Duggan. Leiden: Brill, 2004.

Kirkpatrick, A. F. *The Second Book of Samuel.* Cambridge: Cambridge, 1880.

Kitzinger, Ernst. *Byzantine Art in the Making: Main Lines of Stylistic Development in Mediterranean Art, 3rd–7th Century.* Boston: Harvard, 1977.

Koenig, Sara M. *Isn't This Bathsheba? A Study in Characterization.* Princeton Theological Monograph Series 177. Eugene, Oreg.: Wipf and Stock, 2011.

Kren, Thomas. "Looking at Louis XII's Bathsheba." Pages 41–61 in *A Masterpiece Constructed: The Hours of Louis XII.* Edited by Thomas Kren and Mark Evans. Los Angeles: J. Paul Getty Museum, 2005.

Kuczynski, Michael. *Prophetic Song: The Psalms as Moral Discourse in Late Medieval England.* Philadelphia: University of Pennsylvania Press, 1995.

Kugel, James. *The Bible as It Was.* Cambridge: Belknap Press, 1997.

Kugel, James. "Two Introductions to Midrash," *Prooftexts* 3 (1983): 131–55.

Kugel, James and Rowan Greer. *Early Biblical Interpretation.* Philadelphia: Westminster, 1986.

Kugel, James L. *The Idea of Biblical Poetry: Parallelism and Its History.* New Haven, Conn.: Yale University Press, 1981.

Kunoth-Liefels, Elisabeth. *Über die Darstellungen der «Bathsheba im Bade": Studien zur Gechichte des Bildthemas 4.* Jahrhundert 17. Bacht: Essen, 1962.

Kunz, Andreas. *Die Frauen und der König David: Studien zur Figuration von Frauen in den Daviderzählungen.* Leipzig: Evangelische Verlagsanstalt, 2003.

Labriola, Albert, and John Smeltz. *The Bible of the Poor.* Pittsburgh: Duquesne University Press, 1990.

Lamb, David T. *Prostitutes and Polygamists: A Look at Love, Old Testament Style.* Grand Rapids, Mich.: Zondervan, 2015.

Landy, Francis. "Noah's Ark and Mrs. Monkey," *Biblical Interpretation* 15 (2007): 351–76.

Lange, John Peter. *Commentary on the Holy Scriptures: Critical, Doctrinal and Homiletical: Samuel.* Translated by Philip Schaff. Grand Rapids, Mich.: Zondervan, 1877.

Lawlor, John I. "Theology and Art in the Narrative of the Ammonite War (2 Samuel 10–12)," GTJ 3 (1982): 193–205.

Legaspi, Michael. *The Death of Scripture and the Rise of Biblical Studies.* Oxford: Oxford University Press, 2010.

Lemaire, André. "David, Bethsabée et la maison de David: une approache historique." Pages 41–53 in *L'Historie de David et Bethsabée: Etude interdisciplinaire.* Yod 8. Edited by Daniel Bodi and Masha Itzhaki. Paris: Publications Langues, 2004.

Leneman, Helen. *Love, Lust, and Lunacy: The Stories of David and Saul in Music.* Sheffield: Sheffield Phoenix, 2010.

Leneman, Helen. *The Performed Bible: The Story of Ruth in Opera and Oratorio.* Bible in the Modern World, 11. Sheffield: Sheffield Phoenix, 2007.

Leneman, Helen. "Portrayals of Power in the Stories of Delilah and Bathsheba: Seduction in Song." Pages 139–55 in *Culture, Entertainment and the Bible.* Edited by George Aichele. Sheffield: Sheffield Academic, 2000.

L'Engle, Madeleine. *Certain Women.* 1st HarperCollins ed. San Francisco: Harper San-Francisco, 1993.

Leson, Richard. http://www.themorgan.org/collection/crusader-bible/82. Accessed July 21, 2010.

Lester, Julius. *The Autobiography of God.* New York: St. Martin's Press, 2004.

Létourneau, Anne. "Bathing Beauty: Concealment of Bathsheba's Rape and Counter-Power in 2 Sam 11:1–5." Paper presented at Society of Biblical Literature meeting in Atlanta, Ga., Nov. 21, 2015.

Light, Alan. *The Holy or the Broken: Leonard Cohen, Jeff Buckley, and the Unlikely Ascent of "Hallelujah."* New York: Atria, 2012.

Linafelt, Tod. "Taking Women in Samuel: Readers/Responses/Responsibility." Pages 99–113 in *Reading Between Texts: Intertextuality and the Hebrew Bible.* Edited by Danna Nolan Fewell. Louisville: Westminster/John Knox, 1992.

Lowth, Robert. *Lectures on the Sacred Poetry of the Hebrews (1787).* Hildesheim: Georg Olms Verlag, 1969.

Ludwig, Dean, and Longenecker, Clinton. "The Bathsheba Syndrome: The Ethical Failure of Successful Leaders." *Journal of Business Ethics* 12 (1993): 265–73.

Lumby, J. Rawson. *The First Book of the Kings.* Cambridge: University Press, 1898.

Luther, Martin. *Career of the Reformer III.* Luther's Works 33. Minneapolis: Fortress, 1972.

Luther, Martin. *The Christian in Society IV.* Edited by Franklin Sherman and Helmut T. Lehman. Luther's Works 47. Philadelphia: Fortress, 1971.

Luther, Martin. *Church and Ministry I.* Edited by Eric W. Gritsch. Luther's Works, vol. 39. Minneapolis: Fortress, 1970.

Luther, Martin. *A Commentary on Galatians.* Translated by Theodore Graebner. Grand Rapids, Mich.: Zondervan, 1937.

Luther, Martin. *Lectures on Galatians 5–6.* Edited by Jaroslav Pelikan and Daniel Poellot. Luther's Works, vol. 27. St. Louis: Concordia, 1963.

Luther, Martin. *Lectures on Genesis 15–20.* Edited by Jaroslav Pelikan. Luther's Works, vol. 3. St. Louis: Concordia, 1961.

Luther, Martin. *Lectures on Genesis 31–37.* Edited by Paul D. Pahl. Luther's Works, vol. 35. St. Louis: Concordia, 1969

Luther, Martin. *Lectures on Genesis Chapters 38–44.* Edited by Jaroslav Pelikan and Walter Hansen. Luther's Works, vol. 7. St. Louis: Concordia, 1965.

Luther, Martin. *Schriften, 4. Band, Psalmenvorlesung 1513/15 (Ps. 85–150).* Weimar: Herman Böhlau, 1866.

Luther, Martin. *Selected Psalms II.* Edited by Jaroslav Pelikan. Luther's Works, vol. 13. St. Louis: Concordia, 1956.

Luther, Martin. *Selected Psalms III.* Edited by Jaroslav Pelikan and Daniel Poellot. Luther's Works, vol. 14. St. Louis: Concordia, 1958.

Mann, Griffith. "Picturing the Bible in the Thirteenth Century." Pages 38–59 in *The Book of Kings: Art, War and the Morgan Library's Medieval Picture Bible.* Edited by William Noel and Daniel H. Weiss. London: Third Millennium Publishing, 2006.

Marcus, David. "David the Deceiver and David the Dupe." *Prooftexts* 6 (1986): 163–83.

Marinella, Lucrezia. *The Nobility and Excellence of Women and the Defects and Vices of Men.* Translated Anne Dunhill. Chicago: University of Chicago Press, 2000.

Martin, Dale. *Pedagogy of the Bible.* Philadelphia: Westminster/John Knox, 2009.

Martin, Gary. *Multiple Originals: New Approaches to Hebrew Bible Textual Criticism (Society of Biblical Literature Text-Critical Studies).* Atlanta: SBL, 2010.

Massie, Allan. *King David.* London: Sceptre, 1995.

Maurus, Rabanus. *Expositio in Matthaeum.* Translated B. Lofstedt. CCCM CLXXIV. Turnhout: Brepols, 2000.

May, Simon. *Love: A History.* New Haven, Conn.: Yale University Press, 2011.

McKenzie, Stephen L. *King David: A Biography.* Oxford: Oxford University Press, 2000.

McLeod, Frederick G. *Theodore of Mopsuestia.* London: Routledge, 2009.

Meyer, Mati. "Theologizing or Indulging Desire: Bathers in the Sacra Parallela (Paris, BnF, gr. 923)." *Different Visions: A Journal of New Perspectives on Medieval Art.* Issue Five. http://differentvisions.org/theologizing-indulging-desire-bathers-sacra-parallela-paris-bnf-gr-923/. Accessed Apr. 11, 2016.

Midrash Rabbah Exodus. Translated by S. M. Lehrman. 3rd ed. London; New York: Soncino, 1983.

Midrash Rabbah Leviticus. Translated by J. Israelstam and Judah Slotki. 3rd ed. London; New York: Soncino, 1983.

Midrash Rabbah Numbers. Translated by Judah Slotki. 3rd ed. London; New York: Soncino, 1983.

Midrash Rabbah Song of Songs. Translated by Maurice Simon. 3rd ed. London; New York: Soncino, 1983.

Miller, Patrick D. and J. J. M. Roberts. *The Hand of the Lord: A Reassessment of the "Ark Narrative" of 1 Samuel.* Baltimore: Johns Hopkins University Press, 1977.

Mitchell, Margaret, "Allegory, Christianity." Cols. 796–800 in *Encyclopedia of the Bible and Its Reception 1.* Berlin/New York: De Gruyter, 2009.

Mohammed, Khaleel. *David in the Muslim Tradition: The Bathsheba Affair.* Lanham, Md.: Lexington, 2014.

Montgomery, James. *A Critical and Exegetical Commentary on the Books of Kings.* Edited by H. S. Gehman. The International Critical Commentary. Edinburgh: T. & T. Clark, 1952.

Moore, Stephen, and Yvonne Sherwood. *The Invention of the Biblical Scholar: A Critical Manifesto.* Minneapolis: Fortress, 2011.

Moos, Peter von. *Hildebert von Lavardin, 1056–1133: Humanitas an der Schwelle des höfischen Zeitalters.* Stuttgart: Anton Hiersemann, 1965.

Morson, Gary Saul, and Caryl Emerson. *Mikhail Bakhtin: Creation of a Prosaics.* Stanford, Calif.: Stanford University Press, 1990.

Mount Shoop, Marcia. "The David Syndrome?" *Feminism and Religion.* Nov. 17, 2012. http://feminismandreligion.com/2012/11/17/the-david-syndrome-by-marcia-mount-shoop/. Accessed June 20, 2014.

Muivah, Bienhome "Are Women as Powerless as They Appear? Part 2" Jan. 31, 2014. *E-Pao.* http://e-pao.net/epSubPageExtractor.asp?src=leisure.Essays. Essay_on_Faith _Spirituality. Are_Women_As_Powerless_As_They_Appear_Part_2_By_Bienhome_ Muivah. Accessed Jan. 31, 2014.

Mulvey, Laura. "Visual Pleasure and Narrative Cinema," *Screen* 16 (1975): 6–18.

Morris, Richard. *Legends of the Holy Rood.* New York: Greenwood Press, 1969.

Nienhuis, David R. *Not By Paul Alone: The Formation of the Catholic Epistle Collection and the Christian Canon.* Waco: Baylor University Press, 2007.

Neusner, Jacob. *Midrash in Context.* Philadelphia: Fortress, 1983

Nicol, George. "The Alleged Rape of Bathsheba: Some Observations on Ambiguity in Biblical Narrative." *JSOT* 22 no. 73 (1997): 43–54.

Nicholls, Rachel. *Walking on Water: Reading Mt. 14:22–33 in the Light of its Wirkungsgeschichte.* Leiden: Brill, 2006.

Norris, R. A. "Antiochene Interpretation." Pages 29–32 in *A Dictionary of Biblical Interpretation.* Edited by R. J. Coggins and J. L. Houlden. London: SCM, 1990.

O'Loughlin, Thomas. "A Woman's Plight and the Western Fathers." Pages 83–104 in *Ciphers in the Sand: Interpretations of The Woman Taken in Adultery (John 7:53–8:11).* Edited by Larry Joseph Kreitzer and Deborah Rooke. Sheffield: Sheffield Academic Press, 2000.

Owen, Mackubin Thomas. "Petraeus's Bathsheba Syndrome: Why did a Man We So Respected Succumb to Temptation?" *National Review Online,* Nov. 13, 2012. http://www.nationalreview.com/article/333325/petraeuss-bathsheba-syndrome-mackubin-thomas-owens. Accessed June 20, 2014.

Pacian of Barcelona, *The Fathers of the Church, a new translation, vol 99.* "Iberian Fathers volume 3, Pacian of Barcelona, Orosius of Braga." Translated by Craig Hanson. Washington, D.C.: Catholic University of America Press, 1999.

Panizza, Letizia. Introduction to *Paternal Tyranny.* "The Other Voice in Early Modern Europe," Chicago: University of Chicago Press, 2007.

Pardes, Ilana. "Moses Goes Down to Hollywood: Miracles and Special Effects." *Semeia* 74 (1996): 15–32.

Patrick, Simon. *A Commentary Upon the Two Books of Samuel.* London: Chiswell, 1703.

Pelikan, Jaroslav. *The Reformation of the Bible: The Bible of the Reformation.* New Haven, Conn.: Yale University Press, 1996.

Perpetua, Matthew. "Cee Lo Green Outrages John Lennon Fans by Changing Lyrics to 'Imagine.'" Jan. 2, 2012. http://www.rollingstone.com/music/news/cee-lo-green-outrages -john-lennon-fans-by-changing-lyrics-to-imagine-20120102. Accessed Apr. 7, 2014.

Petersen, Erik. "*Sucispere Digneris:* Et fund og nogle hypoteser om Københavnerpsalteret Thott 143 2° og dets historie." Pages 21–63 in *Fund og Forskning i det Kongelige Biblioteks Samlinger.* Copenhagen: Det Kongelige Bibliotek, 2011.

Pitkin, Barbara. "John Calvin and the Interpretation of the Bible." Pages 341–371 in *A History of Biblical Interpretation.* Grand Rapids, Mich.: Eerdmans, 2003.

Polliack, Meira. "Concepts of Scripture among the Jews of the Medieval Islamic World." Pages 80–101 in *Jewish Concepts of Scripture: A Comparative Introduction.* New York: New York University Press, 2012.

Polzin, Robert. *David and the Deuteronomist: 2 Samuel.* Literary Study of the Deuteronomic History, Pt. 3. Bloomington: Indiana University Press, 1993.

Pressler, Caroline. *The View of Women Found in the Deuteronomic Laws.* New York: De Gruyter, 1993.

Pseudo-Clementine, "Two Epistles Concerning Virginity." *Anti-Nicene Fathers.* Vol. 8. Edited by Alexander Roberts and James Donaldson. Grand Rapids, Mich.: Eerdmans, 1954.

Quick, Matthew. *Love May Fail.* New York: HarperCollins, 2015.

Ramsey, Boniface. *Beginning to Read the Fathers.* New York: Paulist, 1985.

Reno, Rusty, and John O'Keefe. *Sanctified Vision.* Baltimore, Md.: Johns Hopkins, 2005.

Repphun, Eric, Deane Galbraith, Will Sweetman, and James Harding. "Beyond Christianity, the Bible and the Text: Urgent Tasks and New Orientations for Reception History." *Relegere* 1 (2011): 1–11.

Rimmon-Kenan, Shlomith. *Narrative Fiction.* New York: Routledge, 2002.

Rivers, Francine. *Unspoken.* Wheaton, Ill.: Tyndale, 2001.

Roberts, Alexander, and James Donaldson. *The Twelve Patriarchs, excerpts and epistles, the Clementina, Apocrypha, Decretals, Memoirs of Edessa and Syriac documents, Remains of the first ages.* Ante-Nicene Fathers, Volume 8. Grand Rapids, Mich.: Eerdmans, 1951.

Römer, Thomas and Albert de Pury. "Deuteronomistic Historiography (DH): History of Research and Debated Issues." Pages

Rosenberg, A. J., ed. *Book of Samuel 2.* Mikraoth Gedoloth. Judaica Books of the Holy Writings. New York: Judaica Press, 1982.

Rosenberg, A. J., ed. *Psalms, Volume 2, A New English Translation.* Mikraoth Gedoloth. Judaica Books of the Holy Writings. New York: Judaica Press, 1991.

Rosenberg, A. J., and Reuven Hochberg, eds. *Book of Kings 1.* Mikraoth Gedoloth. Judaica Books of the Holy Writings. New York: Judaica Press, 1980.

Rosenberg, Joel. "Meanings, Morals, and Mysteries: Literary Approaches to the Torah." *Response* 9.2 (1975): 67–94.

Rudloff Stanton, Anne. "Motherhood in the Queen Mary Psalter." Pages 172–189 in *Women and the Book: Assessing the Visual Evidence.* British Library Studies in Medieval Culture. London: British Library; Toronto and Buffalo: University of Toronto Press, 1997.

Said, Edward. *Orientalism.* London: Penguin Books, 2003.

Saltow, Michael. *Tasting the Dish: Rabbinic Rhetorics of Sexuality.* Atlanta: Scholars, 1995.

Savage, Anne, and Nicholas Watson. *Anchoritic Spirituality: Ancrene Wisse and Associated Works.* New York: Paulist, 1991.

Schmitt, Gladys. *David the King.* New York: Dial, 1946.

Schroeder, Joy. *Dinah's Lament: The Biblical Legacy of Sexual Violence in Christian Interpretation.* Philadelphia: Fortress, 2007.

Seebass, Horst. "Nathan und David in 2 Sam 12." *ZAW* 86 (1974): 203–11.

Segovia, Fernando. "Cultural Criticism." Pages 307–336 in *The Future of the Biblical Past: Envisioning Biblical Studies on a Global Key.* Edited by Roland Boer and Fernando F. Segovia. Atlanta: SBL, 2012.

Seitz, Christopher, "History, Figural History, and Providence in the Dual Witness of Prophet and Apostle." Pages 1–6 in *Go Figure! Figuration in Biblical Interpretation.* Edited by Stan Walters. Princeton Theological Monograph, Ser. 81. Eugene: Pickwick, 2008.

Seow, Choon-Leong. "1 & 2 Kings," *The New Interpreter's Bible,* Vol. 3. Nashville: Abingdon, 1999.

Seow, Leong. *Job 1–21.* Grand Rapids, Mich.: Eerdmans, 2013.

Shanker, Thom. "Concern Grows Over Top Military Officer's Ethics," *New York Times,* Nov. 12, 2012. http://www.nytimes.com/2012/11/13/us/petraeuss-resignation-highlights -concern-over-military-officers-ethics.html?pagewanted=all&_r=0. Accessed June 20, 2014.

Sheehan, Jonathan. *The Enlightenment Bible Translation, Scholarship, Culture.* Princeton, N.J.: Princeton University Press, 2013.

Sherwood, Yvonne. *A Biblical Text and Its Afterlives: The Survival of Jonah in Western Culture.* Cambridge: Cambridge University Press, 2000.

Shields, Christopher. "Aristotle's Psychology." *The Stanford Encyclopedia of Philosophy,* Spring 2015 Edition. Edited by Edward N. Zalta. http://plato.stanford.edu/archives/ spr2015/entries/aristotle-psychology/. Accessed Dec. 3, 2015.

Shimoff, Sandra. "David and Bathsheba: The Political Function of Rabbinic Aggada," *Journal for the Study of Judaism in the Persian, Hellenistic and Roman Periods.* 24 (1993): 246–56.

Simonetti, Manlio. *Biblical Interpretation in the Early Church.* Edinburgh: T. & T. Clark, 1994.

Smith, Henry P. *A Critical and Exegetical Commentary on the Books of Samuel.* International Critical Commentary on the Holy Scriptures of the Old and New Testaments. New York: Charles Scribner's Sons, 1899.

Smith, Jill Eileen. *Bathsheba: A Novel.* The Wives of King David Series, Volume 3. Grand Rapids, Mich.: Revell, 2011.

Sommer, Benjamin. "Concepts of Scriptural Language in Midrash," Pages 64–79 in *Jewish Concepts of Scripture: A Comparative Introduction.* Edited by Benjamin Sommers. New York: New York University Press, 2012.

Stanton, Elizabeth Cady. *The Woman's Bible.* Seattle: Coalition Task Force on Women and Religion, 1974.

Sternberg, Meir. *The Poetics of Biblical Narrative*. Bloomington: Indiana University Press, 1987.

Steussy, Marti J. *David: Biblical Portraits of Power*. Columbia: University of South Carolina Press, 1999.

Sting. http://www.sting.com/discography/index/album/albumId/208/tagName/studio _albums. Accessed Mar. 18, 2014.

Sting. *Lyrics,* New York: Dial, 2007.

Stones, Allison. "Questions of Style and Provenance in the Morgan Bible." Pages 112–21 in *Between the Picture and the Word: Manuscript Studies from the Index of Christian Art*. Edited by Colum Hourihane. University Park: Pennsylvania State University Press, 2005.

Sun, Chloe. "Bathsheba Transformed: From Silence to Voice." Pages 30–42 in *Mirrored Reflections: Reframing Biblical Characters*. Edited by Young Lee Hertig and Chloe Sun. Eugene, Oreg.: Wipf and Stock, 2010.

Tentler, Thomas. *Sin and Confession on the Eve of the Reformation*. Princeton, N.J.: Princeton University Press, 1977.

Thompson, John Lee. "General Introduction," *Genesis 1–11*. Reformation Commentary on Scripture. Old Testament. Downers Grove, Ill.: IVP Academic, 2012.

Thompson, Mark. "Biblical Interpretation in the Works of Martin Luther." Pages 299–318 in *A History of Biblical Interpretation*. Grand Rapids, Mich.: Eerdmans, 2003.

Trapp, Joseph. *The Royal Sin: Or Adultery Rebuk'd in a Great King*. London: Huggonson, 1738.

Thornton, T. C. G. "Solomonic Apologetic in Samuel and Kings." *Church Quarterly Review* 169 (1968): 159–166.

Trible, Phyllis. "Exegesis for Storytellers and Other Strangers." *JBL* 114/1 (1995): 3–19.

Tumanov, Vladimir. "Divine Silence in Stefan Heym's *The King David Report*." *Neophilologus* 93 (2009): 499–509.

Valler, Shulamit. "King David and 'His' Women." Pages 129–42 in *A Feminist Companion to Samuel and Kings*. Sheffield: Sheffield Academic Press, 1994.

van Liere, Frans. *An Introduction to the Medieval Bible*. Cambridge: Cambridge University Press, 2014.

van Liere, Frans. "The Literal Sense of the Books of Samuel and Kings; From Andrew of St. Victor to Nicholas of Lyra." Pages 59–81 in *Nicholas of Lyra: The Senses of Scripture*. Edited by Philip D. W. Krey and Lesley Smith. Leiden: Brill, 2000.

Vander Stichele, Caroline, and Hugh Pyper. *Text, Image, and Otherness in Children's Bibles: What Is in the Picture?* Semeia Studies 56. Atlanta: Society of Biblical Literature, 2012.

von Moos, Peter. *Hildebert von Lavardin, 1056–1133*. Stuttgart: Hiersemann, 1965.

Walker Vadillo, Monica. *Bathsheba in Late Medieval French Manuscript Illumination: Innocent Object of Desire or Agent of Sin?* Lewiston: Edwin Mellen, 2008.

Wall, Robert W. "The 'Rule of Faith' and Biblical Hermeneutics," *Catalyst* 36/1 (Nov. 2009): 1–3.

Weiss, Daniel. "Portraying the Past, Illuminating the Present: The Art of the Morgan Library Picture Bible." Pages 10–35 in *The Book of Kings: Art, War, and the Morgan*

Library's Medieval Picture Bible. Edited by William Noel and Daniel Weiss. London: Third Millennium, 2002.

Weitzmann, Kurt. *The Miniatures of the Sacra Parallela, Parisinus Graecus 923.* Princeton, N.J.: Princeton University Press, 1979.

Wenzel, Siegfried, trans. *Fasciculus Morum: A Fourteenth-Century Preacher's Handbook.* University Park: Pennsylvania State University Press, 1989.

Wesley, John. Sermon 19, "The Great Privilege of Those That are Born of God," http://wesley.nnu.edu/john-wesley/the-sermons-of-john-wesley-1872-edition/sermon-19-the-great-privilege-of-those-that-are-born-of-god/. Accessed Oct. 25, 2012.

Wesselius, Jan W. "Joab's Death and the Central Theme of the Sucession Narrative (2 Samuel IX- 1 Kings II)." *Vetus Testamentum* 40 (1990): 336–351.

West, Jim. "Reception History: A Simple Definition." July 15, 2011. Zwinglius Redivivus (blog). http://zwingliusredivivus.wordpress.com/2011/07/15/reception-history-a-simple-definition. Accessed Jan. 18, 2015.

White, Timothy, interview, http://www.sting.com/discography/index/album/albumId/17/tagname/albums. Accessed March 18, 2014.

Whybray, R. N. *The Succession Narrative; a Study of II Samuel 9–20, [and] I Kings 1 and 2.* Studies in Biblical Theology. Ser. 9. Naperville, Ill.: Allenson, 1968.

Wieck, Roger. *Painted Prayers: The Book of Hours in Medieval and Renaissance Art.* New York: George Braziller, 1997.

Witek, Maria A. G. "Anatomy of A Dance Hit: Why We Love to Boogie With Pharrell." NPR.com. June 2, 2014. http://www.npr.org/blogs/health/2014/05/30/317019212/anatomy-of-a-dance-hit-why-we-love-to-boogie-with-pharrell. Accessed Jan. 18, 2015.

Witek, Maria A. G., Eric F. Clarke, Mikkel Wallentin, Morten L. Kringelbach, and Peter Vuust. "Syncopation, Body-Movement and Pleasure in Groove Music." Apr. 16, 2014. DOI: 10.1371/journal.pone.0094446. Accessed Jan. 18, 2015.

Wolfthal, Diane. *Images of Rape: The "Heroic" Tradition and Its Alternatives.* Cambridge: Cambridge University Press, 1999.

Wolfthal, Diane. "The Sexuality of the Medieval Comb." Pages 176–94 in *Thresholds of Medieval Visual Culture: Liminal Spaces.* Edited by Elina Gertsman and Jill Stevenson. Boydell, 2012.

Wormald, Francis. "Bible Illustration in Medieval Manuscripts." Pages 307–37 in *The Cambridge History of the Bible: The West from the Reformation to the Present Day.* Edited by G. W. H. Lampe. Cambridge: Cambridge University Press, 1963.

Yamada, Frank M. *Configurations of Rape in the Hebrew Bible: A Literary Analysis of Three Rape Narratives.* Studies in Biblical Literature. New York: Peter Lang, 2008.

Yee, Gail. "'Fraught with Background': Literary Ambiguity in II Samuel 11." *Interpretation* 42 (1988): 240–53.

Young, Frances. "Alexandrian School." Pages 10–12 in *A Dictionary of Biblical Interpretation.* Edited by R. J. Coggins and J. L. Houlden. London: SCM, 1992.

Zetterholm, Karin. *Jewish Interpretation of the Bible: Ancient and Contemporary.* Minneapolis: Fortress, 2012.

Zhixiong, Niu. *The King Lifted Up His Voice and Wept: David's Mourning in the Second Book of Samuel.* Rome: Georgian and Biblical Press, 2013.

Zwingli, Ulrich. *Writings, Volume 2: In Search of True Religion: Reformation, Pastoral and Eucharistic Writings.* Translated by Wayne H. Pipkin. Eugene, Oreg.: Pickwick, 1984.

———. "500 Greatest Albums of All Time." May 31, 2012. http://www.rollingstone.com/music/lists/500-greatest-albums-of-all-time-20120531/pixies-doolittle-20120524#ixzz2yKRH7MHY. Accessed Mar. 20, 2014.

———. "Bathsheba—the Bible Series." https://www.youtube.com/watch?v=W5fEIkgijE8 Accessed Aug. 25, 2015.

———. "How I Stole Him Away." Feb. 23, 2015. http://www.jamaicaobserver.com/magazines/allwoman/How-I-stole-him-away_18429049. Accessed Feb. 24, 2015.

———. http://www.outreach.com/campaigns/the-bible-resources.aspx. Accessed Aug. 25, 2015.

INDEX